THE
DEATH CAMP
TREBLINKA

A DOCUMENTARY

THE DEATH CAMP
TREBLINKA

A DOCUMENTARY

Edited by
ALEXANDER DONAT

HOLOCAUST LIBRARY
NEW YORK

Publication of this book was made possible
by a grant from Benjamin and Stefa Wald

Cover design by Eric Gluckman
Printed in the United States of America
by Waldon Press, Inc., New York City.

ACKNOWLEDGMENTS

Grateful acknowledgment is made to the following institutions and persons for their assistance in the preparation of this volume:

Yad Vashem, Martyrs' and Heroes' Remembrance Authority, Jerusalem;

Ghetto Fighters House, Kibbutz Lohamei Haghetaot, Israel;

Moreshet Archives, Israel;

Center for Holocaust Studies, Documentation and Research, Brooklyn, N.Y., and Asher Reiss, staff member of the Center;

Bund Archives of the Jewish Labor Movement, New York;

Miriam Novitch, renowned Holocaust researcher and writer, Israel;

Samuel Rajzman, the nestor of the Treblinka survivors, Montreal, Canada;

Gertrude Hirschler, New York.

CONTENTS

The Scroll of Treblinka

HUMAN REASON will never make peace with the reality of Treblinka. The human mind cannot accept the soulless rationale of this "scientific" enterprise. We can understand pogroms, explosions of religious fanaticism, of nationalist, political or racial hatred, incited mobs running amok — all these things, albeit terrifying, are *human*. But the cold, prearranged carnage, without passion or hate, planned and organized by a modern government in the heart of Europe, and followed by a "civilized" nation in a fit of collective rabies — this is beyond human comprehension. No wonder that a weird fascination hovers above this Polish hamlet which became the graveyard of over a million Jews not only of Warsaw but also of 150 other cities and towns, in ten European countries.

It is incredible. And still, it did happen, we know it did. It happened in our time, in the time of Albert Einstein, Sigmund Freud and Max Born. How did it happen? Let's refresh our memory by a terse summary of the series of events that led to the transmutation of the unthinkable into the commonplace. It started with the rise of Adolf Hitler, the new leader of Germany, a wicked and demented man. He decided that the people who had given Moses, Jesus, Spinoza and Marx to humanity, were the worst enemies of the nation of Goethe, Schiller and Beethoven. Germany would never be free and happy, said he, until and unless the kin of Heinrich Heine were eradicated from its midst — men, women and children. And when this German *Führer* unleashed a predatory war against other peoples, he called together his faithful and issued the order: "Now, under the cloak of wartime secrecy, while our adversaries are busy defending themselves against the blows of our powerful cohorts, is the time to obliterate the tribe of Judah." His henchmen: Hermann Göring, Heinrich Himmler, Reinhard Heydrich, were put in charge of this nefarious task, to which they gave the name "The Final Solution of the Jewish Problem." They sought to slaughter the Jews and to inherit their possessions and their place beneath the sun.

Special schools for murderers were organized in Germany. Hand-picked hangmen were trained in the art of killing, and a new, modern technology was adapted for the manufacture of death. Several basic methods were used by the Nazis to bring about the "Final Solution."

The earliest technique consisted of pogrom-like massacres and lootings of entire Jewish neighborhoods and communities by *Einsatzgruppen*, mobile killing squads that followed the fighting troops, waging their own dastardly war on defenseless men, women and children. In May, 1940, the police schools in Pretsch-on-the-Elbe, in Dünen and in Schmiedeberg were utilized to organize the four *Einsatzgruppen*, A, B, C and D, and prepared them for the mass murder of Jews in the occupied territories. They claimed over a million victims, mostly in the parts of Poland and U.S.S.R. invaded by the German troops. But soon Himmler became unhappy with the results of this technique. The massacres had caused misgivings not only among some old-fashioned *Wehrmacht* generals, but even Wilhelm Kube, the cruel *Generalkommissar* of Byelorussia, who was later killed by partisans, protested against the slaughters. They undermined, he claimed, "the honor of our *Reich* and our party," and he asked that "whatever had to be done should be done in a humane form." The "chaotic killings" were carried out in broad daylight and could not be kept secret. Some of the victims might survive as unwanted eyewitnesses and — perhaps most important — this procedure did not guarantee a total expropriation of Jewish property.

Accordingly, the *Einsatzgruppen* pogroms gave way to institutionalized murder schemes, carried out in two stages: first, locking up the Jews in ghettos, and then extermination in death camps expressly set up for this purpose. These camps borrowed their techniques — and their technicians — from the Nazi euthanasia program (code-named T-4.) This euthanasia operation had killed over 100,000 mentally-ill, crippled, incurably-sick Germans whom the Nazi regime had ruled to be "not worthy to live." It had to be discontinued in August, 1941, due to heavy pressure from the Church.

The command to adopt this new way of killing came from no less a source than the *Führer's* Chancellery itself. Philip Bouhler, the chief of Hitler's personal Chancellery, discovered Christian Wirth, the specialist in gassing, and Wirth did his work so well that he became known as "the technocrat of destruction." His method of killing was amazingly economical and horribly efficient. The advantages of gassing versus shooting became obvious: it was not only technically "tadellos" (perfect), but also, as Martin Broszat, the head of the Munich Institute of Contemporary History, puts it: "Asphyxiation by gas was technological genocide without a pogrom mood, without feelings of religious, nationalist or racial hostility on the part of the perpetrators . . ."[1] And what was no less important: it was ideally suited to the Nazi aim that *the murderers should inherit all the possessions of their victims*. The Polish judge Z. Łukaszkiewicz, who after the war conducted an investigation of Treblinka on behalf of the Polish government, explains: "In addition to its political objectives, the systematic destruction of the Jewish people was simply meant to fulfill certain economic aims. Their liquidation was a very good source of income."[2]

It is generally assumed that the Wannsee Conference (January 20, 1942) was the official start of the "Final Solution." Historical facts seem to indicate that Wannsee was simply an official rubber stamp on a *fait accompli* rather than a beginning of a new era. Göring's order to Heydrich was dated July 31, 1941 (six weeks after the start of the war against Russia, and six months before Wannsee), and it read:

"Complementing the task that was assigned to you on January 21, 1939, which was to solve the Jewish problem by emigration and evacuation in the most effective manner in accordance with the conditions of that time, I hereby charge you with making all necessary organizational, practical and financial preparations for bringing about the final solution of the Jewish problem in the territories within the German sphere of influence in Europe."[3]

And so the orders were given and the executions began. It was all on a strictly business basis. A commercial deal was concluded between Eichmann and the German Ministry of Transport: 4 pfennig per kilometer of railroad track per person. Children under ten at half rate, those under four traveled free. The rate was cut in half if at least 400 people were being shipped in one transport. The minimum charge per transport was 200 reichsmarks, with no charge for the return of the trains after they had been emptied of their human cargo. A cargo of 1,000 deportees per train. But for the Jewish *Sonderzüge* the norm of deportees was raised to 2,000, and to 5,000 for short hauls, as within Poland. Cargo space was less than two square feet per person. It was good business. That is why there never was a shortage of trains for Jewish transports.[4]

11

Christian Wirth's first step was to organize a pilot extermination camp at Chełmno-on-the-Ner, in Western Poland. Early in December, 1941, the first transports of Jews began to arrive in Chełmno. They were killed in hermetically-sealed mobile vans by exhaust fumes of the vans' own engines fed into the inside through pipes. (In the Ukraine the population nicknamed these vans *dushegubki*, "soul destroyers.") From December 5, 1941, until the end of its existence Chełmno killed (according to Dr. Richard Korherr, Hitler's official statistician) no less than 145,000 Jews (according to other sources, 325,000), and about 5,000 Gypsies, mostly from the Polish territories annexed by the *Reich*. Only four Jews survived.

The next step was "Einsatz [Operation] Reinhard." In the spring of 1942 Reinhard Heydrich, the mastermind of the "Final Solution" and at the same time the Nazi governor of Bohemia and Moravia, was assassinated by Czech patriots. To honor his memory the execution of the "Final Solution" in the *Generalgouvernement* was code-named "Operation Reinhard." It was placed under the overall command of SS Brigadeführer (Brigadier General) Odilo Globocnik, the SS and Police Chief of Lublin. Christian Wirth became the organizer and inspector of "Operation Reinhard." The "Operation" comprised three camps: Bełżec, Sobibór and Treblinka, which were responsible for more than two million Jewish lives.

These camps differed from the dual-capacity concentration camps of the Auschwitz and Maidanek type in one important respect: Auschwitz and Maidanek were not just death camps and were not intended only for Jews; they were also an inexhaustible reservoir of slave labor for the surrounding industrial complexes. Even though more than two and one-half million Jews perished there as a result of outright murder, there were many who survived. The "Operation Reinhard" camps were strictly death camps for Jews. No forced labor, no Gentiles, no survivors. That is why Auschwitz and Maidanek were under the jurisdiction of the SS-WVHA (Main Office of Economic Administration), while "Operation Reinhard" camps under Globocnik were subject directly to the *Führer*'s Chancellery.

The first of the "Operation Reinhard" camps was Bełżec. This camp was in operation from March to November, 1942. At least 390,000 victims died there during this period; according to Polish sources the total was 600,000. There was one survivor.

Sobibór was opened in April, 1942, and was active until the uprising of the inmates on October 14, 1942. The total number of victims, according to the expert Dr. Wolfgang Scheffler, confirms the estimate submitted by Judge Łukaszkiewicz: 250,000. There were fifty survivors.

Treblinka, the largest of the "Operation Reinhard" camps, entered the annals of Jewish martyrdom on July 22, 1942. On July 7, 1942 Dr. Irmfried Eberle, the constructor and first commandant of Treblinka, had notified the commissar of the Warsaw Ghetto, Dr. Heinz Auerswald, that Treblinka was ready to accept "resettlers." On July 22, 1942, SS Sturmbannführer (Major) Hermann Hoefle appeared at the office of Adam Czerniakow, the *Judenälteste* in Warsaw, and notified him that the "resettlement" of the Jews of Warsaw "to the East" had begun. He ordered him to deliver a quota of 6,000 Jews on that very day and for each day thereafter. Six thousand destitute and homeless Jews were gathered from the refugee centers and prisons, and the first Treblinka-bound train left the Warsaw *Umschlagplatz* that very evening. It arrived in Treblinka at 9:30 the next morning, July 23, 1942. Despite some initial apprehensions, most of the Jews of Warsaw really believed that this was no more than a bona fide resettlement. This belief was enhanced by the fact that at one point every Jew who volunteered for "resettlement" received three kilograms of bread and one kilogram of marmalade. People were starved and desperate, and 20,000 hungry souls appeared of their own accord. But after a while dark forebodings awoke in the minds of the people. The few fortunates who managed to escape from Treblinka had tales of horror to tell. Zalman Frydrych, an underground activist with "Aryan" looks, contacted Polish railroad workers and with their help was able to follow one of the transports. When he reached Sokołów, not far from Treblinka, he learned that the trains went to Treblinka crammed with people but returned empty. He also learned that no food had ever been shipped there. Finally he learned the whole terrible truth from two escapees. On his return to Warsaw he told the facts about Treblinka in *Oif der Vakh* (On Guard), the clandestine publication of the socialist *Bund*. Even though some details of the report were not entirely accurate, the total picture was clear: Treblinka was not a resettlement camp but a death camp. "Resettlement" was merely a Nazi euphemism for death. Unfortunately, the publication did not appear until late in September, 1942, and by that time the *Aktion* in which over 310,000 Warsaw Jews had been deported to their death had been completed. In addition, the circulation of the paper was very limited. Still there is no doubt that the impact of the news and the revelations of Abraham Krzepicki and other escapees contributed to that change of mood in the Warsaw ghetto which made armed resistance possible in January, 1943, followed by the uprising in April-May, 1943. From January to May, 1943, 19,000 additional Jews from Warsaw were deported to Treblinka, so that Treblinka became the grave of 329,000 Warsaw Jews. Subsequently, Jews from other Polish cities also arrived; they came from Kielce, Międzyrzec, Białystok, Tomaszów, Grodno, Łuków, Włoszczowa, Sędziszów, Częstochowa, Łochów, Kozienice, Radom, Węgrów, and many, many others, not only from Poland but also from nine other countries.

The estimates of the total of Treblinka victims vary. According to the official German court expert, the director of the Munich Institute for Contemporary History Dr. Helmut Krausnick, at least 700,000 — including the 329,000 Jews from Warsaw — died there. At the second Treblinka trial, another expert, Dr. Wolfgang Scheffler, raised this figure to 900,000 victims. The official Polish figure as given by Z. Łukaszkiewicz is 800,000; Rachel Auerbach puts it at 1,074,000. Franciszek Ząbecki, a Pole who was traffic controller at the Treblinka railroad station and on behalf of the Polish Home Army (AK) kept a daily record of all train transports, insisted that it could not possibly have been less than 1,200,000, "beyond the shadow of a doubt." The most convincing evidence was given to me personally by Samuel Rajzman, the senior of the Treblinka survivors: he had been eyewitness to an SS party celebrating the one-millionth arrival in Treblinka. That party was held long before the end of the camp's operations.

* * *

Treblinka was the reign of ultimate undiluted evil, the mesmerizing dread of unmitigated terror, combined with masterly delusion and camouflage. Let us meet the protagonists of this eerie drama. There are the hangmen: Kurt Franz, nicknamed "The Doll" because of his physical beauty behind which hid a beast in human disguise. He remembered Treblinka as "the best years of my life." His dog, Barry, was expressly trained to maul the genitals of the helpless inmates. Franz Stangl, who was sober enough to realize that behind the smokescreen of propaganda and racist mystique there was no sacred mission but only naked greed ("all they wanted was their money"). Yet, though he knew all this, he was a willing accomplice to one of the most abominable crimes in the annals of mankind. And, of course, Christian Wirth, nicknamed "Christian the Terrible," the roving bestial inspector of "Operation Reinhard," who had nothing but the most abusive epithets for the hapless victims, and who went out of his way to see that not one Jewish child should survive.

And then there are the victims who rose from the depths of despair and dehumanization to the height of selfless devotion and heroism, the leaders and fighters in the conspiracy and in the incredible revolt of the downtrodden wretches of Treblinka. Says Rachel Auerbach: "Under conditions of a terror exceeding even the terrors of Maidanek or Auschwitz, in a place where psychic depression was harder to withstand than anywhere else on earth — a plan of revolt was conceived and successfully carried out. This was perhaps the only instance of this dimension in any camp in the entire area under German occupation."[5]

We see them all in their grim, macabre heroism: the physician from Warsaw, Dr. Julian Chorążycki, the heart and brain of the revolt, who unhesitatingly offered his life when he was discovered by Kurt Franz; the Lodz engineer Galewski who fell in combat; Zev Kurland, the tragic kapo of the *lazaret*, to whom the plotters made their vow of secrecy and who, every night, under cover of darkness, tearfully recited the mourner's Kaddish for the countless victims of the day; the heroic Czech officers Zelo Bloch and Rudolf Masarek, the military brains of the conspiracy who gave their lives in the revolt; the agronomist Sudowicz, and the 14-year old boy Zalcberg who did not live to see the day of freedom.

Finally, there are those few who survived: Jankiel Wiernik, Samuel Rajzman, Shalom Kohn, Tanhum Grinberg, Samuel Willenberg, Richard Glazar, Karel Unger, the brothers Oscar and Zygmunt Strawczynski, and others, who lived to bear the unbearable burden of remembrance, and fell heir to the duty to tell the unbelievable tale of Treblinka.

One million souls entered the gates of Treblinka. Only one thousand were still alive on that memorable August 2, 1942 when they inscribed the name of Treblinka in the book of Jewish heroism. Two hundred of them broke through the barbed-wire fences. Only three score survived.

This book is their story. It consists mainly of the authentic eyewitness accounts of six survivors — undramatized, unadorned, without fabrications and hollow verbiage. The nightmare of Treblinka's hell is portrayed in simple words. Most of the material appears here in English for the first time. Nothing can give a truer picture of Treblinka than Samuel Rajzman's conclusion: "In writing about the Holocaust, we don't need authors with great imaginations. We need people who can depict the reality as it was. It was so overpowering that the facts speak for themselves."

* * *

On the site where for 400 ghastly days the blasphemy of Treblinka tormented human history there is now a monument. It shows in the center an enormous rock topped by a menorah to symbolize the 300,000 martyred Jews of Warsaw. This rock is surrounded by huge slabs of concrete from which rises a forest of thousands of granite pillars of varying shapes and sizes, representing cities, villages, and *shtetlach* lost in the Holocaust. On 150 of them are carved the names of the localities from which the murdered Jews came. The massive pillars bear the names of the countries of the victims' origin.

There is yet another monument to Treblinka not confined to stone or to geographical site. It lives in the hearts of millions of Jews, the people with the longest historical memory. It shall remain forever in our remembrance, from family to family, from generation to generation, in all our habitations.

For Jews, Treblinka is more than an unforgettable page of their thorny history. But for the non-Jewish world, it is an apocalyptic disaster. In spite of the Nazis' frenzied endeavors, the infamy of Treblinka can never be obliterated from German history. It is an indelible symbol of the bankruptcy of European civilization and of two thousand years of Christian teachings.

As a survivor of the Warsaw ghetto, I feel an affinity for Treblinka. My family and I were condemned to share the fate of Treblinka with our Jewish brothers and sisters in Warsaw. By miracle we escaped this horrible fate, but in spirit I consider myself a Treblinka survivor, and I dedicate this Scroll of mourning and anger to the memory of the men, women and children who became the ashes of Treblinka.

Alexander Donat

1. A. Rückerl, p. 11.
2. Z. Łukaszkiewicz, p. 42.
3. R. Ainsztein, *Jewish Resistance*, p. 233.
4. R. Hilberg, "German Railroads/Jewish Souls," *Society*, 1976, pp. 60-76.
5. R. Auerbach, *see* p. 59 of this volume.

IN THE FIELDS
OF TREBLINKA

IN THE FIELDS
OF TREBLINKA

RACHEL AUERBACH

The Yiddish writer RACHEL AUERBACH (1903–1976) was one of the most devoted chroniclers and eulogists of the Warsaw ghetto. She became one of the first members of the clandestine ghetto archives organized by the historian Emanuel Ringelblum, and in this capacity she recorded the testimony of Abraham Jacob Krzepicki, one of the earliest escapees from Treblinka. On the "Aryan" side she cooperated closely with Dr. A. Berman and Dr. Leon Feiner, the leaders of the Jewish underground. After the liberation she was one of the first active members of the Jewish Historical Committee in Poland.

Even though not herself a survivor of Treblinka, she was one of the group which, on the initiative of the Central State Commission for the Investigation of German Crimes in Poland, made an official inspection tour of Treblinka on November 7, 1945. She and (Captain) Dr. Joseph Kermish represented the Central Jewish Historical Commission. The other participants in the tour included Examining Magistrate Z. Łukaszkiewicz of the Siedlce Court; Prosecutor Maciejewski; Licensed Surveyor M. Tratsald; Samuel Rajzman, Tanhum Grinberg, Shimon Friedman, and M. Mittelberg, representing the "Circle of Former Treblinka Inmates." Also present at the tour of inspection were J. Szlebzak, chairman of the Siedlce District Council; Mayor Kucharek of the neighboring village of Wólka Okrąglik, and the press photographer Jacob Byk.

The literary result of the tour was the book In the Fields of Treblinka, *the most poignant report on Treblinka ever published. Then followed the editing of* The Death Brigade, *based on the experiences of Leon Wieliczker-Wells;* Der Yiddisher Oifshtand in Varshe *(The Jewish Revolt in Warsaw), and – after her emigration to Israel, where she became a permanent research staff member of the Yad Vashem Holocaust Memorial Institution – she wrote a series of books devoted to the martyrdom and destruction of Warsaw:* Baim Letztn Veg *(The Last Road),* Varshever Tzavoes *(Warsaw Heritage),* BeHutsot Varsha *(In the Streets of Warsaw),* Undzer Heshbn mitn Daitchn Folk *(Our Account With the German People), and* In Land Isroel *(In the Land of Israel).*

Her contribution to the monumental task of gathering and preserving historical

19

material of this period for posterity is very substantial. She managed to bury her material in two sealed jars under the ruins of the ghetto, where they were recovered after the war.

In the Fields of Treblinka *is published here in English for the first time. Even though not all of her judgments can be accepted without reservation, the editor considers her book as a "must" introduction for everybody who wants to understand Treblinka.*

FOREWORD

I KNOW THAT what I am now sending off for publication is far from easy reading, and definitely not for people with weak nerves. But if something like this could happen to Jews, if Jews who witnessed such things were able to tell about it and I was able to write it down, then other Jews should not spare their own feelings but should acquaint themselves with what in fact is only an infinitesimal fraction of that which was done to Jews.

Let all Jews know it: it is their national duty *to know the truth!*

And whether they want to know it or not, every effort should be made to bring the truth also to the Gentile world.

Let the full awareness of the results of fascism, totalitarianism and the political indifference and inertia of the masses spread at last to all people of all lands!

Let them know to what horrors the reconstitution of German power could lead! It is to this goal that my sad little book is dedicated.

This reportage, or whatever I could call this work of mine, represents a full picture of Treblinka. It is far from complete.

I do not say this because I want to forestall criticism. I merely wish to point out the shortcomings which I can see myself, without implying that I could have corrected them even if I had wanted to do so. I have more than one reason why I could not have written differently than I did.

There is more reflection here than description; more is *said* than is *shown*. The realism of the concrete experience of the death camp is not portrayed.

20

Several important themes have been omitted. Some of the pain is included, but not the exaltation of the Jewish individual.

Among those missing from my account are Halinka Czechowicz, the seven-year-old girl in Treblinka, the little Jewish girl who grew up only minutes before she died. As she parted from her father, she put her head on his shoulder, not because she herself wanted consolation or in order to hide her eyes for a moment from the death they had already seen. No, it was to him that she wanted to give comfort and strength. "Daddy, have no fear! Daddy, don't worry!" she said, and, "Here's my watch. Take it! You'll remain alive and so you'll have it."

Her father did indeed remain alive, and when he finishes telling his story and withdraws into himself, you can see on his face how he still constantly listens to the voice of his child, how he still feels her little fingers on the palm of his hands, giving him that little piece of gold which she had been told to guard like the apple of her eye in case she would manage to save herself. But she knew that she would no longer have any use for her watch.

I, too, can hear and see the little girl. The tears that she never shed because she did not want to make her father suffer will flow within my heart until the end of my days.

I can see hundreds and thousands of other little girls like Halinka, who blossomed like flowers confined in the ghetto, though there was no green grass amidst which to flourish. I would come upon them every day in the crowded streets and look upon their springtime in the Jewish courtyards, until all at once they vanished from view. Sometimes now, I can see a tiny hint of their shadow again in a familiar-looking face I meet today on new streets, in new cities that have become strange to me because they have no more Jews.

Where before had I seen a little redhead with eyes like that, greenish-gold and deep, with chubby cheeks, a pink little nose and tiny freckles? Where before had I gazed spellbound at a blending of Slavic and Jewish charm in the shy smile of a little child's face?

I stop in my tracks: Could this be one of our own who had been saved? Or is it merely a misplaced vestige of the past which will float about as a pale memory in the bloodstream of future generations?

Who is that man with the blond eyebrows who keeps surfacing in my memory again and again? He looks frightened, and he needs a shave, but his face seems strangely familiar. He is not too tall; his movements are furtive and his green raincoat looks worn. Was he a neighbor from Lvov or Warsaw I had never known? Perhaps he was the man who sold me beans when I managed the public soup kitchen in the ghetto. Or perhaps he once stood, one Jew among other Jews, behind a heap of vegetables laid out for sale in the market place. I've sat for hours at a time thinking about him; I've awakened at night and strained to remember him, but I still do not know who he is.

However, there is one thing I know for sure: I will never, never meet that man again. I will never be able to stop him in the street, to single him out from among a crowd of others. It would be like a weight taken from my heart if only I would be able to ask him, "Say, Mr. Jew, who are you? You look so familiar."

And who is that heavy fellow muttering under his breath, half youth, half child, with a matted head of hair like the fur of a young wild animal, wearing a frayed blue scarf, rushing about as if he had no time to stop and rest?

Who are you, little boy? Whose child are you, to make you roam so persistently through the graveyards of my memory?

I could have pointed them all out in Treblinka. That's where they were uprooted, all of them.

And I have not pointed out that tall Jewish woman—the precentress. She was a rabbi's wife or perhaps a stallkeeper who had come to Treblinka from some small town. She stood in front of a crowd of women in the disrobing barrack of the camp and led them, in a loud, clear voice, in the Hebrew and Yiddish words of the *Vidduy*, the final confession which Jews recite when death is near. She raised her arms high and cried out to God to look, to hear and to avenge.

The images of other Jewish men and women flared up like candles, with all their Jewish and human essence, seconds before they were snuffed out.

How much would my words about the prisoners of Treblinka be worth if I were not to mention Dr. Chorążycki, the heart of the Treblinka underground, who is missing? Or other principal characters in the incredible drama of the Treblinka uprising, heroes who ascended heavenward even as they fell in battle: Galewski the engineer, Moshe Ohrland and Captain Zelo Bloch from Czechoslovakia? Faces and characters which peel off from a vast camp of nameless faces, revealed to the world in the final hour of their lives—great Jews all.

The picture of the conspiracy and uprising in Treblinka could not be made to fit into such a small frame. It will have to be set aside for presentation all by itself.

And in fact even these words which I am about to submit for publication do not encompass the true picture of Treblinka as I have seen and known it.

It is no more than a sketch, a fragment of a picture, which I would like to paint during the few years that are still left to me: how a whole living, shouting, roaring world was swept away into oblivion.

Again and again, dozens of times, I will try to do this. I do not know whether I will succeed. But I will try.

Rachel Auerbach

Lodz, January, 1946

THE ROAD TO TREBLINKA. Here it is, the saddest of all roads ever to be trod by Jews, the journey made by so many hundreds of thousands of Jews in boxcars wired shut and packed beyond all limits, under conditions worse than any ever imposed upon calves shipped to the slaughterhouses.

"Water!!" we could hear the people shout from the transports as they passed by, and if anyone who could lay claim to the title of human being heard them, he could never have forgotten it. Inside the boxcar, the Jews licked the sweat from each other's skins to slake their thirst. Terror dried up the milk in the breasts of nursing mothers who begged in vain for something with which to moisten their own parched lips or those of their babies just one more time before they died. These people who were condemned to death had no right to make last requests. The rush to do away with millions of human beings within a span of months was too great for that. Whole communities died of suffocation while they were still on the road, or of asphyxiation from the fumes that rose from chlorine powder scattered in the cars, supposedly for purposes of "disinfection."

When we revisited Treblinka, we, too, should have gone there by train, or perhaps even walked, like pious pilgrims to a sacred shrine, reliving every stage of the Jewish death march, but the milestones of that particular Golgotha have yet to be set in place. At this point, we were not yet going to Treblinka to pay homage to our dead; we were going there only with a commission of inquiry to inspect the site, and the only penance we took upon ourselves was the act of enduring the cold wind which slapped our faces black and blue as we sped along in our car.

The Veterans of Treblinka. There were eight Jews in our car: two members of the Jewish Historical Commission, one press photographer, and five former Treblinka inmates: Three of these five were survivors of the Treblinka uprising; one had been transferred to other camps (incidentally, he witnessed the death of Dr. Isaac Schipper in Maidanek) and one more had been in Treblinka I, the "penal camp," not in Treblinka II, the notorious "death camp." He had been "liquidated" there in the summer of 1944, with two bullets in his body, but he had risen from the dead that night and, aided by a local peasant, had survived until the arrival of the Red Army.

Each of the Treblinka veterans, and even the three of us who had never been there, had a story all his own: veritably wheels within wheels, an entire fabric of stories, which could easily fill volumes of adventure tales. These tales would be spell-binding and gruesome, and very weird. We ourselves, today, would find them very strange and far-fetched—had we not known that they were nothing but the plain and simple truth.

At every tavern where our car stopped, at the inn where we spent the night, at the stops we made to meet our connections, the Treblinka people kept telling their stories without cease. They were driven by a mighty urge to relate the tragic and monstrous things they had seen and experienced, and to set them down in fixed form. A macabre cycle of narrative evolved from the four days that the eight of us spent together.

It is high time that the world, which is ready to start forgetting more than one thing that has happened, should become a little better acquainted with stories like these.

Memories. Once again, the picture of the death camp rises before me, as I have heard it portrayed dozens and dozens of times before: the modern, organized factory of corpses, the German murder plant, in which over a million Jewish lives were reduced to ashes, gold teeth, mattress hair and old clothes. I am gazing at the five Treblinka veterans, but in my mind I see and hear the very first man who had escaped from there. He was the one whose memoirs of eighteen days spent in Treblinka took me weeks to record and to edit back in the winter of 1942–43.

His name was Abraham Krzepicki.[1]

We both worked at a factory where "synthetic honey" was produced, and we both lived in the same apartment building. I can see him now in my memory, still alive, standing in my room: short, black-haired, with young eyes gleaming like black diamonds. Twenty-five years old, blood and milk, sheer fire, but already very wise, firm and resolute, a mature man. It was this resolution that impelled him to escape from the death camp.

His face is shining with happiness. He is holding in his hand a revolver which a Jewish girl has smuggled into the ghetto from the Polish side of town, concealed in a loaf of bread. This was one of the first weapons intended for the underground "Fighting Organization."

Already the first results have materialized: Germans were shot down by Jews during the second "resettlement" *Aktion* in January, 1943. Almost choking with excitement, he tells me incidents of the first battles with the Germans.

He uses military terminology because he served in the Polish army. His fondest dream is to join the underground groups in the woods and to organize an attack on Treblinka. Now I learn that the Jewish workers inside the death camp had cherished the same dream. They were hoping that Soviet partisans would descend upon the camp. They figured that the partisans would be tempted by the large amounts of money which they could seize there to use for their work. But unfortunately these hopes did not materialize.

Krzepicki was planning to join a group which would fight its way through to Hungary. After I had exited from the ghetto to the "Aryan" side in March, I wanted to help him get there too. I felt it would be important to save him, so that he could testify as a witness after the war, but it did not work. For by that time he had become a full-fledged member of the Fighting Organization, subject to underground discipline. His place was to remain inside the ghetto and his fate was to die as a fighter in the uprising.

And thus it happened that Abraham Krzepicki, one of the pioneers of armed resistance, did not live to see the Treblinka uprising or the collapse of Hitler's Germany, which came too late for us. He did not live to act as a guide for our inspection tour of Treblinka. He lived to do only one thing—to exchange the passive, meek death of a martyr in Treblinka for the active, heroic and beautiful death of a fighter in the Warsaw ghetto uprising.

May his name be remembered forever among the names of all the other fighters!

The Literature on Treblinka. As far back as 1942, we knew the basic facts about the Treblinka murder enterprise; we had the information from Krzepicki and other escapees. The material which was gathered in the fall and winter of 1942–43 and which I discussed under the title "I Escaped From Treblinka" now lies buried beneath the ruins of the Warsaw ghetto.[2]

Later, we received a clandestinely-published Polish pamphlet by Jankiel Wiernik, entitled *A Year in Treblinka*, which was carried out of the country by an underground courier, printed in the Yiddish and Hebrew press and subsequently published in New York in Yiddish and English translations.[3]

A series of publications about Treblinka appeared after the liberation of Poland. A pamphlet entitled *The Treblinka Hell*, by Vassili Grossman, was published in the Soviet Union; so was a series of reports in *Nowe Widnokręgi* and other periodicals. The Cracow periodical *Odrodzenie* carried two articles by S. Rajzman. A description of the Treblinka uprising was reprinted in *Dos Naye Lebn* [a Yiddish newspaper which appeared in Lodz during the period immediately following the war]. A literary treatment of the conspiracy and the revolt was prepared for publication by Public Prosecutor J. Leszczyński. Articles of varying length about the Treblinka death camp were printed also in various Polish periodicals.

In the summer of 1945, there was organized in Lodz a "Circle of Former Treblinka Inmates," which for a time assisted the Jewish Historical Commission in all the research work connected with the Treblinka death camp. Their main task was to record the testimony of individuals who had been in Treblinka. The interviews with witnesses were conducted by the Polish psychologist Janina Bukolska, who had been known as a friend of the Jews and did much good work saving Jews on the so-called "Aryan" side in Warsaw during the war.[4]

Jankiel Wiernik is working on a project to construct a scale model of the camp, displaying all the details of the annihilation machinery.[5]

The Central Jewish Historical Commission now possesses several dozen testimonies from former Treblinka inmates, maps of the camp, songs which were sung in or about Treblinka, and various other material, which will be edited and published as a separate volume in due course.

In the meantime, a Polish pamphlet, *Obóz Straceń w Treblince* (The Extermination Camp in Treblinka: Government Publishing House, Warsaw, 1946), has been published by Judge Zdzisław Łukaszkiewicz, of the court in Siedlce, who conducted an investigation and participated in our tour of inspection on November 7, 1945.

In other words, the name of this camp, which is the greatest symbolic and actual mass-grave of Polish Jewry, the site of the most heinous of German mass murders, has achieved great notoriety.

"Treblinka, there it is—
A holy place for every Jew—"

This is what a Jewish folk song, composed after the first Warsaw *Aktion* in the fall of 1942, said of Treblinka. "The Song of the Boxcars" was sung in the Jewish workshops and factories between the first and second deportations, and again between the second and the third. This song of the Warsaw Jews, their final contribution to Jewish folklore, also should be included in the literature of Treblinka.

"It's Nothing, Nothing, Nothing." Of all the Treblinka people alive or no longer living to whom I have spoken, there is one whom I particularly remember now.

This Jew was hard and shrewd, perhaps even dangerous. But his hardness was of the kind that revives and refreshes the soul.

He was skeptical, sarcastic, taciturn, and yet he could say a great deal just by the way in which he exhaled the smoke of his cigarette.

If I am not mistaken, he was a butcher by trade, a very ordinary fellow.

I came upon him shortly after the liberation, a good two years after his escape from the death camp. But the wound of Treblinka was still far from healed in his mind. His manner was still that of a hunted animal, and probably would never be any different. But unlike most of the others, he did not want to talk about what he had lived through. He had no desire to tell his story.

"You were never there? Well, good for you. So why do you need to know about it? You want to write about it?! So write all you want. Whoever wasn't there himself will never understand."

And he added something: "Treblinka is not over yet. Treblinka hasn't ended. It follows us wherever we go, just as it has been following us up until now, in the woods, in the fields, in all the nooks and crannies we had to abandon for fear that someone might give us away. Now, it's in the streets, in this restaurant where I'm still sitting with my Jewish nose, even though by right I should have been in the other world a long time ago.

"*Every man* is a murderer and so am I. I, too, would like to beat and kill, beat and kill. . . .

"It's nothing, nothing, nothing . . .

"There's neither woods nor trees in the wilderness."

He probably meant the wilderness within his own soul, which had been gouged out by the typhoon.

Will we ever attain that moral stage at which we will be able to claim reparations for the damage that was done to souls?

"Forget Your Smile, if You Want to Take a Look in Here!"
Forget your smile forever! And also forget your title of "man," if it was indeed men who have brought such things to pass!

The epic poem of Gilgamesh tells how the divinely handsome, mighty hero Enkidu, King of Babylon, consoled himself after descending into the Netherworld in search of his dead father's shadow. When he returned to the world of the living, he could no longer take pleasure in water from the springs, or satisfy his heart with the sweetness of fruit. He stopped kissing the breasts of women and no longer took a young and wild delight in the beauty of young girls. He became angry with the gods and goddesses and fell into a mood of black depression.

This happened because at long last, once and for all, he had grasped the true meaning of death, just like our own Jewish king from the Book of Ecclesiastes.

On the walls of Dante's medieval inferno there was an inscription reading, "Abandon all hope, ye who enter here!" What, then, should have been inscribed over the entrance to Treblinka?

There were only signs about depositing valuables and turning in clothing for disinfection. . . .

When the Jews arrived in the death transports, half suffocated from crowding and lack of air and from being jammed together with those who had died on the way, they were pounced upon by a mob of German and Ukrainian SS men armed with automatics, clubs and whips, who immediately began to drive them out of the boxcars and to beat them without mercy.

The new arrivals did not have a moment's chance to come to their senses. Nevertheless, they noticed some strange things. They had been told they would be "resettled" somewhere far away in the "East," where they would be put to work. But even though there had been many delays on the way, they could see that they had not traveled very far. They could see the whole structure of barbed wire fences, camouflaged with green branches, the heavy machine guns on the roofs of the barracks and in the watchtowers, ready to release a stream of bullets at a moment's notice . . .

Was this how a resettlement place was supposed to look? Could this be a labor camp or a *Ka-Tset* [concentration camp]?

No. At this point the pretense took on another form. They wanted the people to think that this was just a transfer point. Deliberate mystification was one of the most accepted tactical principles of the authorities, to be applied to every aspect of life. Later on,

German and Polish signs were put up, with instructions about changing trains.

"*Station Obermajdan! Umsteigen nach Bialystok und Wolkowysk!* [Obermajdan Station! Change here for Bialystok and Volkovisk!]"

The name "Treblinka" had already been compromised, so they kept it hidden. Painted on the lower walls of the barracks were baggage-check windows, ticket windows and a large clock, all just like a stage set. Earlier, in the summer of 1942, the masses getting out of the boxcars could look at odd signboards hanging from a high wire, with a whole list of instructions about bathing and disinfection, about what to do with money, jewelry and documents.

On some days, when transports were fewer, the comedy was carried even further. When the new arrivals turned in their valuables at the cashier's windows they were actually handed receipts. Some of the Jews, especially "Yekkes" from Germany, attached great importance to these "receipts," making sure that they had listed all their possessions so they would get back everything "later on." Nevertheless, many people got the idea very quickly and stopped fooling themselves. They could see for themselves that the signboards were fakes, intended to deceive the newcomers. Before all else, they saw piles of clothes and shoes at every turn. Almost everyone recalling his first impressions of Treblinka will tell of the pang he felt at his heart when he saw these things piled up on the ground. "So many clothes! But where are the people?"

The air gave a partial answer to that question. Even before they started burning the corpses, the stench of death hung over the murder factory. Later on, it became commingled with the smell of roasted flesh . . .

"Later on," after the fall of 1942, the Polish Jews, at least, no longer had any illusions.

No—perhaps they did hold on to some of their illusions.

Deliberately blocking out the horror stories they had heard, they still seized on every straw, on every shred of hope, just to keep themselves from having to believe that the unthinkable and the unnatural was really the truth. This even applied to what they had seen with their own eyes. Such is the law of healthy self-preservation, the law of the healthy soul, which uses this means to save itself from madness, from blank despair. Or perhaps this is just another form of subconscious resignation to fate.

The Germans had a brilliant aptitude for exploiting the situation. In their strategy of genocide, as it is now termed, psychological manipulation was just as important as ordinary technology. The psychic and psychosocial mechanisms of the victims themselves were utilized to bring about their destruction. The same guidelines were used in the preparations, in the *Aktionen* in the ghettos, on the way to the camp and in the camp itself, to destroy the greatest possible number of victims in the shortest possible span of time; to achieve the greatest gain at the least expense, with the minimum of danger and loss to their own people! This was their goal. Everything else was a means to that end: to destroy both the masses and the individual physically and mentally, to inhibit all defensive reflexes; to gull most of the people into the clutches of death almost of their own free will; to scatter, disorient, split, and divide every group and every family. Starvation, thirst, crowding, haste, terror—all these served the greater goal of murdering Jews on a gigantic scale. But the most conspicuous instrument employed to serve these ends was the big lie.

In order to silence their natural fears and to lull their healthy urge of self-defense, the victims were told that they would not be harmed; the energies of the most active among them were dissipated in a wild-goose chase after mirages of security, after papers and slips, after new numbers and stamps every day . . .

The Germans understood the power of desperation and the threat of Jewish resistance long before we ourselves did. But they also knew how to hold it down for as long as possible. Utilizing their psychological discoveries in the field of human annihilation, they brought into play methods which had never been known before and which yielded the desired results. By the time that means of neutralizing these new psychosocial methods had been discovered, ninety percent of the Jews were already dead. Those who survived had not been able to salvage anything but their personal dignity. Consistent in self-deception, no one wanted to call the thing by its real name until the end. And even on the grounds of the death camp, a few hundred meters away from the machinery of the corpse factory, there were some who refused to face the facts.

Half of the Jews were worked over with whips; the other half were bombarded with speeches from "sympathetic" SS men, with promises of employment and job offers to skilled craftsmen. Women were often asked to take towels with them into the "bathhouse."

Of course, all these ruses were applied only on days when there was more time to do so. As a rule, the rush was too great for such

31

niceties. The job was of burning urgency; there was no time to play around. August-September, 1942 was the height of the season. From six to ten thousand souls were taken out of Warsaw and other cities every day. A transport of 60 boxcars arrived; it was divided into three sections of 20 cars each and every section had to be processed in the short period allowed by the schedule. Several transports arrived every day.

Hitler was in a hurry. He was determined to get rid of the Jews of Europe even if he would come to a bad end himself. As Stefan Szende put it in the title of his book, this was "The Promise Hitler Kept."[6]

Preliminaries. "Men to the right! Women and children to the left!"

Women and children were not put through a separate "selection"; all of them were consigned to the flames.

Women and children were the first to go into the fire. But first they went into the barracks to undress. They had to leave behind whatever they still possessed, taking off everything they had on, down to the last stitch. They tied their own shoes together with laces prepared especially for that purpose, so that no right or left shoes should remain without mates. The staff also had to see to it that no part of the victims' possessions should remain concealed in the secret places of their bodies, back or front, under the arms or beneath the tongue. Gold teeth were yanked out of the victims' mouths only after they were dead. Of course, the intention was not to spare the Jews pain; it was only to save time.

Later on, when the commercial exploitation of the corpse business achieved its full scope, they also started shearing off the hair of female inmates. The hair would be steamed in kettles, dried out and finally put aboard freight trains for delivery to furniture factories as first-class mattress stuffing. Others said that the hair was sent to Germany for use as insulation mats in submarines. Treblinka exported 25 boxcars of this merchandise. . . .

Polish people still talk about the way soap was manufactured from the bodies of Jews. "Sent away for soap!" was the expression the Poles would use when they spoke of transports to Treblinka, Bełżec and Sobibor. The discovery of Professor Spanner's soap factory in Langfuhr near Danzig proved that their suspicions had been well founded. Witnesses tell us that when the corpses were burned on pyres, pans would be placed beneath the racks to catch the fat as it ran off, but this has not been confirmed. But even if the

Germans in Treblinka or at any of the other death factories failed to do this, and allowed so many tons of precious fat to go to waste, it could only have been an oversight on their part. They were fully capable of doing things like that. It was entirely in keeping with their proclivities. Only the newness of this branch of manufacturing was to blame for this omission. If the Germans ever would make another drive across Europe, they would not make this mistake again.[7]

The male inmates would undress in front of the barracks. The Germans did not bother to cut off their hair. It was not worth the trouble! Here and there, perhaps, there were a few hundred, or a few thousand, queer Jews with long, "artistic" locks of hair! Maybe there were a couple of oddball poets or professors! But the Germans did not think it worth while to look for them. So they used the men for other things. The men were driven away naked from the disrobing area, carrying their clothes in their hands to yet another assembly place. They were not allowed to leave anything behind in the disrobing area. One shift was not allowed to mingle with the next. The boxcars at the platform also had to be cleaned with lightning speed; bodies. knapsacks, bundles and human excrement had to be removed. The cars had to be nice and clean when they went back to pick up new "raw material." The next shift that entered was not supposed to notice anything "suspicious" in the cars. Whether this had any real significance or not, a principle was still a principle. This is just another example of the famous German punctiliousness.

The three categories of Jews on the camp staff, identified by red, blue and pink insignia, were responsible for upholding this principle in the boxcars, on the platform, and in the disrobing area. This is division of labor. This is organization!

The "Road to Heaven." The work proceeded without cease, smoothly and quickly.

Stripped. Inspected. Clipped. "Forward, March! *Los*!!!"

A small gate was opened at the other end of the disrobing area, and the crowd was herded onto a road which twisted along between two barbed wire fences. This road was about 300 meters long. It passed through a group of pine trees, through the famous "grove" which had been left standing when this part of the forest was cut down to build the camp. This road was called the "Schlauch" [tube]. The Germans had humorously dubbed it "Himmelstrasse" [Road to Heaven]. The journey on this road made by the stark naked

33

victims was given an equally humorous designation: "Himmel-fahrt" [Trip to Heaven, Ascension].

At the end of the "Road to Heaven," where Jews went straight into the next world, there was yet another door; this door led to the "bathing establishment." This was a gray-white building with all the accoutrements of a regular public bath in the inside: "cabins," plus a few chimneys protruding from the roof.

You entered the cabins from a corridor through doors just big enough to admit one person at a time. The door had been made so narrow on purpose, so that people who were already inside would not attempt to break down the door and escape. The cabins were lined with white tiles halfway up the walls. The floor sloped down to wide, hermetically sealed chutes facing the entrance gate. Real shower heads were set in the ceilings of the rooms, but they were not connected to any water pipe. They were connected to something else.

Initially, in the first building, there were three such cabins. Later, when the enterprise had proven "viable," it was expanded. A second "bathhouse" of the same type was constructed, bigger and nicer than the first one, with 10 cabins inside.

German and Ukrainian SS men stood on guard at either side of the "Road to Heaven" with their dogs. Unique among the dogs was Barry, a beast which had been trained to seize male inmates by their sexual organs. The SS men, too, when beating prisoners, had a predilection for hitting their victims' sexual organs; heads, breasts, bellies—all those places most sensitive to pain. Smacks from whips and canes on the naked skin, blows from clubs, and sometimes also stabs from bayonets, particularly when the victims were being shoved inside for good. The doomed Jews had to travel their last road in double time, amidst shouts, insults and indignities.

Not the smallest hint of respect in the face of the mystery of death! It was not enough that they robbed the Jews of their lives and of all else they possessed, including what was left of their bodies. They robbed them even of their last bit of human dignity, of their last right to human respect.

Total robbery! Total murder! Total brutality!!!

The entire "Trip to Heaven" was somewhat stylized on the pattern of medieval Jew-baiting. It has also been suggested that having the victims arrive at the gas chamber exhausted would help speed up the effects of the gas, and permit them to give up the ghost more quickly. "Humanitarian," wasn't it?

The Final Act. The "Trip to Heaven" is soon over.
Blows rain down from all sides, on heads, backs . . .
The Jews hurry even without being told to do so. The gas
chamber is the only place where one is safe from the smacks of
canes on the naked skin, from indignities, from the cold in the
winter time. And so they run and leap over one another, just to
experience the moment of death a little faster. Death, the great
redeemer. . . .

A witness has told us that when Jewish men were executed by
shooting, they neither groaned nor whined. They were only in a
terrible hurry. They threw off their clothing while they were still on
the way. Those who were always first in life wanted to be first here
too, to be released from life as soon as possible.

This was true also in the case of the people in Treblinka. They
were already resigned, free of all illusions. If they had any illusions
left until then, they certainly lost them during the "trip to Heaven."

But arrival at the gas chambers was not yet the final act. The Jews
had to endure the terror and agony of death under conditions of
terrible crowding. The crowd was driven forward with cries of
"Faster! Faster!" and the chambers were jammed with three times
as many people as they could hold. Those who could not be fitted
into the chambers had to stand outside and wait their turn to be
gassed. The floor of the gas chamber was sloping and slippery. The
first ones in would slip and fall, never to rise again. Those who
followed would topple over them. The chamber was packed to the
brim. The people were jammed together so closely that they
pushed each other into a standing position. Some witnesses report
that the people inside the chambers had to raise their arms and pull
in their stomachs so that more could be fitted in. And then, when
they stood pressed together, little children were slipped in above
their heads like so many bundles.

Gas was costly and therefore had to be used economically.
At last, the doors were slammed shut.
The shift was ready to die.
The motor, installed in a workshop near the bathhouse, could be
started now. First, a suction pump was brought into play to draw
the pure air from the chamber. After that, the pipe to the reservoir
of exhaust gas from the motor could be opened.

"A few minutes later," Jews who had worked in that part of the
camp recalled, "we would hear terrible screams from that building." The screams of human pain, terror and despair. At the last

moment, it seems, when the pump started to suck out breatheable air, all self-control broke and there was an outbreak of collective hysteria inside the gas chamber.

Later . . . in due time . . . all was quiet again. . . .

About 25 to 45 minutes later, the chutes on the other side could be opened and the corpses tumbled out. The bodies were naked; some of them were white, others were blue and bloated. They were always wet, covered with their final sweat, befouled with the filth of their final defecation, with rivulets of blood running from their mouths and noses.

"When they ran into the building on the entrance side," Jankiel Wiernik, who spent more time than the others as witness to these happenings, recalled, "I heard them shouting all sorts of things: 'Sh'ma Yisroel!' 'Down with Hitler!' 'Away with Hitler!' 'Oy vey, Mama!' But when the chutes on the opposite side were opened, they were all quiet, all still, all—equal in death."

Now the gravediggers came running up to grab the corpses and carry them off.

Sometimes, when the chutes were opened, the corpses were found standing erect like so many dolls, their dead eyes wide-open. They were usually tangled in a mass, their arms and legs wrapped so tightly around each other that it took a great effort to drag out the first batch. The others then tumbled down the ramps by their sheer weight. Meanwhile, the gravediggers were driven and beaten without mercy. This was the hardest and most dangerous work in the entire camp. The corpse carriers generally lasted only a few days at their jobs. When they could no longer carry on, they were liquidated and replacements were taken from among the new arrivals.

Even while the corpses were dragged away in double time by the gravediggers, their mouths were examined. Their false teeth and gold caps were quickly yanked out by Jewish "dentists" and the corpses laid out, end to end, in the mass graves which had been prepared for them. Later, during the winter of 1943, they were taken straight to the pyres to be burned. It sometimes happened that one of the people regained consciousness on the way, and then the Ukrainian SS men would finish him off with a bullet.

If not, he had to be buried anyway.

The gas chamber was cleaned out.

This shift was finished; a new shift could be admitted.

The "Lazaret." To keep the chase along the "Road to Heaven" from being held up in any way, those who were too weak to run were ordered liquidated in the area in the front section of the camp known as the "lazaret" [infirmary].

This witty designation had been bestowed upon a long, always open ditch near the ditches into which those who were dead on arrival were tossed. These ditches were used also for the garbage and refuse from the barracks, and a fire was kept burning in them at all times. Even during the early months of Treblinka's operations this had been the camp pyre. Those who had become sick, or had been "selected" at work or at roll call, whether or not they had been found guilty of some "transgression," were taken here to be shot, next to the ever-burning flames. "You are going to the *lazaret*" meant, in camp slang, that you were going to be shot. (In the Lvov death brigade, a similar arrangement was referred to as "the hospital.")[8] But to give added emphasis to the joke, something original was added at Treblinka. Since a lazaret may be expected to have a doctor on hand, an individual with a Red Cross armband was stationed there. His task was to lead the old and the sick to the ditch, sit them down facing the fire, and make sure that they dropped straight into the ditch when they got their bullet in the back of the head. Before going to their "treatment," which cured them forever of all their ills, whether chronic or not, the sick people passed through a reception room set up in a special barrack. A Red Cross flag flew from the roof of this building. Inside, there was regular furniture, including sofas upholstered with red plush, and an infirmary window. This was where the sick people took off all their clothes.

Children, too, were often liquidated in the *lazaret* rather than in the gas chambers. These were the toddlers too little to be able to run, children who had no mothers to undress them and lead them by the hand on their "trip to Heaven," or children of large families whose mothers had their hands full. These children were separated from those bound for the gas chambers—in order to "make things easier on the way to the bathhouses." All children of this category were processed in the *lazaret*. If the "caretaker" was kind, he would smash the child's head against the wall before throwing him into the burning ditch; if not, he would toss him straight in alive. There was no danger that small children would climb out of the ditch and would have to be dealt with all over again. Therefore, in Treblinka as in other places, children were often thrown live into the fire, or

37

into the regular mass grave. The most important consideration was to conserve bullets or gas wherever possible. It was also believed that children did not die as easily and quickly from a bullet or from gas as adults did. Doctors had given some thought to this matter, and they had concluded that children have better circulation because their blood vessels were not yet hardened.

Divertimento: The Science of Annihilation. In Treblinka, as in other such places, significant advances were made in the science of annihilation, such as the highly original discovery that the bodies of women burned better than those of men.

"Men won't burn without women."

This is not an inelegant joke, a bad pun with a macabre theme. It is an authentic quotation from conversations actually conducted at Treblinka. The statement was based on fact.

It is all very simple. In women the layer of subcutaneous fat is better developed than in men. For this reason, the bodies of women were used to kindle, or, more accurately put, to build the fires among the piles of corpses, much as coals are utilized to get coke to burn . . . Blood, too, was found to be first-class combustion material.

Another discovery in this field: Young corpses burn up quicker than old ones. Obviously, their flesh is softer. The difference between young humans and older ones is the same as that between veal and beef. But it took the German corpse industry to make us aware of this fact.

It took some time for the technology and terminology of this new industry to reach full development, and for specialists to complete their training in the annihilation of humans, and in the destruction of the dead bodies. One Treblinka document stated: "The burning of corpses received the proper incentive only after an instructor had come down from Auschwitz." The specialists in this new profession were businesslike, practical and conscientious. The instructor in incineration at Treblinka was nicknamed by the Jews as "Tadellos" (perfect); that was his favorite expression. "Thank God, now the fire's perfect," he used to say when, with the help of gasoline and the bodies of the fatter females, the pile of corpses finally burst into flames. In the Lvov sandpile the camp commandant would reward the Jewish gravediggers' brigade on such occasions with a keg of beer. His pet phrase was *"Nur anständig und sauber"* [only do it clean and proper]. The corpses themselves were always referred to as *"Figuren,"* and it is significant to note that this euphemism was not restricted to Jews who had already died. In many camps, this term was used also with reference to Jews who were still alive. It seems that the Germans already regarded the Jews who still lived as corpses, except that for the time being they were still capable of carrying out certain functions because the Germans commanded them to do so. After that, again on command, they would undress, receive their bullet or their portion of gas, and lie down dead along with the other "figures."

How queer, how odd is this new German reality! All you need to do is block out certain psychological reflexes in order to enter that German "beyond"—beyond the barbed wire and beyond normal human feelings. Nietzsche's *Beyond Good and Evil* finally has been translated into reality. During those few years of war the German annihilation industry certainly made some impressive strides toward that end.

A constant exchange of discoveries went on between the bases of annihilation. They were forever rationalizing and coordinating their working methods.

In addition to familiarizing themselves in theory with all the general principles of terror and destruction, the SS men in the *Sonderkommandos* took practical courses in bestiality. Such celebrated units as the "Einsatz Reinhard" in Central Poland, or the "Rollkommando" in Galicia, with their first-rate experts in all the rules for conducting *Aktionen*, "liquidations" and shootings, and with methods of setting up death camps, also saw to the training of new cadres of specialists who would succeed them.

The branch concerned with the cremation of the dead really came into full flower after the defeat at Stalingrad. Beginning with February, 1943, when the Germans first started making preparations for the eventuality that they would have to quit the areas they had occupied in Eastern Europe, they tried to erase all the traces of their mass murder operations. This new branch, which took its orders directly from Berlin, was set up in all the important places where there was a significant number of mass graves by a personal visit from Heinrich Himmler. Himmler exerted his influence to alter the methods of liquidating the remnants of Jewry in the occupied areas. Jews were no longer to be buried in mass graves or shot into open ditches. So that no one would have to drag the corpses, and thus have to do the same work twice, the Jews were shot right next to the burning garbage dumps, facing the fire. The victim received a kick from the rear so that he would not fall sideways, but rather straight forward, directly into the flames. Larger groups were also shot near the fires, and the staff had a special procedure for tossing the bodies into the flames. In the newer establishments gassing was also done on the pattern of Auschwitz, just a step away from the crematorium. "Going to one's death" was no longer referred to as "going to the gas" or "going into the chamber," but rather as "going up the chimney." In Treblinka, where there were no crematoria, but only giant open pyres, no bodies were buried anymore. Those who went into the chambers arrived in time to watch the flames that would consume them that very day.

Psychological Digression. Two years after World War I, there appeared in Germany a detailed *History of the War*; if I'm not mistaken, the work consisted of two volumes. Its author was the German-Jewish psychiatrist and sexologist Magnus Hirschfeld. A large part of the work was devoted to an analysis of the murders perpetrated during World War I—most of them, incidentally, by the Germans.

German scholars would do well to take an interest in certain phenomena of World War II as well. They are closer to the subject matter and perhaps it would be easier for them to explain certain psychological and sociopsychological mechanisms of the German mass murders. It is easier for us to ask questions than to answer them.

Let us note some facts:

Altogether, there were in Treblinka approximately 30 to 40 SS men, and 200 to 300 Ukrainian guards; that was all. This was the entire staff of hangmen in that mechanized automatic murder factory, which did not need too much personnel to do its work.

What manner of people were these?

How could they do what they did?

Fact: the sight of this terrible, elemental catastrophe, the picture of the most shattering mass tragedy which no human eye had ever seen before, did not have much of an effect on the Germans who were working there. The depths of human suffering which were revealed every minute, the tragic family scenes which were played out here at every step, left them indifferent. The simple, elemental feeling of pity appeared to have completely atrophied in them. All through the greatest horrors their nerves remained unruffled.

And one must remember that they were not only passive spectators at this tragedy.

The catastrophe never touched them, and this alone was enough to give them a splendid self-confidence. Precisely in the face of this abyss of human degradation into which they watched masses of Jews drowning, they saw themselves as masterful and exalted.

Such epithets as "sadists" or "outcasts," "degenerates" and "criminals" don't supply much of an explanation. It is true that criminal tendencies were thoroughly exploited by the Nazi regime. Underworld figures afflicted with the weirdest antisocial sicknesses, from every kind of actual and potential criminality, were harnessed as a source of energy for the regime, just as water power is harnessed for driving turbines. They were indeed a reservoir of annihilation energy essential to the service of the state and the war effort, a national treasury of evil.

In most of the camps and prisons of Nazi-occupied Europe, German professional criminals were brought in and appointed as "kapos," *Stubenälteste* and the like. Their job was to terrorize the Jewish prisoners who had been "recruited" for work from among the local population. They were given a free hand to do this and needed no special incentives for the job . . . Their zeal came along with the power and also from their own enthusiasm. They far exceeded the required "quota" of murder and mayhem.

It also was not too hard to involve German "political criminals" in a working team of terror; many of them, just like the professional criminals, did the dirty work of spying upon, torturing and terrorizing the non-Germans in the prisons and camps. Initially, they did this out of cowardice; later, they were driven by a newly-awakened taste for sadism and power. Needless to say, the chief victims in every instance were the Jews.

Local underworld elements, too, emerged in Nazi-occupied countries and became the most important collaborators of the "New Order"—the agent, the informer, the spy, the instrument of terror, the truncheon raised over the head of the population. Even the Jews had such an individual; the pimp and professional criminal Shmaye Grauer, who, in his role as the "Jewish Dictator" in the community, became the hangman and liquidator of the Lublin ghetto. Nor was this an isolated instance. Almost every ghetto, every camp, every Jewish labor brigade, had its own Shmaye Grauer, big or small. The Germans knew how to mobilize underworld elements, even among the Jews, who, in this wild orgy of murder and robbery, finally got their chance to settle accounts once and for all with those whom they considered "the simpletons": to vent all their jealousy and hatred against the intellectuals and against those who were socially productive and established. It was at the expense of such people that they tried to survive.

But the main psychological and sociopsychological problems in explaining the death camps and mass executions are not posed by the professional criminals, and not by the born or trained sadists who did their dirty work primarily inside the prisons and concentration camps. *The big question mark is represented by the ordinary, simple, normal Germans who, with the self-awareness and calm deliberation of respectable functionaries of the state, committed the most heinous crimes ever perpetrated in this world.*

Percentagewise, their participation in the mass murder was the greatest. They did it without any emotion, in full, cold-blooded awareness of what they were doing. And that is why they were the most dangerous and the most difficult to understand.

We read and we hear about the things which even these supposedly "normal" Germans did and we wonder whether their racial theorists were not right after all. Perhaps the German really are made of a different sort of flesh and blood than the rest of mankind.

Clearly, the refrains of Rosenberg's theories and the smooth phrases of Goebbels' propaganda alone could not have brought about such a basic change in human nature. Their pat phrases about the "mission of the German spirit" and other things German were only a transparent thieves' cant into which every German could read his own meaning, and a very simple one at that. They deliberately appealed not to some sort of idealism but to the predatory urge, to national and personal egotism and megalomania. These, too, are elemental human emotions. Just as Hitler based his power on the lowest, most depraved elements in the collective social organism, so, too, he influenced individuals by appealing to their basest instincts and impulses.

The enslavement of the German individual to the regime, on the one hand, and the Nazi system's unlimited power over whole populations in the occupied territories, over the life and death of hundreds of thousands of victims, on the other—all this created a unique psychological climate which could not fail to have its effects. The Nazi propaganda of limitless national egotism and megalomania, of training in satanism, or at least in carrying out the basest and most depraved orders with cowardly obedience, had its effect *on almost every German.*

It appears that the more one kills, the greater is the desire to remain alive oneself. One's own small, mean existence becomes all the more important.

In Treblinka, there was nothing more banal than death. But not the death of the hangmen themselves—oh, no! They feared more for their lives in Treblinka than anywhere else. All their zeal for their "work" derived in large measure from the fact that, by virtue of their participation in the "Treblinka *Sonderkommando*," they were exempt from front-line duty. That was the main thing. But just being in the *Kommando* wasn't everything; one had to demonstrate one's worthiness to be part of such a *Kommando*. If one could prove that he was a particularly proficient and dedicated worker at the job of annihilation, then he could stay on and get promoted. This was an opportunity for which SS men vied with one another in bestiality.

Fear is one of the most powerful and generally most corrupting instincts. Hitler's hold on the German people was based on fear, or rather, on fear above all else. One can think of the Nazi system as a structure, or a hierarchy, founded on primitive fear.

In that vast sea of boundless brutality, sadism, and cynicism, I have heard of only one instance where a German actually declared that he would rather to the front lines than stand by and look upon what was going on at the camp. But this probably happened at the beginning of his career. After a week or so, he had become one of the most evil among the evil. I know of one such metamorphosis in a Protestant minister, and also in a schoolteacher. The German nobility, and the intellectual elite, too, was represented in the ranks of the murderers. There was a Baron von Eupen in Treblinka, and there were some noted physicians and scientists in other camps. (Baron von Eupen, who was commandant of Penal Camp Treblinka I, was one of the best-known personalities among the camp commanders. Some witnesses report that he was not only a baron but also a writer; others say that he had been a lawyer before the war. What is certain is that he distinguished himself by his sadistic imagination and ingenuity. He kept fine saddle-horses and hounds at the camp, and one of his most frequent pleasures was to have his horse ride over a prisoner and trample him beneath its hooves.) These members of Germany's elite quickly made their peace with the "new German reality" and, in fact, soon felt quite at home in it.

If these individuals all had been convinced anti-Semites, Hitlerites, demons and murderers, it might have been easier to understand. But this was not so. The demonic and macabre became everyday trifles here. The greatest shame of the German people is that they persecuted innocent, defenseless human beings, that they killed men and women, the old and the sick, and snatched little children from their mothers' arms—all, in the great majority of cases, for petty, trivial motives. They were cowardly and mean in the extreme—twisted little screws in a giant machine of crime.

And it is we who became the objects of this machine; we stood eyeball to eyeball with a mad, depraved devil. Powerless and disarmed, outlawed, isolated, abandoned, with fettered hands and feet and paralyzed souls.

The German Idyll. Always cheerful, always spry and lusting for life. That's how the Germans were at Treblinka. "A young nation of instinctive vigor, biologically sound." This is how they were characterized in their own idiom.

In order to enliven the monotony of their murderous work, the Germans installed at Treblinka a Jewish orchestra. This was in keeping with the established procedure in other camps. The orchestra had a twofold purpose: first, to drown out, as much as that was possible, the screams and moans of the people being driven to their death in the gas chambers; second, to provide musical entertainment for the camp staff, who represented two music-loving nations—Germany and the Ukraine! A band was needed also for the frequent entertainments which were arranged here. In time, a choir was organized and there were even amateur theater performances, but unfortunately the outbreak of the uprising frustrated the great plans for the advancement of culture and art which had been concocted for Treblinka.

Among the doomed "Judenscheisse" [Jewish shit] one could find all the talent one's heart desired. No general in ancient times could have found so much talent among a conquered people to delight his heart. A true lotus land full of slaves with specialized skills.

If musicians were wanted, musicians were on hand; if singers were needed, these were available, too. (After all, the Jews are a musical people also!) Even sculptors came in handy for decorating gateposts and watchtowers with symbolic reliefs. Or perhaps tailors, shoemakers, or saddlers were required—one whistle was sufficient to round up as many of the best craftsmen as were needed. During the *Aktionen* in the ghettos, the Jews actually paid for the privilege of being used as slave labor, particularly where

Jewish lives and bodies were not worth a penny. And if at any time one of the German bosses took it into his head to liquidate one or another of the craftsmen, he could pick out a replacement from the very next transport to arrive. When there was a letup in transports, as happened during the winter of 1943, and several hundreds of additional workers were needed for the camp highway in Treblinka I, a few of the "boys" from the *Sonderkommando* were sent into Warsaw [to get more personnel]. The rest of the personnel and the hardware that were needed for a small-scale *Aktion* could be found right in the camp. They brought in over 7,000 or 8,000 additional Jews, so there would be plenty to choose from. After all, by the end of the year they would have to put all that "Scheisse" into the gas chambers anyway. What's the difference, sooner or later? Herr von Eupen needed the workers, so he personally went along with the expedition and placed himself at its head. For him such a ride was like a winter hunting trip, for his special sort of game. Some think that this was the reason for the "January *Aktion*" in the Warsaw ghetto.[9]

Jews put up a stiff resistance to this *Aktion*. This was the first time they took the opportunity to put up a fight against the German "hunters."

In Lvov, the commandant of the Jewish gravediggers' detail wanted to find some clothes for "his" Jews so they would be able to change after they had completed their odoriferous job. He therefore brought in two shipments of wealthy Jews from town and liquidated them; that was how he got the needed clothes.[10]

At the head of the band in Treblinka was Arthur Gold, the former conductor of one of the best chamber music groups in prewar Warsaw. Before him, there had been another band. (According to Abraham Krzepicki's testimony, a band of four musicians from the nearby town of Stoczek used to perform at Treblinka during August, 1942.) Many musicians passed through Treblinka; most of them had brought their instruments with them. They had seen their own families disappear in the gas chambers and now they remained alive here for a brief period. Every day they stood up and performed; this was the Treblinka "concert in the square." The music had a devastating effect on the Jewish workers and on the people who were being driven to their deaths. It shattered what was left of their emotional stamina. But for the Germans, it was a "boost," a tonic for tired nerves.

The music flourished. Treblinka even had its own special march, a Treblinka anthem. Both the text and its musical arrangement were local products. The Jews sang the Treblinka song at the roll calls and every time they marched out to work. Here is the last stanza of the Treblinka anthem:

> Work, obedience and duty
> Must be our whole existence,
> Until we, too, will catch a glimpse
> Of a modest bit of luck.

The "modest bit of luck," you understand, refers to a bullet in the back of the head at the lazaret . . .

The SS men were fairly generous to the musicians in the orchestra. They let them have shorter working hours, or even excused them from work altogether, so that they could have time to practice. When it came time to liquidate them, the SS did it, of course, without so much as a blink of an eyelid. Entertainment and liquidation were two completely separate things: Suppose a householder raises a calf or a pig. When it comes time for him to slaughter the animal, won't he go ahead and do it?

There were sports too, at Treblinka; light athletics and boxing. The people who engaged in these sports also enjoyed certain privileges—of course only up to a point, that is, up to their "regrettable" liquidation. They got better food, and had to do less work than the others. Tournaments were arranged.

Oh, the Germans certainly felt at home in Treblinka! Their habits and ways were catered to assiduously. And how hard the Germans worked at relaxing and having a good time! Treblinka stood out among the other camps chiefly due to the fun one could have there, and the novel amusements that were devised all the time.

Here, the creativity in human nature found expression in a myriad little details.

The following is just one case in point:

In other camps, too, answering the call of nature entailed all sorts of threats and chicanery, particularly in the matter of time limits. In the Janowska camp at Lvov, for example, there were "Scheisskarten" [shit cards] and people risked death for "misuse" of these cards. In various camps, there were special "Scheissmeister" [shit masters] who were responsible for seeing that nobody should stay in the toilet longer than allowed . . . But in Treblinka, there

46

was an "Oberscheissmeister" [head shit master]. The originality here consisted mainly in this man's attire: he was dressed half like a Circassian and half like a rabbi, with a big alarm clock suspended from his neck. He looked so funny that, according to witnesses, even the Jews, who felt sorry for him, had to laugh whenever he came into view. The office of "head shit master" was held by a merchant from Czestochowa who had a typically Jewish face; this in fact was the reason he had been chosen for the job. I could tell dozens of tragicomic stories involving this man, but, O God, it isn't my intention to compile a collection of anecdotes about a death camp! I merely want to show how the Germans' minds worked in relation to such matters and how much they hankered after some fun.

"What's so surprising about that?" one simple Jew, who had seen all this with his own eyes, once asked me. "They were young, healthy, well-fed, had plenty to drink, wallowed in Jewish money, their pockets stuffed with diamonds from Jews, and they were exempt from front-line duty. What more could they have wanted? So they amused themselves at the expense of the Jews and poked fun at our shame and our suffering."

This was the psychological explanation given by a Jew, and it was probably correct.

In the morning, when new transports of Jews arrived, the entire staff of SS men, well rested and freshly shaven, in top condition inside and out, would be on hand to receive the newcomers. You could tell the camp commandant by his white gloves and by his fine patent leather whip. Indian summer in Poland can be beautiful. When the weather was good during the September days of the "Warsaw cauldron,"[11] the sun was broiling hot, just like in mid-summer. The commandant would then come out into the yard in a white uniform. He was a captain on active duty. Since the weather was so nice, it was a good idea to give his summer wardrobe one last airing.

In the German section of the camp there was a corner in which rabbits, foxes and squirrels were kept. There was also a pond in which ducks swam around, and there was even talk of bringing in a deer. This corner with its tame animals was referred to, with provincial pretentiousness, as the "zoo," and the Germans were very proud of it. They also planted a garden in the sandy soil, with flowers—lots of flowers.

Some Jews were expressly assigned to the task of cultivating and pampering the flower beds. The most beautiful and variegated ones were located at the entrance to the new gas chambers.[12] From time to time, Treblinka received distinguished visitors: Wehrmacht generals from Małkinia, SS officers from Lublin, Białystok and other places. First, the SS visitors were given a tour of the operation. They were shown the workings of the various phases of production and were smugly permitted to admire its "efficiency." It is said that when Himmler visited Treblinka late in February, 1943, a special "attraction" was prepared for him: a party of young women, who had been specially selected for this purpose so that the supreme SS and police chief of the Reich could take aesthetic pleasure in looking at their nude bodies as they demonstrated the workings of the camp, being driven into the "bathhouse" and then dumped out as corpses. . . .

As the Italian saying goes, "*Se non è vero, è ben trovato.*" [Even if it's not true, it's well invented.] It is certain that Himmler favored the workshops with a visit and that he was recognized there by witnesses who had known him from newspaper photographs.

Witness Samuel Rajzman tells us that in April, 1943, the Treblinka plant received a visit from Governor General Hans Frank. After a tour of the death factory, the distinguished visitors were invited to a meal. They ate, drank, talked and smoked cigarettes. Afterwards, the guests were escorted to their fine limousines which were waiting to take them home. There were handshakes, military salutes, and arms raised in the Nazi salute: "Heil Hitler!"

After the visitors had gone, the German staff might be a little tired, but there was still some work left for them to do before they could retire for the day. There was the roll call square to be inspected; there might be a chance to shoot a couple of Jews. Perhaps a Jewish swindler would be turned up among the workers with a piece of moldy bread in his pocket. In that case there would be a public trial; he would be given 50 to 100 lashes and then strung up with his head down as a good object lesson for the other Jews. Or perhaps, on that particular day, he'd simply be finished off by a bullet because everybody was in a good mood. There had been better reports from the front. A major counter-offensive at Kerch. . . . In any event, nobody would be permitted to leave the square until after a little speech had been delivered. If you happened to be tipsy, your speeches would be that much better. True, that whole gang of Jews wouldn't be left around to muck up this world much longer. Nevertheless, every opportunity had to be used to educate them. As everybody knew, the education of inferior individuals and peoples in the virtues of order and duty was one of the noblest duties of an SS man.

Afterwards, the staff would stroll back to the German barracks and stretch out for a nap or perhaps even turn in early. After all, the work was a grind, even if it was not unpleasant.

In short, life at Treblinka was idyllic.

For the German staff, Treblinka, a duty post far behind the front lines, was literally a country resort. The trouble is just that we cannot spend too much time in the German section of the camp where this sunny mood prevailed! We must return to the *raison d'être* of this country estate, to the place where the greatest "Höllenspektakel [inferno show]" of the whole operation unfolded.

Only the German language has a word like "Höllenspektakel." "Galgenhumor" [literally "gallows humor" i.e., macabre humor] too, is a word from the German lexicon.

The Little Peepholes. No matter how much we have heard or read about Treblinka, we will always learn something new: something to rekindle unbearable pain and anger in our hearts, something to keep us awake at night.

For instance, we had believed for a long time that the final agony in the gas chambers, where most of our relatives and friends were asphyxiated, lasted just 20 to 25 minutes, or half an hour at the most. We have now learned from Jankiel Wiernik's account that the death throes in the new, larger gas chambers (in Treblinka) took longer than it had in the old chambers. In fact, they often went on for as long as one hour because the Russian tank motor which supplied the chambers with exhaust fumes did not put out gas sufficient to fill the larger space and the wider pipes. The output was not sufficiently large and effective. Wiernik also mentions in passing that sometimes the Jews would be made to stand packed in the chamber all night long without any gas ever being let in. In these cases the victims would use up all the air, so that many died from lack of oxygen even before the gassing had begun. Recently one more witness has turned up: Yekhiel Reichman, who worked side by side with Wiernik in the strictly off-limits area where the gas chambers were located. Reichman has related additional details about how long it took to die in the gas chambers.

During the early winter of 1943, when the transports to Treblinka became less frequent, totalling two or three a week at most, the Jewish workers in the camp began to starve, because they no longer had the food packages brought in by new Jewish arrivals to fall back upon. The German and Ukrainian SS men found themselves with not enough to do. For this reason, the German and Ukrainian staff, led by Ivan, who ran the motor for the gas chamber, instituted a novel "amusement" for times when no new transports were scheduled to arrive.

There were little glass peepholes set into the walls of the corridor alongside the gas chambers. These little windows had been put there for a practical purpose: it enabled one to look inside the chambers. Perhaps more gas was needed. Was this particular shift finished, so that the chutes could be opened to dump out the bodies and an order could be phoned in to send along the next shift? But now, in addition to this strictly utilitarian purpose, the windows could be used to satisfy another sort of German curiosity.

Curiosity, as we know, is the mother of knowledge. Now often, SS men pressed their noses to these little windows to watch the mass agony that was going on inside the chamber.

They considered it a special treat when Ivan took the time to pump out the pure air and to let in the exhaust fumes either gradually or not at all, while the Jews stood packed inside the chamber, as the oxygen behind the hermetically sealed doors became less and less. ... They could watch eyes begin to bulge, tongues begin to protrude and mouths begin to twist. They could observe how a child, held high above the heads of the others by its mother so that it should not be crushed, remained alive while the mother stood erect, wedged among the others, her head drooping and her arms going rigid in the stiffness of death. ...

It was interesting to see how long the Jews would be able to hold out.

This experiment, by the way, could be a very serious and significant thing. Perhaps in time it could yield a method in which no exhaust fumes would have to be used at all and asphyxiation would take place with no need to spend money on chemicals. Mechanics would then replace chemistry. Treblinka was ambitious. In this way Treblinka could bring about a true revolution and create a new era in the technology of mass murder. The problem was how to keep the chamber hermetically sealed. The motorless procedure still took too long because some oxygen always kept seeping in.

Sometimes as long as 48 hours passed before all signs of life in the chambers would cease.

Imagine what the faces of these observers in the little windows must have looked like to the Jews who were being asphyxiated inside.

Such ideas—naturally just pale, dim reflections of all this—must have been portrayed by our preachers in olden times when they frightened sinners with the agonies suffered by the soul as it left the body after burial.

The Barber Shop. Yekhiel Reichman worked near the gas chambers, first as a "barber" and later as a "dentist," yanking the gold teeth from the mouths of the corpses. Reichman worked as a "barber" for only three days. But even though he spent quite a few more months in Treblinka, and witnessed and survived a good deal more than an American or English reader would believe, he still thinks that these three days which he spent as a "barber" were the most horrible of all.

"Every time I think about it, I feel like I'm going crazy," Yekhiel recalls. And as a rule this fair-haired man is even-tempered and calm. "I must not think about it."

He would cut off the women's hair before they went to their death. Some of them were naive enough to ask him what was going to happen to them.

"Yehudi, what are they going to do with us?"

They would stare him in the face, waiting for him to allay their fears and make them feel better. . . .

Some of them, particularly young girls, asked the "barber" not to shave them down to the skin but to leave them at least some short curls. Perhaps they were just trying to lull themselves into believing that they were being shaven only for reasons of hygiene and cleanliness before being taken to the "bathhouse." They remembered similar insults from the "good old days" when Jews still had been able to obtain official permits to travel on trains but had to produce a "delousing certificate" for this purpose. Some of the fanciest ladies had had to let their heads be shaven because they were suspected of having lice . . . But by now most of the women in Treblinka knew very well . . . all too well . . . After September, 1942, in Poland, it was difficult not to know. . . .

Can you understand what it means for a woman to have her hair cut off? That was how the Jewish "brides" of Treblinka were readied for a macabre marriage.[13] The devil himself held the black candles for the ceremony, and the reflection of the flickering candlelight was frozen in the deathly green eyes of the "barber."

I have read in Stefan Zweig's biography of Marie Antoinette how

51

they came to the queen's prison cell to cut off her hair on the morning of her execution. And I have read elsewhere how the hair of unfortunates about to be beheaded turned white the moment it was touched by the razor of the executioner, to be shaven off before their heads were chopped off.

There were hundreds of thousands of Jewish Marie Antoinettes in Treblinka and elsewhere, starting with little girls, six years old, who had just finished growing their first pigtails.

In the Light of Statistics. How many Jews were killed in Treblinka? In all likelihood, it will never be possible to establish the figures with scientific accuracy. There are two sources upon which estimates can be based: The testimony of Jewish survivors and railway documents from the Treblinka station. Unfortunately, only a very few of the documents have survived. The rest have been lost in the confusion of war. Nevertheless, the investigating commission set up by the Polish government has been able to establish, on the basis of extant papers, the probable minimum number of Jews who perished in Treblinka.

On the basis of the commission's findings and of our own calculations, we believe that the figure of over 3,000,000 Jews killed in Treblinka, which has been cited by various authors, is definitely too high. The true figure was probably a little over one million.

The mass executions in Treblinka began on July 23, 1942, which that year happened to be the date of Tisha b'Av [the traditional Jewish day of mourning and fasting for the Temple in Jerusalem], and definitely ended in the middle of September, 1943. The largest number of transports were brought in during the months of August, September, October, November, and the first half of December, 1942. At the end of August there was a hiatus of one week because too many corpses and too much clothing had accumulated and the camp staff was unable to cope with the work load. Subtracting that one week, there still remain four and one half months, with 144 days of full "production," in the gas chambers. According to all the testimony that has been heard, one to three transports would arrive at Treblinka each day. Each transport consisted of an average of 60 boxcars, and each boxcar held between 80 and 150 people. According to a number of witnesses, there were days when the transports had above-average passenger loads, and the number of transports arriving was more than three. On such days the gas chambers were in operation until 1 a.m. and finished off more than 20,000 corpses within 24 hours. But on the other hand there were days when the transports were much smaller, particularly those from Germany, Czechoslovakia, and other West European countries, with the deportees arriving in passenger trains which were not as crowded (except that there were many trunks and special baggage cars). Besides, we must take into account the possibility that the witnesses might have counted each 20-car section which was brought onto the camp siding from the Treblinka station as a separate transport. As I have already stated, each transport, after pulling into the Treblinka station, would be split up into sections, with each section moved by a special locomotive to the unloading platform in the front section of the camp. (The reason for this procedure was that the platform at the end of the Treblinka siding, which was behind the gate inside the fenced-off camp grounds, could accommodate no more than 20 cars at a time.)

Thus, we are assuming an average of one transport daily with 60 boxcars each, and 100 people in each car, for the "busy season" of Treblinka "production." This would be equivalent to an average of 6,000 people per day. Multiplied by 144 days this would yield a total of 864,000 souls.

From the middle of December, 1942 until the middle of January, 1943—the Gentile holiday season—there was a pause in transports, a vacation of sorts. After this pause, the shipments became much less frequent. Two, or at most three, transports would arrive each week. During March and April hardly any transports arrived. The last transport seen by the Jewish witnesses arrived in mid-May, 1943; it consisted mainly of people deported from Warsaw after the Warsaw ghetto uprising.

After February, 1943, the emphasis in Treblinka's "production" program was shifted to the cremation of the corpses, which were dragged out of the mass graves during that period. In the Treblinka uprising on August 2, 1943 most of the camp's buildings were burned down; some of the Germans and Ukrainians were killed and most of the Jewish inmates either were killed in the fighting or managed to escape. However, a few of the buildings survived, notably the masonry building which housed the gas chambers and in which transports of Jews were gassed until as late as September, 1943. We know for certain that transports of Jews from Białystok arrived during that period. Taking into account all the information available to us, we figure that at least 25 transports of Jews perished in Treblinka between mid-January and September, 1943 (or about the time of the uprising) and about 10 transports after the uprising—or about 35 transports in all. According to our previous estimate of average numbers of cars per train and deportees per car, this makes a total of 210,000 souls. Added to the total for the "busy season" of transports, this would yield a grand total of 1,074,000; in other words, just over one million Jews. (Judge Łukaszkiewicz in the work cited above estimates that a total of 800,000 Jews perished in Treblinka.)

This is the most likely figure. The Germans certainly kept an accurate record of the number of bodies removed from the gas chambers. We know this from the testimony of a Jewish locksmith named Turowski, who recalls a safe in the German barracks were documents were stored, with a button with which a short circuit could be created in order to incinerate the safe's contents. We also know that in the early days the Jews were told as they undressed and turned in their money to keep 1 złoty in order to pay "for the bath." A Ukrainian guard would sit in a wooden hut at the entrance to the "Road to Heaven" and collect the złotys. Aside from gulling the Jews into believing that they were really going for a shower, this procedure also served statistical purposes. But this was soon abandoned because of the commotion it created. Also, all the German papers and invoices in Treblinka were burned during the uprising.

Until just recently, the figure of over 3,000,000 Jews killed was widely assumed for Treblinka. But this is definitely an exaggeration. Treblinka received Jews from Central Poland, partly also from other districts in Poland, and from other countries, and it was undoubtedly one of the biggest mass graves for Jews in Europe. But we must not forget about the death factories in Bełzec and Sobibór. We also must not forget about the shootings in the towns of Galicia, Lithuania, Volhynia and the Ukraine; in Ponary, near Vilna; at the Janowska camp in Lvov, and so forth; about the tens of thousands who were shot in Stanisławów, in Tarnopol, in Kolomyja, in Rovno, in Baranowicz, and elsewhere. Also consider the gas vans,[14] which were used in western Poland in 1941. In a very conservative estimate, the Polish government's investigation commission has established that a total of 350,000 Jews were killed in such vans used at Camp Chełmno. Their calculations are based on the invoices submitted by the drivers of these vans, who were paid for each trip. Aside from this, we must remember that Jews represented the largest contingent of corpses in the other huge murder centers of Poland and Germany — Auschwitz, Maidanek, Dachau, Buchenwald, Bergen-Belsen, and so on. We were always the leading characters in the Germans' black comedy. Now, how many Jews perished of starvation and typhus? How many were killed in the "blitz pogroms" of the early years of the Nazi occupation?

How many died of "natural" causes, as compared to people of other nations in the regular labor camps and concentration camps? In our calculations, we must also keep in mind the total number of Jews killed, and, above all, the total number of Jews who were living in Europe up to the outbreak of the war. The great majority of the Jewish masses of eastern and southeastern Europe was killed off. But let no one, under the impact of our catastrophe, go to the extreme of citing a larger number of Jews killed than ever lived in Europe at any one time. . . .

Such places as Treblinka, with their huge mass graves, do not need the kind of odd local patriotism which is expressed by exaggerating the number of victims in order to depict the monstrosity of the mass murders committed there. Believe me, over a million people killed in the course of one year in one little place is a million times more than a million human brains could grasp. And even half a million would be much more than enough.

In his pamphlet, *The Treblinka Hell*, Vassili Grossman attempts to draw statistical conclusions on the basis of the number of victims which the gas chambers were capable of processing and which, according to his calculations, corresponds to the figures obtained in estimating the size of the transports. He, too, arrives at the figure of three million. However, this statistical procedure does not stand up to critical examination. The basic fact is that no conclusions can be drawn from the size of the gas chambers. Initially, there were three gas chambers. Later there were ten more. We don't know how many of the chambers were in use, and since when, and how many times a day they were in use, or the total number of Jews the gas chambers could hold at a time, or whether all the chambers were in operation simultaneously. In short, we can derive no figures from data about the gas chambers. We only know that many, many—oh, how terribly many were destroyed in them.

Several thousand Gypsies and several hundred Poles also perished in Treblinka.

According to the testimony of Samuel Rajzman, transports arrived in Treblinka from the localities as follows: most of them came from Central Poland (Warsaw and the Warsaw district, Radom, Czestochowa, Kielce, Siedlce, etc.); about 120,000 Jews came from the eastern and northeastern areas of Poland (Białystok, Grodno and Wołkowysk districts); 40,000 came from Austria, 10,000 from Czechoslovakia and 14–15,000 Jews from Bulgaria and Greece.

The report that Jews came to Treblinka from all the countries mentioned above was confirmed officially when the investigating commission excavated on the Treblinka grounds a large number of banknotes and other documents originating from those countries.

During the Treblinka uprising, several hundred Jewish inmates escaped, but most of these perished later. After the liberation, about 50 Treblinka veterans gathered together in Poland. For a time, these people banded together as a "Circle of Former Treblinka Inmates," with headquarters in Lodz. But in time, most of them emigrated.

Eyeglasses, Hairbrushes and Gold Pens. Our impressions of a toll of many hundreds of thousands, or even a million souls, is derived not only from the count of people, but also from incidental circumstances which were recorded *en passant*. The testimonies quoted below are now in the archives of the Jewish Historical Commission in Lodz.

Here is a statement excerpted from a Treblinka testimony about such personal valuables as pens, eyeglasses and hairbrushes.

Alexander Kudlik, a former inmate of Treblinka, relates: "From the sorting of garments, we proceeded to the sorting of gold pens. I spent about six months going through gold pens—ten hours a day, for six months, just sorting pens."

In testimony taken by Judge Łukaszkiewicz from Samuel Rajzman, we read:

"The property of the Jews who were killed in the camp was systematically assorted. Various specialists had been trained for the purpose of sorting personal property. I was one of these. I spent about three months doing nothing but sorting eyeglasses. A huge number of eyeglasses passed through my hands during that period. I also recall a story involving women's hairbrushes. Initially, these brushes (I mean the kind not backed with precious metals) would be shipped to Germany. Then, one day, orders came that all synthetic stones should be removed from the metal-backed brushes and only the bare metal should be packed and sent on to Germany. In this manner, several thousand kilograms of raw material were expedited to Germany."

In the statistical notes recorded by the secret Committee of Prisoners consisting of Engineer Galewski, Kurland, and Rajzman, we find the following statistics:

"The following items were shipped out: About 25 carloads of hair packed in bales, 248 carloads of men's suits, about 100 carloads of shoes, 22 carloads of ready-made textile goods. Jews from other countries (especially Bulgaria) would bring whole carloads of material here. Over 40 carloads of medicines, medical equipment, and dentists' metal were sent off. Twelve carloads of artisans' tools, 260 carloads of bedding, feathers, down, quilts, blankets. In addition, about 400 carloads of miscellaneous items, such as dishes, baby carriages, ladies' handbags, valises, pens, eyeglasses, shaving gear, toilet articles and other small items. Several hundred carloads of various types of clothing, underwear, and other used textile items."

According to information given to Rajzman by a Jew who worked at packing valuables, gold and foreign currency, over 14,000 carats in diamonds alone were sent out [from Treblinka]. We see, then, that in no small degree the German murder of the Jews was a mammoth operation of armed robbery.

The "Kopachke." The technical equipment of the murder plant, included, among other things, a mechanical digging machine, the excavator or, as the inmates of Treblinka called it, the "Kopachke." Initially, when the dead were still buried in the ground, this machine was forever digging ditches in the front section of the camp, next to the *lazaret*, and also behind the gas chambers. It would excavate many cubic meters of dirt at a time from the ditches. Later on, when they started to cremate the corpses in an attempt to erase every trace of the killings, the excavation was used to exhumate piles of corpses for cremation.

One way or another, the German robot of Treblinka was constantly on the go. Its hammering was the characteristic sound of the death camp and could be heard for miles around. Those who escaped from the camp could orient themselves at night by this sound and know whether they were moving away from the camp or wandering around in circles.

In time, two more excavators appeared in Treblinka. If Hitler had won the war, one of these machines probably would have been rewarded for its services by being placed into a German war museum, side by side with models of German tanks and artillery. It had performed a real service. It worked day and night, digging ditches, banging away — the "Kopachke," iron robot, mechanical heart of the mechanical business of killing Jews.

The Prisoners of Treblinka. We have already analyzed the data and defined the phenomena. The Germans created a science of annihilation and we are creating a science of perishing.

The German crime would not have been perfect if the Germans would not have been able to use Jewish workers to help them attain their purpose.

The masses of inmates in Treblinka died in one way—death being the chief product of the camp, but the death of the Jewish operators at the murder factory was of quite a different sort. Their final agony lasted longer and was interspersed with intervals of hope. Transformed into a delirium of conflicting emotions, it was perhaps even more difficult, in the last analysis, than death in the gas chambers.

There were about 1,000 of the Jewish workers: from 500 to 600 in the first section of the camp and about 300 near the "chambers." Their main duties were to clear away what was left by those killed, to take away the corpses and then to mask and clear away the traces of the killings. Each area had its own special functions. The camp was divided up into *Kommandos* [details] which were constantly decimated by selections or suicides but were quickly replenished by new transports. The skilled artisans in the workshops, and the construction workers lasted the longest. The latter were employed in the construction and maintenance of the camp buildings. After Himmler's visit in February, 1943, when they began to exhume the corpses from the mass graves and cremate them, the "corpse detail" was augmented to four times its original size.

The most important of all the details throughout was the "camouflage detail." Its function was to cut down branches in the woods and interweave them into the barbed wire fences. It was forbidden to come closer than one kilometer to these fences. In the fall of 1942, the field of mass graves, which was surrounded with pine trees, came to be referred to humorously as the "Kindergarten." The purpose of the trees was to hide the interior of the camp from outside observers.

How did the Jews behave in that hell, where everyone knew he would not get out alive, where it took unique spiritual strength not to succumb to the spell of death at the sight of so many corpses, where it was a major achievement just to keep on wanting to live? How, indeed, did those Jews who worked here hold out? Were they gruesome living specters whose words and thoughts are frightening to approach, just as one is filled with disgust at the thought of having to touch a corpse? No, these doomed people who had death as their constant companion, who walked among tens of thousands of corpses at every turn, themselves threatened by dozens of deaths—these people preserved their little flame of humanity, their little flame of "self," and even their little flame of Judaism, in this place of a thousand horrors.

How uncanny are the mechanisms of human nature! How terrifying is their impact even in conjunctures far less dramatic than the hangman-victim complex!

What the Jewish workers lived through in Treblinka was identical with the drama played out in other camps of the same type.

Out of fear of the German scum, some of the Jews became scum themselves; they beat other Jews and informed on them. Others became robots. But there were some—and by no means few—who remained human beings, as before. As a matter of fact, they became better human beings than before. Under conditions of a terror exceeding even the terrors of Maidanek or Auschwitz, in a place where psychic depression was harder to withstand than anywhere else on earth—a plan of revolt was conceived and successfully carried out. This was perhaps the only instance of this dimension in any camp in the entire area under German occupation.

Sporadic assassination attempts and acts of vengeance, both in Treblinka and in other camps of all kinds, were far more frequent than we know now and than we will ever know. An act of especially great courage was the planned and premeditated deed of Meir Berliner, a citizen of Argentina, who stabbed the SS man Max Biel[as] to death on September 10, 1942. Later, this Hitlerite "martyr" had the German barracks in Treblinka named "Max Biel[as] Kaserne" after him.

The revolt, or better, the uprising, in Treblinka, took place, after protracted preparations, on August 2, 1943. That fall, a revolt was organized in Sobibór. Attacks on German guards, along with attempts, successful or otherwise, to escape were organized in many places. The positive effect of the Treblinka revolt consisted in the fact that it stood under the powerful spiritual influence of the Warsaw ghetto uprising and that it placed the emphasis not so much on saving the lives of the participants as on carrying out definite tasks: to destroy the camp, to kill the SS men, and even to free the Jewish and Polish prisoners in the nearby penal camp of Treblinka.

It would be hard to imagine anything more thrilling and grand than the development of the conspiracy in Treblinka, the outbreak of the rebellion, and the escape of part of the prisoners. The results were not, and could not have been, one hundred percent effective; but even so, the Treblinka conspiracy and revolt comprises one of the brightest chapters of the dark history of Jewish death in Poland, and one of the most thrilling victories of human courage, intelligence, and willpower over terror, perfidy, and brute force.

"Kiewe" and "Berish." Aside from their true German surnames—like Stangl, Franz, Miete, Spetzinger, Post, and so forth—which were pronounced with a gnashing of teeth, the Germans at Treblinka had nicknames too. These were derived partly from secret communications between prisoners, and partly from Jewish folk wisdom, or even folk humor, macabre perhaps, but humor just the same. There were Jews who managed to incorporate memories of home in these nicknames.

One of the sadists in Treblinka was dubbed "Kiewe."[15] "Why 'Kiewe'?" I ask, and I learn that this character really was named Küwe in German, but when Jews called him Küwe they gave it in the Yiddish pronunciation. But that didn't make him kosher; it only made him ludicrous.

Another degenerate was dubbed "Berish." Why "Berish"? He got that name from a Jew who hailed from Otwock. This fellow would beat his victims to death if he had the slightest occasion to lay a hand on them. The Otwock gravedigger's name was also "Berish." The only difference between the two Berishes was that the Berish from Otwock had been the town undertaker, who had given a sendoff to people who died on their own accord, while the "Berish" of Treblinka would speed them along on their journey with his whip and grin.

The super-sadist in the camp, Kurt Franz, who, because of his demonstrated abilities, was promoted from Unterscharführer all the way to Untersturmführer and deputy commandant of the camp, was called *Lalka* ("The Doll") by the Jews, because physically he was as beautiful as a doll. As beautiful as an angel but as wicked as the devil. Perhaps he was given his nickname to emphasize this contrast.

There was also a local "Frankenstein." The name of this movie monster, the dangerous *golem* of the screen, was very popular in the camps and in the ghettos. But the Treblinka name was probably second-hand, the original bearer having been a Warsaw gendarme, who had been in the habit of shooting a few Jews every time he had duty at a ghetto exit, in the days before the mass deportation.[16]

The occupations of surviving Treblinka inmates include one traveling salesman, one forwarding agent, one cutter, one shoemaker, and one bookkeeper.

The prewar occupations of the hangmen had included one electrical technician, one storekeeper, one baker and one retail clerk. "Lalka" had been a waiter.

And these two groups of people, representatives of such modest, everyday, socially proper categories of people came to be locked into a demonic circle in a uniquely created constellation and played out such a weird hellish drama among themselves.

This is the practical consequence of a system where some men are totally enslaved and robbed of all their possessions, while others are totally depraved. This is the practical outcome of Hitlerite totalitarianism.

The Treblinka underground and revolt represented a great moral victory of the Jews over this system.

A Jew Tells His Story. Among the Treblinka veterans who were riding along with us on our inspection trip was a rare bird, a witness who had not yet been interviewed. His name was Tanhum Grinberg,[17] a shoemaker from Błonie, the prototype of the Jewish man-in-the-street, warts and all. Every time he opened his mouth, out came the authentic accents and nuances of the Jewish masses. And what I'd like to tell about him is a personal note rather than the macabre details of what he told me.

In 1941, Tanhum was evacuated from Błonie and forced to move into the Warsaw ghetto. He was still a young man then, but he was already the head of his family, the provider for his mother, three younger brothers and a sister. In order to protect himself against dragnets for forced labor, he had gone to work at Schultz's shop even before the mass *Aktion* of July-September, 1942. He worked three days a week "for the German" and three days a week "for himself." Somehow, he managed to get by. When the blockades began (the Germans combed the ghetto building by building and deported everyone who did not have working papers), Tanhum managed to secure passes for his family from his place of employment. These papers were supposed to protect them from deportation. But about a week later, when he came home from Schultz, he found his apartment empty. Some of his neighbors were still there, because they had hidden, but Tanhum's family,

61

who had relied on their "Ausweis" [pass] to protect them, had been taken away.

Tanhum goes into great detail to paint the picture of his empty home. "A pot of potatoes was still on the kitchen stove; the potatoes were half-cooked and cold. The fire had gone out . . ."

He sat down in his room all by himself and cried.

"I've only cried three times in my life," Tanhum told us parenthetically. "The first time was when my father died. He had been 46 years old and sick with cancer. The second time was when they took away my mother and the children. And the third time . . .

"The third time was when, after having gone through everything, I was liberated.

"A whole group of us Jews had gathered in the little town of Sterdyń, right near where we are now, in the immediate vicinity of Sokołów and Treblinka. I had been hiding in that town ever since the uprising. So we had a little celebration, right after the liberation. There were some Soviet soldiers—also Jews—with us. One of them was an officer from near Kharkov, another was a girl who played the violin. She played very nicely. We drank some liquor. The Jewish first lieutenant got a little drunk. As the girl went on playing, he became very sad. Finally he got up, strode to the middle of the room and delivered the following little speech:

"'I, too, once had a home. I had a wife and a child, a little boy, five years old. When the Germans started their killing, somebody hid them, but someone else betrayed them and delivered them up. They were killed and so was the man who had hidden them. The one who betrayed them is still alive today. I ought to go back to our town, take my pistol, and shoot him, along with his whole family. But I mustn't do it and I don't want to do it because it wouldn't do any good. I'll never go back home. The only thing left for me is liquor and more liquor.'

"With that, he went back to the table and drank some more. And as the girl played on and the Soviet officer talked, I realized that all of us Jews are in the same position today, and I was seized with weeping, such weeping. . . . I went into another room and, I tell you, I cried like a baby."

Tanhum was an eyewitness to Meir Berliner's attack on Max Biel[as] on September 10, 1942. He had been working in the shoemaker's shop in Treblinka. He worked for the Germans, as he says, as if "for Pharaoh in Egypt." In Treblinka, he says, you felt each day like Isaac being offered upon the sacrificial altar.

Meir Kapo. Tanhum also tells us about a young man—the others talk of him, too, whom they called "Meir Kapo." He was the son of a scribe of parchment scrolls, and he had a beautiful singing voice. A pious Jew, he introduced the custom of having the prisoners hold regular evening prayer services every night, after the barracks were closed. Afterwards, they would recite the "El Maleh Rahamim" and the mourners' Kaddish for those who had died.

"What about the Germans and the Ukrainians?" I asked. "Didn't they try to stop you?"

"There's a story for you," Tanhum replied. "You probably haven't heard about the music in Treblinka. (What a question! Do I know about it?) Did you know that the Germans loved to hear Jewish melodies? They would pass by and stand near the windows of our barracks when we held our services. That's why they thought so highly of Meir—until they shot him. They made him a kapo, even though he never did us any harm."

I was amazed at this tableau of Germans standing near the window to listen to the "El Maleh Rahamim" being chanted in memory of the very people whom they themselves had just murdered that day.

There was a forest not far away, with a field—a field of corpses—in between.

Chaim'l and his Pony. Meir's story triggered a new flood of reminiscences from the Treblinka veterans. One of them told about Yom Kippur, in 1942, in Treblinka (that year, the holiday fell on September 21) and about those who insisted on fasting on that day. Another tells us that matzos were actually baked inside the death camp for Passover. And a third told us this story, which is worth recording here.

It sounds just like one of the old folktales of Jewish martyrdom. "On Hanukkah," says Shimon Friedman of Penal Camp Treblinka I, "one of the Jews managed to get a few candles from somewhere that night in the barracks, and he lit the Hanukkah candles. A Ukrainian guard who was passing by saw the candles, and burst into the barracks. 'Who lit those candles?' he wanted to know. Of course, the candles were snuffed out when he opened the door and nobody wanted to admit having done it. So the Ukrainian said, 'Now just a moment. You don't want to confess? With me, you would have gotten away with just a punishment, but now I'll tell the Germans and we'll see what will happen.'"

There was no reason not to take his threats seriously. This was serious business. The Jews started to discuss what they should do. Neither the "guilty" party nor any of the other prisoners came forward to assume the burden of guilt. Then a 15-year-old boy named Chaim'l moved out of his corner. His job at the camp had been to go around the camp with a little pony, hitch it to a wagon at mealtime, and take food to a group of women who worked in the laundry. He was an orphan, and everyone liked him.

"It was me! I lit the candles!" Chaim'l cried. "Today is the anniversary of my mother's death and that's when we light *Yahrzeit* candles."

The boy accepted 25 lashes in order to save a whole group of Jews from terror.

A Pole Tells a Story. From Siedlce we drove in the official car of the county office. I got the seat next to the driver. The driver, a man named Marzec, was a likable fellow, a tough young guy who during the Nazi occupation had kept at his place a radio and—a Jewish woman and child. He, too, had stories to tell about Jews and about Treblinka.

His stories were simple, factual, and short. He told about the days of the *Aktion* in Siedlce, when the Germans set up tables in the marketplace, "And that's how the ceremony began." The staff sat down at the tables, ate and drank their fill, and then they got to work. "They shot the old and the weak right then and there, on the spot. And if somebody was told to go to the left, with the women and children, he was obviously a goner." He had gotten a perfect grasp of the German tactics: women, children, the old and the sick, were sure to be the worst off.

People tried to escape from the transports and many corpses lay strewn along the railroad tracks at every stop.

Then they made a pause in Siedlce. They promised that those Jews who worked would not be bothered. They were told to go back to their homes. "What they wanted to do," Marzec comments, "was to have the Jews who had scattered to the woods and the villages gather together in one place. And when the people got back into town, right on Rosh Hashanah (the Jewish New Year), the Krauts came in and loaded them on the train, too, despite the jobs and all the papers that they had. They told them to close up shop, and that was the end of the story."

Men and Monsters. All the Poles of that area, the Siedlce and particularly the Sokołów districts, had seen a lot and knew plenty. The Germans and Ukrainians of Treblinka were very well known in the town of Kosów, where they used to come to have a good time, get drunk, and have their pictures taken. Judge Łukaszkiewicz recorded many testimonies from Poles of that area; notably from railroad employees at the stations through which the transports passed. The peasants of the area were able to see the flames of the Treblinka funeral pyres at night. All those who escaped from Treblinka of necessity turned to them for help. Some of the Jews found help, but others only found robbery, betrayal, and death.

"There are men and there are monsters," sighed our driver and the Treblinka veterans joined in. But the fact remains that each of these survivors had found a Pole who had risked his life to help him. In the case of Friedman, it had been a peasant woman who had heated up a kettle of water one morning, washed his wounds and bandaged them with clean strips of linen. She gave him a chunk of bread and a cane to lean on. Then she showed him the way he should go: "Go on, and good luck!" At the edge of another village, not far from where he had lain all day hidden in a haystack, burning up with fever from his wounds, he found another householder who would bring him some food from his home every night and even a cigarette to smoke. Our man recalls that cigarette with even more gratitude than he does the food which had kept him alive! Eventually, that same peasant was the first to bring him the news that he was a free man and that the "Russkis" had already entered the neighboring village.

Another member of our company, Yekhiel Reichman, would have liked to make a detour of a few miles with our car to visit "his" peasant and to give him a new shirt, with thanks, to replace the shirt which the man had given him when he was a fugitive, wounded and bleeding, after the uprising, with the manhunt pursuing him from all sides . . . One other man, Samuel Rajzman, also had been helped by a man who was supposedly a peasant but was in fact a judge, who had settled down with his family in the village during the occupation. Himself a member of the underground, he had taken in several Jews after the uprising and kept them for a whole year, until the liberation.

There was also a householder somewhere in the area who had barely managed to save himself when his house and possessions were set on fire as punishment for his having given shelter to Jews.

In another family the father and two sons had been shot for the same crime.

Shrouded in Fog Forever. When we arrived at Kosów, on our trip to Treblinka, it was market day there. There were crowds of peasants, men and women, and wagons, cattle and horses. The local police knew that we were supposed to arrive. The district attorney, the judge and the licensed surveyor, were waiting for us; so was the chairman of the Sokołów National Council, along with a group of militiamen and the mayor of the village of Wólka Okrąglik, in whose territory the Treblinka camp had been located. As we drove past the marketplace, shrill whistles could be heard from somewhere in the crowd. We remembered that eleven Jews had been killed in Kosów-Lacki not long before, that there were many anti-Semites at large in the neighborhood, newly-rich people who had become both prosperous and depraved from having lived near the death camp. We remembered this, but at that moment, we were not thinking about being in danger.

All that morning the weather had been frosty but clear and sunny. But after two o'clock in the afternoon, when we left the town and took a side road for the final ten kilometers to Treblinka, an eerie fog descended on the whole area.

Until that stage of our journey, the Treblinka veterans had kept interrupting each other with running commentaries, and showing off how familiar they were with the area. But now, all at once, they grew quiet, each one absorbed in his own thoughts.

The wheels of our car slid smoothly over the highway, which had been built by Jewish hands. I looked around to see if anyone could hear my heart beating loudly as it always does when one comes face to face with something which has preempted his thoughts, filled him with fear and tortured his imagination. But the actual encounter produced a very different effect than had been anticipated. I tried to recall in my mind's eye the faces of all my near and dear ones for whom this road, on which we now approached our destination, had been the last.

If there really is such a thing as immortality their souls should have been hovering over this place, among the souls that could find no redress, because their physical mass had already vanished. Who could tell—perhaps it was these Jewish souls which constituted that fog which now hung heavy above our heads.

Now we could already see the tracks of the Siedlce-Małkinia railroad line. There it was, right there, next to that little forest.

A leaden fog hung so low in the sky that it seemed as if we would be able to reach out and touch it. The milky-gray fog filled up the entire space. The pine trees stood out from a distance as if shrouded in black veils. The sun had become pale and dim; it looked like a small, round human face gazing down at us from above, like the twisted, suddenly-aged face of someone newly bereaved.

"Where did this fog come from?" someone in our car asked. "There will always be a fog over this place," one of the Treblinka veterans replied. And I could sense that he was trying to say something, something important and profound, something he had never said in his life before. But he couldn't say it.

The Polish Colorado, or, "The Treblinka Gold Rush." I knew that it would be like this one day; I had been writing about it three years before, predicting that the place where the Jews had perished would become the Polish Klondike, where adventurers from all over the country would come to dig in the soil for treasure.

Great treasures had indeed passed through Treblinka. Hundreds upon hundreds of thousands of people had come here, bringing with them their best and most precious possessions. "You will be permitted to bring along gold and foreign currency." That is what was printed on the deportation posters in Warsaw and in other cities, too. The real meaning of these instructions was, "For God's sake, little Jews, don't forget to bring along your money and your gold!" They were doing the Jews a big favor! They were permitting them to take with them things which, according to German law, they should have given up a long time before.

If the Jews had not been trying so hard to avoid looking the truth straight in the eye, this alone should have made them realize what was in store for them. After all, they were not such complete fools that they had actually given away all their valuables, as they had been expected to do under the regulations of 1940. Some had more, some had less, with the exception of those who had already sold everything because they had needed the money (meaning those who had not died of starvation as early as 1942—the very poorest, the refugees, the Jewish proletariat); but most of the Jews had put aside something "for a rainy day," in the hope that they would never need it.

As a people of wanderers over the generations, and especially since the beginning of the war and the deportations, Jews had realized that they could be ordered out of their homes on half an hour's notice and forced to leave all their possessions behind. For this reason, all the Jews tried to convert as much as possible of their immovable property into movable goods. And the most movable of all goods were gold, jewelry and American dollars.

Does this mean that the Jews were really a nation of rich people? Not by any means! But I have no intention today of entering into a debate with anti-Semitic myths of Jewish riches. It is true that there were some very wealthy Jews in Warsaw and other cities, but their wealth could not save them. They were taken to Treblinka together with their fortunes. But taken as a whole, the aggregate property of the middle and lower class Jews, the Jewish "man in the street", was even greater. The strings of pearls, diamond earrings and gold necklaces inherited from grandparents, the gold coins of the previous generation, the Czarist gold rubles, American "hard" gold pieces; the few "soft" dollar bills which a Jew might have received from a relative in America and worn in a little bag around his neck or in a money-belt around his waist—most of these items were given to the women to hide, to sew into their corsets or to conceal in a variety of other ways. Until 1942, it was believed that women would be less liable to be searched than men. This may be the reason, why, actually, the hunt for women during the *Aktionen* was even greater than for men.

All these items were brought to Treblinka. Gold and foreign currency lay literally strewn about, if not in the mud, then in the sand and the dust. Ten and twenty-dollar coins would be trampled down into the ground. In many instances, Jews tore up their dollar bills in the last minute, but they could not tear up gold, and so the Germans were able to carry off millions, indeed billions, in cash from Treblinka and other such places.

We must remember that *the killing of Jews was primarily a crime of robbery with murder*. The utilization of gold and valuables, like that of all the other Jewish property, and the entire process of "Werterfassung"* at Treblinka, was organized in a first-rate manner from the very start. Jewelers were brought in from Germany to supervise the assorting of the cash and the valuables. One of these persons, the Treblinka veterans report, was "quite a decent Yekke"[19] ("decent" because he had never tormented Jews without cause and always tried to see to it that the Jews who worked for him would not be subjected to the selections), who hailed from Leipzig. Together with his "Goldjuden" (literally "gold Jews") he selected, appraised, and weighed and packed suitcase after suitcase of diamonds,

* Organized looting of the deported Jews' possessions.

jewelry, gold pieces and foreign currency. From time to time he would load the valises onto trucks and send them under escort to Lublin, perhaps subject to the order of SS General and Brigadeführer Globocnik, or to be sent on by Globocnik for government requirements, or for the personal use of the cabinet ministers and Reichsführer in Berlin.[20]

It is not difficult to imagine that those who had played a predominant role in procuring this source of revenue were properly rewarded for their troubles.

It is easy to picture how the Globocniks and Himmlers would exchange gifts and favors. Less "official" but no less substantial were the "nice gifts" which the German and Ukrainian SS men gathered up and sent out for their own account; the heavy rings, the fine watches. Such things didn't drop into their pockets just like peanuts!

The ones to benefit the least from property left behind by Jewish deportees were the Jews who arrived after them. It is true that they also tried to get their hands on some of it; with the help of Ukrainians who had been bribed, the Jews who worked in the woods bought food in the neighboring villages for good foreign currency, at skyrocketing prices.

Jews who managed to escape often took something out with them. But most of the time they were robbed of everything on the way—sometimes of life itself. And so plenty of robbers grew rich in that area.

And now that it's all over, that the camp had been burned down and everything carried off, what hope is there for treasure now? Plenty!

Those in the know are aware that not all the dead were cremated and that, aside from those who were buried naked, Jews in some places were buried fully dressed without their pockets being searched, their hidden valuables undiscovered—secret wealth, sewn into their clothes. In some cases the posthumous "Werterfassung" did not include the extraction of gold teeth. And in fact there had been people lying in wait to dig in the soil for gold teeth, clothing and other treasures buried there by Jewish workers.

All kinds of scavengers and marauders come here in droves, shovels in hand. They dig, search and ransack; they sift the sand, they drag parts of half-rotted corpses from the earth, bones and scattered refuse in the hope that they may come upon at least a coin or a gold tooth. These human jackals and hyenas bring along live artillery shells and unexploded bombs. They explode several of them at once, tearing huge craters into the desecrated, blood-drenched soil which is commingled with the ashes of Jews.

The Sandy Soil Yields Up Its Secret. Our car came to a stop. We got out: this was where the camp area began. According to our measurements, it is 15 hectares. A well-paved road runs parallel to the railroad tracks for about 1½ kilometers and then comes to a dead end. Another road branches out from it and comes to an end even sooner. The surface of both roads contains a weird mixture of coals and ashes from the pyres where the corpses of the inmates were cremated. The second road leads in the same direction as the "Road to Heaven," of which no trace is now left. Just a bit of the concrete foundations of a horses' stable — this is all that is left today of the camp buildings, the barbed wire fences, the barracks, the watchtowers, the gas chambers. Some of the buildings were burned down during the uprising, and the rest were carried off by human scavengers from neighboring villages after the arrival of the Red Army.

While the Germans were still here, the whole area had been plowed up and sown with lupine grass. And the lupine grass really grew and covered the whole surface with a green mask. It looked as if all the traces of crime had been wiped away. But since then, during the past year, the human jackals and hyenas have been coming to the burial ground and here is the picture that we saw:

Here and there, like patches of grass near the seashore, half-covered by the shifting sands, there were still little clumps of withered lupine. Not one level place in the whole area. Everything had been torn up and dug up, little hills and holes. And upon them, beneath them, and among them, all sorts of objects. Aluminum kettles and pans, enameled tin pots—blackened, dented, full of holes. Combs with teeth broken off, half-rotted soles from ladies' summer sandals, broken mirrors, leather billfolds. All this is near the station platform where the camp's first barbed wire fences had been.

We began our tour at the place where the transports had been unloaded, and we continued on the road which the Jews who were brought here had followed. What we saw here was the remnants of the Treblinka "Werterfassung." Remnants of the huge piles of Jewish property which had been packed up and sent away, incinerated, cleared off, and yet still could not be completely cleared away. It v ˹s not possible to clear away every trace of what the hundreds of thousands of people who had passed through there had experienced. Here was the *physical evidence*; here were the *corpora delicti*.

Perhaps someone might wonder what sort of people they were who left such plentiful evidence of their truncated lives, to what nation they belonged. Well, look about you and you will see it for yourself:

Twisted Sabbath candlesticks—enough for whole collections. A scrap from a prayer shawl. Just dug out of the ground, lying white and fresh, complete with a blue Star of David, is an elegant Warsaw armband (from the corner of Karmelicka and Leszno—the latest fashion in the ghetto). A whole pile of ladies' marriage wigs.

These must be unburned, stray remnants from some store.

The hair shorn off the living women had been turned into industrial raw materials, but it seems that the ritual wigs of the old, pious Jewish women had been set aside for better uses. Perhaps they could be sold, by way of a friendly "neutral" country, to Jews in America, for a good price, along with the Torah scrolls and Talmudic folios which had been carefully accumulated for this purpose, packed in cases and hidden away?

But the physical evidence was not limited to objects. As we moved further into the grounds, we walked over a field which was sown with human bones.

The bombs had uncovered the contents of the desecrated soil. Leg bones, ribs, pieces of spine, skulls big and small, short and long, round and flat.

Skulls! . . .

If only we could get an ethnologist to come here!

He could have made the most accurate anthropological measurements relating to the racial features of the Jewish people.

Or perhaps what was needed here would be a philosopher; a thinker, a Prince Hamlet of Denmark to stand up and deliver a gravedigger's speech, to look upon those skulls and speak directly to them.

"Anybody have a bag? Is there a bag around here? Let's take a bagful of bones with us!"

In a minute, a pile of bones had been scraped together. But there was no bag around and so we couldn't take any of the bones.

But then how much could one bag have held? What with all the cremations, we could have taken out whole carloads from there. If bones can be classed as relics, then Treblinka held relics sufficient to supply the entire Jewish people.

This Is My Child's Foot! The further we went, the heavier the air became with the smell of death. We had already passed through the famous "grove," the sparse pine trees through which the "Road to Heaven" had run. We were now standing where the gas chambers had been, the huge mass graves and the pyres. In some places, the smell of death was still mingled with the odor of fire. Indeed, here and there we could see little piles of white ashes along with blackened bones, heaps of soot. All this had been buried several meters deep in the soil, mixed with sand and covered with more sand, but the explosions had brought it to the surface again. In one place the simultaneous explosion of several bombs had created a huge crater. Deep down in the hole, some outlines could be dimly seen through the fog.

"Those aren't just bones," says the district attorney. "There are still pieces of half-rotted corpses lying there, bunches of intestines."

By now the district attorney and the judge knew every nook and cranny here. They had been conducting their investigation for some time. They had examined both Jewish and non-Jewish witnesses, taken measurements and carried out minor excavations.

The Treblinka veterans were running back and forth, pointing things out, arguing with one another. They made mistakes and then began to remember the places again. They wanted to do something, to make some extravagant gestures, that would at least reflect their emotions, bound up as they were with this place. They wanted to gather bones. They leaped into ditches, reached their bare hands into rotted masses of corpses to show they were not repelled.

They did the right thing. Now we were just like the Muslim sectarians who carried their dead along in their caravans to Mecca, considering it their sacred duty to bear the smell of death with patience and love as they went along the road. That was how we felt in these fields, where there lay the last remains of our martyrs.

"Look there, at the edge of that hole," said the judge, "these are bones from a child's leg!" One of the Treblinka survivors rushed over. "Be careful!" said another. "There's still some flesh hanging from that leg!" But the one who had taken it was wrapping it up into a newspaper with much the same reverence as a pious Jew wrapping up an *etrog* [the citron fruit which is used in the Feast of Tabernacles and must remain unblemished]. He wrapped it with the skirt of his coat, then put it into his breast pocket and hugged it to his breast.

72

"Perhaps it's the foot of my little boy, whom I brought here with me," he said. And the weird truth is that even though everyone wanted to use some flowery figure of speech, and though figures of speech might have been in order or out of place, this discovery could have chanced to be the plain, unvarnished truth.

Who would be able to recognize the skulls, the ribs, the leg bones, which had not been turned to ashes? As Peretz Markish once said, in his poem, *The Pile*:

"Are you searching for your parents?
"Are you searching for your friend?
"They're here. They're all here."

These bones are the bones of all of us. Let us take a good look: Are these not also our own skulls lying in that sandpit? And we—or is it perhaps some cruel, furious God—aren't we just dreaming on this death-like, dreary, foggy autumn day, that we still have our own heads on our shoulders?

Isn't it only a gratuitous accident that our bones are not also scattered all over this field?

Were we not all condemned together, to perish in the same way, and in the same place?

Night Falls. We were going back now.

Again we came to the place where someone had noticed a little pan for warming milk, half-buried with its mouth in the sand. Had a mother brought it with her in her knapsacks for her baby? Now the pan was lying there all alone, like an orphan. It was getting rusty in the rain; no one would want it any more.

Ashamed and sick at heart, our heads bowed, we left the place.

The time is not yet ripe when we will be able to gather at this place in deep mourning. Could anyone pray here, knowing that here, in this earth, were the remains, the ashy dust, of his loved ones and friends, of hundreds of people he knew and of other hundreds of thousands of Jews whom he had never known? The terrible anger, pain and protest against the gigantic, cosmic crime which was committed here has been blurred and distorted by the repulsive, petty, disgusting things which are now being done here by petty creatures; here, today, after the war and after the downfall of Hitler.

We climb into the car and drive back to Siedlce.

My head starts to ache.

A heavy weariness enfolds us all.

Night has fallen upon the field of Treblinka.

Translated from the Yiddish

1. See his memoir, "Eighteen Days in Treblinka," p. 77 ff. of this volume.

2. Two parts of this archive were uncovered in September, 1946 and December, 1950. There was a part which has never been recovered. Among the material recovered are the memoirs of Abraham Krzepicki's "Eighteen Days in Treblinka."

3. Wiernik's work is reproduced on p. 147 ff. The account from *Dos Naye Lebn* is reproduced on p. 224 ff.

4. These interviews are now in the archives of the Jewish Historical Institue of Poland in Warsaw. Copies are in the Yad Vashem archives in Jerusalem.

5. This model is now on display at Kibbutz Lohamei Ha-Getaot, the ghetto fighters' kibbutz in the Upper Galilee, founded by resistance and ghetto fighters in 1949. See photograph on p. 259.

6. S. Szende, *The Promise Hitler Kept* (London: Gollancz, 1945)

7. We know today that the Germans conducted experiments with soap manufactured from human fat, but they did not manufacture it on a large scale. See Raul Hilberg, *Destruction of the European Jews*, pp. 623–24.

8. See Leon Wells, *"The Death Brigade,"* New York, 1978.

9. The so-called "January *Aktion"* lasted from January 18 to 21, 1943.

10. See L. Wells, *The Death Brigade.*

11. During the final phase of the first *Aktion* in the Warsaw ghetto, the remnants of the ghetto's Jews were herded into an area comprising only a few blocks and were subjected to a general "selection." During this operation, which lasted from September 6 to September 13, 1942, an estimated total of 100,000 Jews was deported. Hence the term "Warsaw cauldron."

12. According to the testimony of Stanisław Kohn, the roof of this building was topped by a Star of David and the inscription *Judenstaat* ("The Jewish State").

13. The author is referring to the custom still practiced among very pious Jews to cut the bride's hair off before the marriage ceremony so that she will not tempt other men. Afterwards her head is covered by a kerchief or a wig.

14. These "mobile gas chambers" were cars in which the victims were asphyxiated by the carbon monoxide fumes generated by the car's own motor.

15. Kiewe, a Yiddish corruption of "Akiba." Actually, the man's name was Küttner.

16. The Treblinka "Frankenstein's" real name was Willy Mentz; he was sentenced to life imprisonment by a German court in 1965.

17. See Tanhum Grinberg, *The Revolt in Treblinka*, p. 214 ff. of this volume.

18. In Europe, whistling is equivalent to the American custom of booing to express derision of disapproval.

19. Yiddish slang for German.

20. This guard, named Franz Suchomel, was to be tried and convicted by a German court in 1965 to seven years.

EYEWITNESS
ACCOUNTS

EIGHTEEN DAYS IN TREBLINKA

ABRAHAM KRZEPICKI

ABRAHAM JACOB KRZEPICKI was in his early twenties when war broke out in Poland in 1939. He was drafted into the Polish army and was taken prisoner by the Germans. After his release, he settled in Warsaw. On August 25, 1942, he was deported to Treblinka. However, he managed to escape 18 days later and returned to the Warsaw ghetto. He joined the ZOB (Jewish Fighting Organization) in the ghetto and was killed in the Warsaw ghetto uprising in April, 1943. He was a member of a Hanoar-Hatzioni group headed by Jacob Praszker. During the shelling of the Brush Workshops he was wounded in the leg. His comrades had to evacuate the burning building and were forced to abandon him and other wounded fighters.

The leaders of the ghetto underground archives (under the historian Emanuel Ringelblum) entrusted Rachel Auerbach with the task of recording the testimony given by Krzepicki (December, 1942–January, 1943). Krzepicki's report–he was then 25 years old–was the first eyewitness account of the crimes perpetrated at Treblinka. The manuscript (in Yiddish) had been buried in the rubble of the ghetto along with other documents from the second part of the Ringelblum archives. It was recovered on December 1, 1950 by Polish construction workers beneath the ruins of 68 Nowolipki Street. The original manuscript is now at the Jewish Historical Institute in Warsaw (File #290). It was first published in the Jan.–June, 1956 issue of the Institute's Yiddish-language publication, Bleter far Geshikhte (Vol. XI, No. 1–2, 1956, Warsaw).

This is the first English translation of Krzepicki's account.

Chapter One

THE BLOCKADE. On August 25 [1942], at about half past six in the evening, the honey factory at 19 Zamenhof Street, where we workers were employed, was surrounded. SS men broke into the factory and drove out all the people. Entreaties and begging were of no help. With guns drawn, they threatened to shoot us. We left everything behind and vacated the factory. We were lined up in rows. Since I knew German, I went up to the Scharführer and asked him to let me take some things with me. I had thought of hiding, but I could see that it would not work. As I was gathering my belongings, a *junak* [non-German auxiliary guard] came up to me pointing his gun at me, but when I shouted "Scharführer!" he refrained from shooting. . . .

As I left, the Scharführer gave me a kick to make me move faster. Several men who had been found hiding in the Toporol[1] garden had been shot at the courtyard. We were taken out to Zamenhof Street. In the group outside in the street there were some more SS men with their sleeves rolled up and carrying whips in their hands. They looked like butchers in a slaughterhouse; we didn't like the looks of this. Jews with blood all over them were coming from Wołyńska Street. Gangs of Ukrainians were going around, looting the abandoned houses. When Brandt[2] came driving up, people said to each other, "Look! Here's Brandt! Maybe he'll get us released because we're working people." After that two hundred more people appeared; they were returning from one of the workshops. They walked along as if they hadn't a care in the world, because they were coming home from work. One of the Ukrainians asked Brandt what he should do with these people. "Take them all in!" Brandt replied, and that whole crowd was taken into our ranks.

Brandt gave an order to Lejkin,[3] "*Alles abmarschieren!*" [Everybody, march off!] and so we began to march off, five abreast. The ghetto police and the Ukrainians formed a cordon on either side, with a Jewish policeman or a Ukrainian standing at intervals of 20 paces and an SS man at intervals of 40–50 meters. And so we marched off. I was the last to move out because I was planning to escape. But it was impossible, there were too many Germans around. I just looked around the streets and told myself that I was now saying good-bye to Warsaw. As I arrived at the *Umschlagplatz*, I heard one of the ghetto policemen telling one of his relatives to "go to the right." I also wanted to go "to the right," toward the hospital, where I thought I might be able to save myself. But this same policeman dragged me back and I went out into the *Umschlagplatz*. I could see that I was done for.

At the Umschlagplatz. We still hoped that some kind of separation would take place at the *Umschlagplatz* and we would be able to show our papers. But unfortunately we never had that chance. As we came closer, we saw the boxcars ready for us and we said to each other, "*Oy vey*, we've had it! We're in trouble!" And in fact, the Lithuanian guards came straight over to us and started hitting us over the head with whips; they did not let anyone go near the Germans. From the *Umschlagplatz* we were moved toward the boxcars. Only two foremen from Waldemar Schmidt's shop managed to get through; they were in uniforms and army caps. They went up to the *Scharführer*, who was the old sadist, but he had a sudden inspiration. He looked them up and down for five minutes, then nodded and told them that they could go. This was how those two men got away, but nobody else was that lucky. We were moving closer to the boxcars. Already we could see elderly people stretched out on the floor of the first car, half-unconscious. We didn't like the looks of this. Then steps were moved up to the boxcars and the Lithuanian auxiliaries started driving us faster with their whips, up into the cars. We had to give up all hope of being able to show our papers to somebody and so we got into the boxcars.

In the Boxcar. Over a hundred people were crammed into our car. The ghetto police closed the doors. When the door shut on me, I felt my whole world vanishing. Some pretty young girls were still standing in front of the cars, next to a German in a gendarme's uniform. This man was the commander of the *shaulis*[4] and the escort for our train. The girls were screaming, weeping, stretching out their hands to the German and crying, "But I'm still young! I want to work! I'm still young! I want to work!" The German just looked at them, and did not say a word. The girls were loaded into the boxcar and they traveled along with us. After the doors had closed on us, some of the people said, "Jews, we're finished!" But I and some others did not want to believe that. "It can't be!" we argued, "They won't kill so many people! Maybe the old people and the children, but not us. We're young. They're taking us to work."

The cars began to move. We were on the way. Where to? We didn't know. Perhaps we were going to work in Russia. But some of the old people didn't want to believe this and, as soon as the train started moving, they started to recite the mourners' Kaddish. "Jews, we're done for!" they said. "It's time to recite the prayer for the dead."

The Jews Recite the Kaddish. It's impossible to imagine the horrors in that closed, airless boxcar. It was one big cesspool. Everybody was pushing toward the window, where there was a little air, but it was impossible to get close to the window. Everybody was lying on the ground. I also lay down. I could feel a crack in the floor. I lay with my nose right up against that crack to grab some air. What a stench all over the car! You couldn't stand it. A real cesspool all over. Filth everywhere, human excrement piled up in every corner of the car. People kept shouting, "A pot! A pot! Give us a pot so we can pour it out the window." But nobody had a pot.

After the train had traveled some distance, it suddenly stopped in the middle of nowhere.

A *shaulis*, revolver in hand, entered our car. He drove the people over to one side of the car and planted himself on the other side facing them with his revolver. I thought he had a poison gas shell in his gun and that we were going to be gassed right there in the car. But then I remembered the window and I couldn't understand what was going on. It turned out that the *shaulis* had come not to kill us but only to rob us. Every one of us had to step up to him and show what he had. Working quickly, the *shaulis* stowed away everything that was not well hidden: money, watches, jewelry. No doubt he was in a hurry to get to other cars. After a while, the train moved on.

"Let's Get Out of Here!" I tried to talk to some of the young people. "Let's get out of here! Let's get out through the windows!" But many of them said, "It's no good! If we jump, we'll get killed anyway." But two people jumped down just the same. The Germans noticed and stopped the train to shoot after them. I don't know what became of these two. I had given up the idea of jumping and got back down on the floor, together with the others.

The train stopped at some little depot. One by one, we dropped off to sleep, and we slept for a few hours. At about 5 a.m., we saw many other transports of Jews passing by our window.

Things got very bad in the cars. "Water!" we shouted through the window to the railroad men; we offered them a lot of money to bring us water. We were willing to pay a lot for a drink of water. It was very bad, but we couldn't manage to get all the water we needed for all the money we had; 500 to 1000 złotys were paid for one single portion of water. The railroad men and the *shaulises* took the money. Those who have not lived through this will not believe what happened then. We were lying one on top of the other, without air. Those who had been able to get some water got no great pleasure from it. One person cried that his father had fainted; another, that his mother had passed out, and a third that his child

80

was unconscious, and so the water was divided into such small portions that no one got much benefit from it, even though under such circumstances people ordinarily are quite selfish. Various important people, professors and doctors, were riding in our car. They took off their shirts and lay on the floor, gasping. "A little water for the doctor, he's fainting!" someone cried out. I didn't know the names of these people. I paid 500 złotys, over half the cash I possessed, for a cupful of water (about half a pint.) As I started to drink my water, a woman came up to me and said that her child had fainted. I was in the middle of drinking and simply couldn't tear the cup away from my lips. Then the woman sank her teeth into my hand with all her might, to get me to stop drinking and leave her some of my water. I wouldn't have minded being bitten again, just as long as I could have more water. But I left over some of the water in the cup and saw that the child got to drink it.

Things got worse in the boxcars from minute to minute. It was only about 7 a.m., but the sun was already hot and the temperature kept climbing. All the men had taken off their shirts and were lying half-naked, clad only in their pants or underpants. Some of the women, too, had thrown off their clothes and were lying in their underwear. People lay on the floor groaning, tossing from one side to another, twisting their heads and their whole bodies, this way and that, gasping for air. Others lay quietly, resigned, semiconscious, no longer able to move. We were willing to pay the *shaulises* anything they wanted for a little water.

A little later, at about 10 a.m., we could see through the window the German who was in command. One of us asked him through the window to give orders that we should get some water. The German replied that we should be patient, because in an hour's time we would arrive at our destination, Camp Treblinka, where everyone would get water. He also told us to be calm. In Treblinka, we would be divided into groups and put to work. But our train did not move again until 4 p.m.

While the German officer had been speaking, everyone had been satisfied. The Jew at the window who had been talking with the German calmed us down and repeated what the officer had told him: that we wouldn't have to be afraid because everybody would be put to work at his own occupation. Some of the people applauded, bravo! Others tried to figure out what kind of work they would be given. This one was a ditchdigger, another a car-

81

penter, a third, a locksmith. Everybody in the car was now in a good mood.

At 4 p.m., the train began to move again. We moved a short distance; then we saw the Treblinka station. As the train moved on, we saw whole mountains of *smattes*.[5] The Jew at the window who was the first to see the rags again tried to calm the crowd, saying that this would be our work. We would be put to work sorting out these rags. Others wanted to know where the rags could have come from. They were told that in Maidanek near Lublin and in other camps the Jews had been given paper clothing and that the clothing with which they had come had been gathered together, sorted out, and forwarded to Germany to be reconditioned. Others volunteered that in Warsaw there was also a special shop at 52 Nowolipki Street, known as Hoffmann's shop, where old clothes were reconditioned. Minutes before the train pulled into Treblinka station, we saw Jews being taken to work. This, too, was reported to the others, and everybody was glad. Everybody was told that Jews were being taken to work, led by a Ukrainian.

After passing the Treblinka station, the train went on a few hundred meters to the camp. In the camp there was a platform to which the train ran through a separate gate, guarded by a Ukrainian. He opened the gate for us. After the train had entered, the gate was closed again. As I was later able to note, this gate was made of wooden slats, interwoven with barbed wire, camouflaged by green branches.

When the train stopped, the doors of all the cars were suddenly flung open. We were now on the grounds of the charnel house that is Treblinka.

Chapter Two

The doors of the cars were opened by Ukrainians. There were also German SS men, standing around with whips in their hands. Many of the people in the car were still lying on the floor, unconscious; some of them were probably no longer alive. We had been on the way for about 20 hours. If the trip had gone on for another half day, the number of dead would have been a great deal larger. We would have perished from heat and lack of air. As I later learned, when some of the transports arrived at Treblinka and were unloaded, it was found that all the passengers were dead.

When the doors of our car were opened, some of the people who had been lying half-naked tried to put on some clothing. But not all of them were given a chance to throw on their clothes. At the command of the SS men, Ukrainians jumped onto the cars and used their whips to drive the crowd out of the boxcars as quickly as possible.

"So Many Clothes! But Where Are the People?" We left the cars tired and exhausted. After traveling for so many hours in semi-darkness, we were momentarily blinded by the sun. It was 5 p.m., but the day's heat was at full strength. As we looked around, we saw countless piles of rags. The sight stabbed at our hearts. So many clothes! But where were the people? We began to recall stories we had heard of Lublin, Kolo, Turek and we said to each other, "Jews, this is no good! They've got us!" They drove us faster, faster. Through another exit, guarded by a Ukrainian, we left the platform area and entered a fenced-off area where two barracks were located.

One of the Germans rapped out a command: "Women and children to the left! Men to the right!" A little later, two Jews were stationed there as interpreters to show the crowd where to go. We men were told to sit down outside along the length of the barrack on the right. The women all went into the barrack on the left and, as we later learned, they were told at once to strip naked and were driven out of the barrack through another door. From there, they entered a narrow path lined on either side with barbed wire. This path led through a small grove to the building that housed the gas chamber. Only a few minutes later we could hear their terrible screams, but we could not see anything, because the trees of the grove blocked our view.

Beneath Machine Gun Barrels. As we sat there, tired and resigned—some of us lying stretched out on the sand—we could see a heavy machine gun being set up on the roof of the barrack on the left side, with three Ukrainian servicemen stretched out around it. We figured that any minute they would turn the machine gun on us and kill us all. This fear put some new life into me, but then I again felt the terrible thirst which had been torturing me for so many hours. The Ukrainians on the barrack roof had opened an umbrella over their heads to shield them from the sun. My sole thought at that moment was, "A cup of water! *Just one more cup of water before I die!*"

Some of the people I had known from the factory were sitting near to me. Our bookkeeper K., our warehouseman D., and several other young people. "It's no good," they said. "They're going to shoot us! Let's try to get out of here!" We all thought that there was an open field beyond the fence which surrounded both barracks. We didn't know then that a second fence lay further on. When I had revived a little, I followed some of the others through an open door to the barrack on the right. I planned to break down one of the boards in the wall and to run away. But when we got into the barrack, we were overcome by stark depression. There were many dead bodies lying in the barrack, and we could see that they had all been shot. Through a chink in the barrack's wall we could see a Ukrainian guard on the other side, holding a gun. There was nothing we could do. I went back outside.

As I later learned, the corpses were those of a transport of Jews from Kielce who had arrived in Treblinka that morning. Among them were a mother and her son. When it came time to separate them—women to the left and men to the right—the son wanted to say a last good-bye to his mother. When they tried to drive him away, he took out a pocket-knife and stuck it into the Ukrainian. As a punishment, they spent all that day shooting all the Jews from Kielce who were at the camp.

I sat down outside once more. After a while I noticed a Jew with a red triangular patch on his knee, driving a horse and wagon on the other side of the fence. I signaled to him and asked him with my eyes: "What will they do with us?" He answered with a wave of his hand: "Scrap!"

The area between the barracks where we were sitting was guarded on all sides. Leaning against a telephone pole stood two large signs, which I now read for the first time.

"Attention, people from Warsaw!" the signs read in huge letters, followed by detailed instructions for people who supposedly had arrived at a regular labor camp. They were to hand in their clothes to be deloused and disinfected. Our money and our other belongings would be returned to us later on . . .

A little later, an SS man came over to us and delivered a speech. He spoke very cold-bloodedly but here and there his oration was interspersed with humor. "Have no fear!" he repeated every minute, "Nothing will happen to you. The dead bodies lying here," he told us, "arrived in that condition. They died in the train from suffocation. It's nobody's fault. Everyone will be treated well here. Everyone will be employed at his own trade or occupation, tailors in the tailor workshops; cabinetmakers in the furniture shop,

shoemakers as shoemakers. Everyone will get work and bread."
Some people began to call off their occupations. When they went
up to the German, he laughed at them in a friendly way, felt their
muscles and patted them on the back. "*Ja, ja*, that's good! You're
strong, that's what we need." Some people began to applaud the
German. Most of the Jews who heard this sweet talk did indeed feel
better and started to believe that they really were in a labor camp.
"Sit quietly, in order"—the German gently urged them and people
sat up straight in their places, like children in a classroom.

Selection For Work. Afterwards, a second SS man appeared,
with a rifle on his shoulder, and selected ten men from one group.
He didn't want the older ones, only younger people. He lined them
up in a double column and marched them away. Meanwhile, I
hung back. I didn't push forward to be taken, because I was afraid;
it just might be that these people would be taken away and shot.
Later on, I learned that the ten had been put to work clearing away
rags from the railroad tracks.

Still later, a Ukrainian came over and took five more men away to
work. At the time I didn't know for what purpose they were being
taken. But I started to think of joining those who were going off to
work. Another Ukrainian, who came a little later, spoke to us in
Russian. I didn't understand what he was saying; I thought that he
was going to take us for work. He took only three people and said
that when these would return, he would take others in their place.
It turned out that he took us to the outhouse behind the barrack
and since I had come along by mistake, he dubbed me "The
Speculator." He was not the worst in that bunch. A little later, the
SS man who had taken the ten men was back. This time he wanted
60 men, and I was one of them.

The SS man lined us up in double columns, and took us out of
the fenced-off area between the two barracks into the wider yard
through which we had passed when we were first unloaded from
the train. The SS man led us to the right behind the narrower
enclosure and from there into a large, open area.

Ten Thousand Corpses In One Place. Here we beheld a horrible
sight. Countless dead bodies lay there, piled upon each other. I
think that perhaps 10,000 bodies were there. A terrible stench
hovered in the air. Most of the bodies had horribly bloated bellies;
they were covered with brown and black spots, swollen and the
surfaces of their skin already crawling with worms.

The lips of most of the dead were strangely twisted and the tips of their tongues could be seen protruding between the swollen lips. The mouths resembled those of dead fish. I later learned that most of these people had died of suffocation in the boxcar. Their mouths had remained open as if they were still struggling for a little air. Many of the dead still had their eyes open.

We, the new arrivals, were terror-stricken. We looked at each other to confirm that what we were seeing was real. But we were afraid to look around too much, because the guards could start shooting any minute. I still did not want to believe my eyes. I still thought that it was just a dream.

The Corpse Processing Plant at Work. Five hundred meters farther away, a machine was at work digging ditches. This machine, together with its motor, was as big as a railroad car. Its mechanical shovels were digging up piles of dirt. The machine loaded the dirt into little wagons, which turned away and dumped it onto the side. Things were humming out there on that big field. Many Jews had already been working there earlier. They were dragging corpses into the ditches which had been dug for them by the machine. We could also see Jews pushing carts piled with bodies toward the big ditches at the edge of the field.

There it was again, that stench. They were all running, pursued by Germans, Ukrainians, and even Jewish group leaders called kapos (*Kameraden-Polizei*), who kept driving them on: "Faster! Faster!" All the while, we could hear the crack of pistols and rifles and the whine of bullets. But there were no cries or groans from those who were shot because the Germans shot them from the back in the neck. In that way, the person drops dead quick as lightning and never even has a chance to make his voice heard one last time.

There were various kinds of ditches in that place. At a distance, running parallel with the outermost camp fence, there were three giant mass graves, in which the dead were arranged in layers. Closer to the barracks, a somewhat smaller ditch had been dug. This was where our 60 men were put to work. A group of workers walked around the area, dusting the corpses with chlorine powder, which they dipped from big barrels with their buckets. [. . .]

I should point out here that none of the gassing victims were buried in this area; only those who had died in the transports or who had been shot on arrival at the camp, before entering the "showers."

Our team of 60 men was divided into three groups. Since I knew German, I became the leader of my group, and in fact soon had to shout at my people and chase them. If I had not done so, I could have been whipped or shot at any time.

The Young Man With the Eyeglasses and the SS Man. The SS man who had brought us here had a chat with me. I had asked him what the work would be like and he calmly and patiently answered all my questions. "Whoever wants to work," he said, "will get work from us. As for the rest, when you've been here a while you'll be able to figure out everything for yourself." While he was talking to me, he noticed a young man from Warsaw, wearing glasses, who was part of my group. He was standing in the ditch, receiving the bodies which others had been dragging over. It seemed to the German that he was not working fast enough.

"Halt! Turn around!" the SS man ordered the young man. He took his rifle from his shoulder and before the young man could have figured out what was expected from him, he lay dead among the bodies in the ditch. They dragged him farther along and soon additional corpses were piled on top of him.

The German returned the rifle to his shoulder and resumed our conversation, as if nothing had happened.

A chill seized my heart. A few minutes later, when the German had gone away, something similar happened to another Jew. This man was shot by a Ukrainian. The Ukrainian had ordered him searched and had taken a packet of money from his pocket. Before long, our group was missing ten men and we heard continual shooting all around.

A Nap Among the Rags. I could see at every turn that things were bad. I was dead tired and thirsty, barely able to remain on my feet. I was very unhappy about the spot I was in. A little later, about 8 p.m., when it had become darker, I took advantage of the darkness to move closer to the railroad tracks where I had seen the piles of clothing. I no longer cared. I burrowed my whole body and my face into the rags. Unconscious of time and place, I fell asleep almost at once.

When I woke up, it was already completely dark. By the light of electric lamps hanging suspended from poles, I could see a group of Jews not far from me, with red patches on their knees. I recognized one of them who had been a prisoner of war together with me. I went over to him and asked him to do me a favor and let me join his group. He replied that this could be done. While I was talking to this young man, a new transport rolled into the camp. We all went out to meet the boxcars. My world turned black as I looked into the cars. I was stunned by what I saw there. The cars contained only corpses. They had all suffocated on the journey from lack of air. The cars were jam-packed and the corpses lay piled one on top of the other. It is not possible to imagine the impact of the sight of these cars full of dead bodies. I inquired where the transport had come from and I found out that it had come from Międzyrzec (Mezrich). About 6,000 souls, men, women and children. A very few individuals were not dead; they had only fainted. They could have been saved with a little bit of water. But nobody had any water for them. We ourselves had not yet received any water since our arrival in Treblinka.

We were ordered to go over and help unload the dead. The work was very hard and the SS men, as was their custom, kept urging us on with their whips and guns: "Faster! faster!"

We simply had no place to lay out the bodies. The giant piles of clothing were right next to the railroad tracks; beneath them, there were still many unburied bodies left over from before. Meanwhile, we dumped the bodies next to the tracks and arranged them in layers, one on top of the other. From time to time, we heard groans. The sounds came from those who had merely fainted and were now regaining consciousness. These unfortunates were begging with faint voices for a little water, but we were unable to revive them because we ourselves were on the verge of passing out from thirst. We could only separate the ones still alive and put them down a little to the side, near the rags. The Germans didn't notice it because it was so dark.

Among the living I also found a little child, about a year or a year and a half old. The child had regained consciousness and was crying at the top of its voice. I put it down, too, apart from the others, next to the pile of rags. By the next morning the child was dead and it was thrown into the ditch.

We went on working like this until about 2 a.m. When we went up to the SS man and asked for water, he promised us that we would all get water after we had finished up our work. But first we would have to clean out the cars.

After we got through cleaning the cars, we were ordered to move to one side and line up in double columns. The locomotive whistled and the train slowly pulled out of the camp station. A Ukrainian and an SS man stationed themselves at either side of the exit gate and shone flashlights under the wheels to see whether anyone was hiding beneath the cars. A few cars pulled out in good order. But when he got to the third or fourth car, the German shouted, "Halt!" He had discovered two boys lying hunched up between the wheels. One of them got a bullet even before he could crawl out from under the car. The other was able to jump out and started running quick as lightning, trying to lose himself in the crowd of Jews. But the SS man stopped him right away. The young man immediately took his papers out of his pocket and tried to prove that he was a worker. He shouted and pleaded, but this did not impress the German. He started hitting him over the head as hard as he could with his rubber truncheon, until the boy collapsed. Then the Ukrainian came up, turned his rifle upside down and with great force, as if chopping wood, hit his victim over the head with the rifle butt. Finally, they put a bullet in him. Then, at last, they left him alone. The train rolled out.

Now the SS man turned his attention to us. Standing as we were in double columns, he ordered us to sit down in the same order on the ground and took with him one of us to bring water. Coming back with a bucket of water, the German gave each of us a cupful and we drank it greedily. I literally didn't know how to start drinking. I held the cup in front of me with both hands and thought that this water was the most precious thing on earth.

After we had drunk our water, the German led us over to the area between the two barracks and ordered us to sit down near the wall of the barrack at the left. The men from my transport were still sitting in front of the barrack on the right. Some of them wanted to slide over to our group, which had just returned from work, but the SS man would not let them do it.

How We Were Put to Bed. The German went away to ask the commandant what to do with us. When he came back he led us into the barracks on the right side, which was divided down the middle by a wall. He let us into the smaller half and told us to go to sleep. Other Jews were already asleep in the barrack; among them were some whom we had seen at work earlier. We understood that we, too, had gained a temporary reprieve. The rest of the men in our transport were taken to the "showers" that very night.

Chapter Three

Back to the Corpses. The next morning we were put to work on the corpses again. Each one of us received one cup of water for breakfast. We were not given any bread. None of us had his belongings with him. However, we could take as much as we wanted of the food we found in packages that the victims had thrown away. Packages, bundles, valises and knapsacks were scattered at every turn. Some of these packages contained the finest foods, but none of us felt like eating just then; all we wanted was water.

The first task assigned to my group (20 people) was to clear away the murdered Jews from Kielce, who were still lying in our barrack on the other side of the partition, behind which we had spent the night.

Teams of four men each picked up one corpse after another, carried the bodies out to the other side of the fence and laid them out next to the bodies which we had unloaded from the Międzyrzec transport. The Międzyrzec and Kielce corpses could have exchanged greetings. Here, in the area next to the railroad tracks, a second group was at work, loading the bodies onto carts and pushing the carts to the big mass graves which I had seen the day before, running alongside the outermost fence of the camp. The people from the barrack who had been gunned down and those who had suffocated inside the boxcars were buried fully clothed. Apparently, it was considered too much trouble to undress Jews who were already dead. As a rule, the Germans tried as far as possible to see to it that the bodies of Jews were brought in naked, and if someone dropped dead with his clothes on, the Germans magnanimously forwent the *Werterfassung*. This may not have been in accordance with the regulations, but simply the result of daily practice, due to lack of time. At this point we weren't even ordered to search their pockets for money or jewelry. At about 12 noon we were through clearing out the barrack, and were assigned to other work.

The 35 Corpses in the Well. Next to the watchtower in our fence there was a well. Many corpses had accumulated in this well, and we had to pull them out that day. A Pole from Penal Camp Treblinka No. 1[6] was working with us. He stepped into a bucket which was attached to the well's chain, and we lowered him into the well. He would tie the corpses to the bucket, one by one, and we would turn the crank and pull the bodies up. I counted a total of 35 corpses. I had no way of knowing who the people were and how they had gotten into the well. Some of them were tied with ropes. Perhaps they had tried to get down into the well for a drink of water—who could tell? Others said that they might have taken their own lives.

While I was working at the well, I saw a group of workers approaching. They had with them a bucket filled with water. Hoping to get a chance for a drink of water, I tried to join them, but the German who was guarding our group spotted me and hit me across the face with his rubber truncheon. So I had to go back.

The Personal Effects of the Victims. When we were through with the bodies in the well, we were taken to clear away the things in the left-hand barracks, where the people undressed before entering the gas chamber. Here, piled up in huge mounds, were the garments, underwear, shoes and all sorts of other items left by the men, women and children who had undressed there the day before. Various amounts of cash, large and small, were also lying around on the floor. There was Polish money as well as foreign currency, securities and jewelry. It was our job to pick up the rags as they were, and to add them to the piles of clothing near the railroad tracks.

Suddenly, we heard faint moans from beneath a pile of clothes. We discovered several women who had been hiding beneath the rags. They were alive and afraid to emerge into the light of day. When they saw us Jews, they began to whine, "Water, a little water!" But we had no water ourselves and there was nothing we could do for these women. One of the Ukrainians quickly came over and, seeing the women who had survived, he finished them off with a few bullets. We immediately took them away and added them to the other corpses.

In addition to the women whom we found in the barrack, I saw two women lying on the other side of the barracks. They had been killed. They had tried to slip out through the barbed wire fence, thinking, probably, that an open field lay on the other side. One of them had actually pushed through to the other side, but the other had been caught between the wires, and the bullet hit her there. We took these two bodies also and added them to the pile of corpses.

The Roll Call. Thus, at 7 p.m., the work ended on my second day in Treblinka. At 7 o'clock, a roll call was held and an inmate count made. Altogether, there were about 500 of us, and a Jewish commander (kapo) was appointed to take charge of us. He was G.,[7] an engineer from Lodz, who was a convert to Christianity. The roll call that day (just as on all the days that followed) lasted about two hours. Throughout that time, we had to stand at attention in our ranks; if we didn't, we were savagely beaten. Those who for some reason had fallen from grace had to step out of line and had to lie down and receive 25 lashes right there in front of all the others. Nonetheless, some people were so tired that they sat down on the ground, because they could no longer stand up. After the roll call, we went into the barrack and went to sleep.

Camp Routine. The next morning there was another roll call. After we had been counted, a routine was established in which we had regular roll calls three times a day. A regular meal schedule was also established. A field kitchen was set up near the well, where we got a pint of soup three times a day. We received no bread, but we never missed it, because we could take provisions from the packages which new arrivals had brought in with them. We also took cooking ingredients from these packages. The field kitchen was manned by Jews who ladled out the soup.

It was our third day in Treblinka. We badly wanted to wash ourselves, but there could be no question of using water for that purpose. All the time I was there, a drink of water was the most important thing there could be. So we used to wash ourselves only with the cologne and perfume which we found in the knapsacks.

After roll call, we were taken out to work in the big field with the mass graves, where I had worked on the first day. This time I had to carry the bodies out to the main ditches near the fence.

The Big Ditches. These ditches were 60 or 70 meters long. They were also very deep, but I could not tell how deep they were because the ditches to which we had been assigned were already filled with many layers of corpses. The one thing I found surprising was that, deep though these ditches were, no water got to the corpses. The graves remained open through the night and the next day more bodies were piled into them. While I was in Treblinka, only the small ditch to the left, where I had worked on the first day, was closed.

By the time we came out there in the morning, the excavator was already in operation, and digging out new giant graves. A few days later, the excavation was stopped and a new system was instituted. They started burning the dead in the graves and we used to dump into the graves old clothes, valises, and trash which we had picked up in the yard. These articles were set on fire and kept on burning day and night, filling the camp with billows of smoke and the odor of burning flesh. . . .

Why the Transports Stopped Coming. Many of the dead bodies I had seen a few days earlier were still lying in the yard and near the railroad tracks. Perhaps it was due to the accumulation of so many unburied bodies that no new transports arrived in Treblinka between August 25 and September 2 or 3, 1942. The remains of the earlier transports had to be cleared away first.

Already on the day of my arrival, I had seen that many of the corpses were decomposing, crawling with worms, and half-rotted. Today the scene was even more horrible and repulsive. Many of the bodies were already disintegrating and when we pulled them from the heaps where they had lain piled atop one another, their limbs fell off. Mostly, this happened with the corpses of young children, perhaps because their flesh was more delicate.

Nevertheless, there was no particular lack of "shirkers" who looked precisely for these little corpses, because they were easier to carry. Others could be seen picking up heads, entrails, hands and feet that had fallen from the corpses. Not everyone had the physical strength to carry the very heavy, monstrously bloated corpses of those who had died of suffocation in the boxcars.

"The Doll." Suddenly I felt as if an electric current were passing through the place. Even the biggest loafers and shirkers threw themselves into their work with great haste. The word had flashed through the crowd: "It's the Doll! The Doll is coming!"

A young SS man with the rank of Oberscharführer appeared on the scene. He was extraordinarily handsome. I quickly learned that this was the worst sadist in Treblinka. The commandant of Treblinka was a captain; he was in command of the camp. But it was the Oberscharführer who was really in charge of the murder operations. He was nicknamed Lalka, [Polish for] "The Doll." The Jews had given him that nickname because of his handsome face. It was the habit of this murderer to leave several people behind him every time he took a stroll through the camp. He used to stand off at a distance and observe a group of workers; if by some chance somebody was not working fast enough, or simply happened not to please him, he would come over and beat him with the whip, which he always carried with him, until the blood flowed. Then he would order him to strip naked and put a bullet in his neck. Sometimes, for variety's sake, he would have an Ukrainian do the shooting. On this occasion, the murderer finished off several Jews and then coolly walked away.

We were working very hard. The heat was great almost all the time that I was in Treblinka. The terrible stench of the dead bodies settled in our nostrils. We were sick at heart, sweat poured from our bodies without cease, and we were plagued by thirst. We could not get enough water to quench our thirst. When a bucket of water did materialize there was such pushing and shoving that on more than one occasion the bucket was overturned and then nobody had any water. On such occasions one of the Ukrainians would come over, drive away the crowd with his rifle butt, and hand out the water himself. We did not drink our water; we sipped it as one would the costliest beverage. Not once in the three weeks that I was in Treblinka did I ever really manage to quench my thirst. Even now, I can still feel this craving for water in my gut. Whenever I start to drink a glass of cold water nowadays, I savor it doubly, and at the same time I can feel my fingers tremble; that's how important this drink has become to me.

Aside from the thirst and the backbreaking toil, we were plagued by a terrible fear. We could never have pictured the things we now experienced in the flesh. They were worse than even the most lurid horror stories from our childhood about evil witches, robbers, and seven-headed vipers who dragged off people to their caves to suffocate among the corpses and bones of earlier victims.

There were corpses all over the place, corpses by the tens, hundreds, and thousands. Corpses of men, women and children of all ages, in various postures and facial expressions, as if they had been frozen immediately after they had taken their last breath. Heaven, earth, and corpses! A gigantic enterprise which manufactured corpses. Only a German could get accustomed to a place like that. I could never get used to the sight of the dead.

We worked on the field of corpses until 7 o'clock at night. Tired, thirsty, broken in body and soul, we returned to rest in the barrack, where the roll call and the associated beatings took place. There we lay down to sleep. We had lived through a third day in the killing center of Treblinka.

The days that followed passed a little more quickly and began to fall into a pattern.

"The Doll" Has His Fun. On the fourth day, as I was at work at the graves with my group, the following incident took place involving several young fellows. They had not been working very fast. Suddenly, "The Doll" appeared on the scene, marched them to the open ditch and ordered them to undress. In no time at all, they too, were lying naked and dead with the other corpses.

I learned that before the war Lalka had been a prizefighter.[8] Apparently, he also regarded shooting Jews as a kind of sport. Frequently he would appear on the field in excellent spirits. He would come striding up, with light, springy steps, and give a Jew a few punches from behind with his fists. If the Jew fell down, he would give him a playful kick, like a football player. Then, continuing on his way, he would finish him off, either by himself or through one of the Ukrainians, with a bullet in the neck.

How to Attract the Attention of a German. The most dangerous thing of all was to do anything that might attract the attention of a German. A certain elderly doctor from Warsaw had his hand bandaged. That was sufficient reason to order him to undress and lay him out dead in the ditch . . . An invalid with an injured leg would sit while he was sorting out rags. As soon as Lalka saw this, he was a dead man in the wink of an eye. A Jew who worked in the field kitchen scalded himself. So he got a bullet in the neck because he was now unfit for work. As a result, those who got sick, hurt, or bruised kept it to themselves like the most dangerous secret, so that the Germans would not find out. A boy who slept next to me in the barrack had swollen legs and went to the greatest exertions that this should not be noticed. But he could not keep his legs covered up all the time, and he was soon "cured" with a bullet in the neck.

Naturally, the decimation of the people who had been working side by side with me left me stunned. Here, a person had been standing next to me, we had been straining side by side, dragging the bodies into the graves, and all of a sudden he is lying there, with glassy eyes, naked and dead in a grave where in about a minute's time he will vanish from sight because other bodies will be lying on top of him.

"I Must Get out of Here." Whenever I took a final glance at someone who had been killed I would think that the same fate awaited me, if not today, then tomorrow. I thought of my family across the ocean who would never even find out where my remains would be. Young though I was, I would soon lie dead and rot or be cremated, and those who were still alive would be repelled by the sight of my body, just as I was repelled when I had to wrap my arms around the dead bodies of others.

I greatly regretted that I had not looked for ways to steal across borders and join my family while I still had been free and able to do so. And as I gazed at the bodies in the open graves I began to think more and more intensely about ways to get out of this place. When I got back to other places in the camp, I would cool off and become resigned. Then I would see only the difficulties and the impossibility of escaping from that hell. But once I was back in the field of corpses I would always gather new energy to think up a way of escaping. The idea and the will to take to my heels became stronger within me every time.

Chapter Four

Selection. At last, the number of bodies in the great field of corpses began to grow smaller and finally the day came when the field had been cleared. What would they do with us now? No new transports were coming in; what kind of work would they give us, then? Frightened, we discussed this among ourselves and our hearts told us that our time was drawing near.

One day, in the afternoon, when we came back to the roll call area between the two barracks, they lined us up in rows of five and we sensed that something was about to happen.

First of all, a group of Ukrainians ran over to search the piles of rags to make sure that no one was hiding out beneath them. They found a few men and stabbed them right then and there with the bayonets which some of the Ukrainians used to carry.

Fifty men from Treblinka Penal Camp No. 1 used to work with us. They wore red patches. The Scharführer ordered them to fall out and stationed them to one side. Then he started counting out fives. He counted out 50 men at random and sent them over to join the red patches. There were 100 men in all who were marched off to a special barrack. These men were supposed to remain; the others were supposed to go to the "showers." I was not among the one hundred.

After the roll call, they let us go back to the barrack as usual, but they told us that we would be called that same night and then we would all have to come out. Finally, the Scharführer gave us a speech and took the opportunity to lecture us, saying that we were not a useful element, that we had only ourselves to blame for everything, and so forth. We understood very well what this meant and had no patience to listen to this tripe.

You can imagine the mood in our group after we had been left alone in our barrack.

Was this our last night, or our last hour? We didn't know, but it was obvious that the end was drawing near.

Different people behaved in different ways. The very young, who probably never had been pious, joined with young Hasidim in reciting the mourners' Kaddish. There was no lack of moralists who interpreted our present misery as God's way of punishing the

Jewish people for its sins. And as they preached, some people did indeed feel sinful and guilty and they began to beat their breasts and recite the *Vidduy* [the last confession before death]. Others tried to remember some prayer; they swayed and lulled their fears with a tune from the Psalms. Still others simply bawled like children.

"Feh! You ought to be ashamed of yourselves! You're crying like old women!" Those who had a better grip on themselves said things like that to give the others some courage. They even tried to make us see things in a more cheerful light, saying that the situation wasn't necessarily as bad as all that and that a change could still come.

"If only I could have a drink!" a fat young man whom I knew from Pawia Street cried. Someone else wanted to ease his despair with a cigarette, but it did not occur to anyone to think of ways of saving themselves or of putting up resistance. We were too weakened, too beaten down—and too thirsty.

A Ukrainian Tries to Cheer Us Up. The strangest thing of all was that a Ukrainian was among those who tried to cheer us up. He was on guard duty over the barrack and when he heard the commotion and weeping inside he walked in and spoke to us in Russian, telling us not to take things so hard. Nothing would happen, nothing would be done to us; we would go on working the same as before.

And, wonder of wonders, his prediction came true. A rare miracle occurred. To this day, I don't know why. Some said that there had been a breakdown in the gas chamber. By morning, no one had come for us, and then we had roll call just as usual. It is true that 80 men had been taken out to be shot, but the remainder, a good few hundred people, were assigned new work.

The Lumpenkommando. Those of us who were left were classified again; some of the carpenters were taken out and sent to the woodworking shop in the German sector of the camp. A group of Jews was assigned to chopping down trees in the woods, another group to repair the road leading into the German camp; the largest group of Jews, including myself, was detailed to sorting out the clothes, and other belongings of those who had perished. Each group had its own designation, which was called out at roll calls. There was a *Strassenbaukommando* [road construction detail], a *Holzfellerkommando* [woodcutters' detail], a *Maurerkommando* [bricklayer's detail], a *Flaschensortiererkommando* [bottle sorting detail]. One of the details, the watchmakers, consisted of only six men, who were responsible for sorting out gold and valuables. The most important and numerous detail was our *Lumpenkommando* (rag detail), which had the job of sorting and packing clothing and linens. Each of the details had only one wish: that its job should last as long as possible. We persuaded ourselves that in the meantime help would come to us from somewhere—from overseas, or the war might end, or Russian airplanes . . . There was no lack of naive people.

Clothes Speak Volumes. Lined up in double columns, we were led away through three gates to the far barracks, which were located in a separate enclosure on the other side of the German camp. These barracks were packed full of rags, which had been lying about unsorted for weeks, or even months. We picked up layer after layer. Apparently, these had been the belongings of the Jews from Warsaw, which had been deposited in layers, according to the various types of people who had been brought, one after the other to Treblinka. First had come the poor, the beggars, the inmates of refugee shelters, and then the better types, with better clothes. At first, we had to handle heavily soiled and lice-infested clothing and underwear. The starving lice crawled all over us from head to toe and there was nothing we could do about it. Some said that we would get typhus; others said, "What's the difference which way we die?" But when we had gotten through clearing half of a barrack, the stuff got finer and more elegant. We found papers in their pockets, so that in every instance that seemed interesting to us, we were able to establish the identity of the owner of the clothes. There were things also from German Jews, Jews from Vienna and Berlin, who apparently had been brought to Warsaw prior to the *Aktion*.

Werterfassung: Sorting and Packing the Personal Effects of the Murdered Jews. But who had the stomach to investigate whose possessions these had been? The work would proceed in the following manner:

We would stand in groups next to piles of personal effects, guarded by a Ukrainian, with an SS man at the head. As usual, we were constantly hurried on as we worked. "Faster! Faster!" They were always in a hurry. The SS man would saunter through our ranks as we stood, bent over our work, and dish out quick blows left and right. Later, the practice was introduced to have the Jewish kapo beat us as much as possible while we worked. If he didn't proceed with sufficient vigor and wasn't beating someone new all the time, he himself would get lashes from the SS man. We would empty pockets and knapsacks and sort out the things by categories: linens, clothing, outerwear, and tie them up in separate bundles. The smaller items, too, were carefully sorted: soap separate, matches separate, toothbrushes, lighters, compacts, belts, flashlights, pencils, gold pens, breast pockets, wallets, etc., etc.

The Germans made good use of everything, and if a murdered Jew by some chance had happened to be a famous lawyer or an outstanding medical authority, or had talent and knowledge in some other field, they would inherit from him a finer pen, a nicer shirt, or a platinum watch instead of an ordinary gold one.

Entire luxury boutiques grew up around us as we worked. Everything was packed away in canisters or cases, which we carried over to a central area, where each container was listed, provided with shipping labels, and was expedited to the railroad station for shipment to Germany. It was harder to process the clothes; these had accumulated in such masses that the Germans had to dispense with records and send off this part of the Jewish property without any accounting. It was impossible to speed up the processing of the clothing and as long as I was in Treblinka, I constantly had before my eyes the same mountains of rags, which I had seen when I had first arrived. There was also quite a lot of tea kettles, thermoses, hot-water bottles and especially a plenitude of bottles, all of which we sorted and packed away for shipping. As I have already mentioned, there was a special bottle sorting detail (*Flaschensortierkommando*) and more than one Jew who happened to break a bottle paid for it with a bullet in the neck.

The six watchmakers and jewelers, who were employed at assessing, sorting, and packing the gold, the watches, the other jewelry and the currency which had been found among the personal effects, were working in a corner of their own. Like all the other work details, they, too, worked under a German supervisor, a portly, somewhat elderly SS man who didn't treat them badly. When it came time for a selection, he would keep them late at their work and thereby save their lives. Try to figure out a German! Perhaps his motive was to keep his supply of "soft ones"[9] rustling. Other German group commanders, too, didn't like to change their personnel and sometimes would protect their Jews when they learned that a selection was about to take place. I myself experienced this while I was working in the woods.

I should point out here that the selections were an eternal sword hanging over our heads. We would get up every morning before reveille and wash and make ourselves look as youthful and vigorous as possible. Not even in my best days had I shaved so often as I did in Treblinka. Everybody shaved every morning and washed their faces with cologne taken from packages abandoned by the Jewish prisoners. Some even put on powder or rouge. They would pinch their cheeks—so it was told—so that they should have good color. The prize at stake was a few more days, or perhaps even a few more weeks, of life.

The initial, simpler stages of money sorting were assigned to us. Only individual valises or boxes filled with valuables were taken straight to the jewelers. The money we found in pockets or purses was thrown into separate piles. Coins and bills were separated, as were dollars, pounds, Czarist gold rubles, and the "junk," as we called ordinary Polish currency. Everyone who was taken to the *Umschlagplatz*, no matter how poor, had taken with him some kind of money for a rainy day, whatever iron reserves he possessed, with which he might be able to save his life. In the very first poster the Germans put up in Warsaw, they did us the favor of announcing that we would be permitted to take our valuables with us . . .

We found whole fortunes sewn away in secret pockets, in ladies' corsets, in jacket linings. Valuables often were given to the women to conceal. They would bake diamonds into bread, or place them into little matchboxes and cover them with matches. The foremen ordered us to search everything for valuables, and our so-called sabotage consisted in not putting too much effort into carrying out these orders. For this reason, plenty of hidden treasures probably remained in the clothing; these may or may not be turned up sometime in the future. In this way, huge fortunes were buried or incinerated together with those Jews who were dumped fully clothed into the special mass graves in the death field.

All over Treblinka one would find scattered bits and pieces of money notes including dollar bills and other foreign currencies. These bills had been torn up and thrown away by Jews who finally understood what kind of place this was. This was their final protest and act of revenge before disappearing forever in the "bathhouse." . . . The bosses of Treblinka didn't worry too much about trying to prevent our taking some of the gold and valuables for ourselves because they knew that eventually they would be able to get their hands on it—when they would send us naked to our deaths . . .

The Millionaires of Treblinka. Some of them enjoyed collecting all sorts of "curios." They made no effort to hide this from us, but among themselves the Germans were wary of each other. They would come right over to us and take away a nice gold watch, which they would immediately take to one of the six Jewish watchmakers, to put in working order. Or they would pick out a particularly unusual ring or some other item of women's jewelry, no doubt as gifts for their sweethearts in the Fatherland. All of them—both Germans and Ukrainians—had so much money that they didn't even bother to touch it. I think that they all became millionaires in Treblinka.

We didn't bother about such things. There were few among us who even believed they would ever be able to get out. Nevertheless, temptation would come now and then and, without any specific plan, or intent, one or the other of us would hide a few items, and if someone managed to escape from Treblinka these things came in handy, because both Jews and peasants in the Treblinka area would ask huge sums from Treblinka escapees for the least little favor. If someone was noticed hiding something from among the valuables, his neighbor would say to him, "What do you want that for? You're not going to get out of here alive anyway. The dogcatchers won't leave any living witnesses."

But I kept thinking all the time about escaping and every once in a while I used to take some of the money and valuables and bury them in certain places. Either I'll survive—I thought—and I'll return here some day and take it out, or if not—at least those fiends will not get their hands on it.

From time to time, as we sorted out the clothing, it would happen that one or the other of us might recognize items that had belonged to one of his relatives or friends. If he looked at the documents found with these items, he would soon see whether his assumption had been correct. A few sighs or, more rarely, a few tears, were the only memorials to those who had perished.

After I had been working a few days at sorting personal effects — no new transports had yet arrived — I was assigned along with 14 other men to clean up the road to the gas chamber, or, as they called it, the "bathhouse." That area aroused the greatest fear among all of us. But I had never been there before.

The "Trash" on the Last Road. The road leading from the left-hand barracks or the roll call area to the building in the middle of the woods was concealed by trees. This was the path upon which hundreds of thousands of Jewish men, women and children ran their last race, a narrow sandy winding path bordered on both sides with a barbed wire fence . . .

As we came closer to the path, we saw the "trash" which they wanted us to clean up before new transports arrived. This "trash" consisted of a veritable windfall of banknotes which people had torn up and thrown away before they died. We were given special birch brooms and rakes for the job. With the rakes, we raked up gold coins, jewels and diamonds from the sand. One of us picked up a gold twenty-dollar coin and took it over to the Ukrainian who was standing guard over us, as an inducement to have him get off our backs as we worked.

"What good is this money to me?" answered the Ukrainian. "Don't you know that none of us will get out of here alive, either?" This particular Ukrainian happened to be a fairly decent fellow. He didn't rush us at our work and didn't beat us. Only when a German showed up, he would put on an act and shout at us, "Bystro, bystro!" [Russian for "Quick! Quick!"]. We kept busy this way, cleaning up the ground until the evening roll call and bedtime.

I Already Know the Whole Camp. The next morning, 15 men, including myself, were taken out of our group and escorted once again to the gas chamber area. This time we were given a different job; we were ordered to help put up the walls of a new building. Some said that this would be a crematorium for the bodies of those who had been asphyxiated in the gas chamber because burying them took up too much space. I came to a new area with a separate barrack for the workers—a kingdom unto itself. In this way, I got an opportunity to acquaint myself with the most secret and important part of the camp—the part where the mechanical murder factory itself was located, and also the separate field for the dead where those who were murdered there were buried. One after another, I was able to learn about all the parts of the annihilation camp, Treblinka 2.

Inside the camp as a whole, there were five smaller barbed wire enclosures within the area of one large enclosure.

The area where I had been working on the rags was the center of the *Werterfassung*, that is, the place where the loot taken from those who had perished was gathered and picked over. Two barracks there were packed with the personal effects of Jews. Later, when

102

some of the items had been sent away so that there was more room, the workers employed in the *Werterfassung* were moved in also. I only spent one night in this new place, but I'll get to that later.

Near this area was located the so-called "German camp," through which our column would march every day on the way to work. There were two long barracks which stood facing each other (see plan). The bedrooms, kitchen and mess hall of the SS men was located in one of the barracks. In the barrack facing it was the commandant's apartment and the food storehouse, where the Germans kept the best groceries they had found inside the baggage of the Jews. There was no shortage there of wines, sardines, candy and imported delicacies from food packages which Jews used to receive from overseas, and so forth. We too, would find more than one fine snack or drink there. But as time went by, the food supply from the packages began to dwindle, and, because no new transports were coming in, we began to get hungry.

Behind the food storehouse there was a little house where there lived a special category of Jews. These individuals wore yellow patches. They were a few dozen Jews from the neighboring towns, who had been put to work several months earlier building the camp. In recognition of their services, some of them were allowed to remain alive with the special job of waiting on the Germans and Ukrainians who were quartered here. Most of them were artisans in various fields, and they had been joined by some skilled workers from Warsaw with various trades. Together, they groomed, shaved, barbered, dressed and shod the gang of murderers. Several girls were working in the kitchens. They were the only females who walked the earth of Treblinka for more than 24 hours. Those same barracks also housed the workshop for the Jewish artisans. The yellow patches—they can really be called the yellow survival badges—were worn by the Jews on their right knee. As I have already mentioned, there was one other class of Jews in the camp with a longer life span. These were the privileged characters from the Treblinka No. 1 penal camp; they wore a red patch on their knee as their own badge of survival.

The Gas Chambers. By that time I had already become acquainted with four district parts of the camp, including the big, five-sided field of corpses, which was fenced off next to the railroad tracks, and the roll call square between the two barracks. But I had not yet become acquainted with the most terrible of all the parts of the camp—the gas chambers. That day, I was to come quite close to this, the fifth and last part of the camp. I have forgotten to mention that there were towers at all four corners of the camp, each of them three stories high, in which Ukrainian guards constantly paced back and forth. These were the watchtowers which served as observation posts to make sure that no one could run away from the camp. At the top levels of the watchtowers, there were machine guns, searchlights which sent out broad beacons every few minutes to every part of the camp, making the night as bright as midday. Only on nights when Warsaw was bombed did the searchlights remain dark.

Most of the buildings in the camp were made of wood. The gas chamber and the new building—which was in the process of being built at the time and to which we were assigned as construction helpers—were made of brick.

We were put to work slaking lime in the ditches which had been dug. Barrels of water, drawn from a special well, were standing nearby. It was from these barrels that, for the only time while I was in Treblinka, I was able to satisfy my thirst a little more. But it did not do me any good. Just like others who finally got a chance to grab a little more water, I was seized by diarrhea that same day. It was very debilitating.

Aside from that little bit of water, the workers were no better off in this area than elsewhere in the camp. On the contrary, here in the "Death Camp," as that place was known, the treatment the workers received was even harsher, if that was possible.

Toward noon, when the sun was burning at its strongest, I witnessed a scene which had a most horrible impact on me.

On my way back from the kitchen, I happened to pass by the barrack which housed those who were regularly employed in that area. In general, these people had no contact with the workers in the rest of the camp. There, I came upon three Jews lying on the ground. I didn't know how they got there. Perhaps they hadn't been able to make themselves go on working, or perhaps they had collapsed from exhaustion, and wanted to rest a little, and had been caught by an SS man. Now that sadist was standing over them with a thick whip in his hand, belaboring one of them. The man was lying naked and totally unconscious. But the German still refused to leave him alone and kept whipping him with all his might on his naked belly . . . The others, it seems, had already received their share, since they were lying there bloody and unconscious. As I looked at this scene, I thought to myself that compared to this, the

104

place where I had worked before had been like gold, and I resolved to get out of here no matter what the consequences and go back to the old place.

But the longish, not too large brick building standing in the middle of the "Death Camp" had a strange fascination for me: this was the gas chamber. Before I left the area, I felt I had to obtain a glimpse of this, the most terrible part of the camp where the sinister crime was perpetrated on the Jews.

I had already come quite close to it several times, when I and others had been carrying water for the lime and clay from the well which stood right next to the building. But it had not occurred to me to leave my group and move a little closer to see. Only as we were returning from our midday meal and our column halted for a while, did I sneak away from them and move toward the open door of the gas chamber.

I think I have already noted that this building was surrounded by a wooded area. Now I noticed that, spread over the flat roof of the building, there was a green wire net whose edges extended slightly beyond the building's walls. This may have been for protection against air attacks. Beneath the net, on top of the roof, I could see a tangle of pipes. . . .

The walls of the building were covered with concrete. The gas chamber had not been operating for a week. I was able to look inside through one of the two strong whitewashed iron exits which happened to be open.

I saw before me a room which was not too large. It looked like a regular shower room with all the accoutrements of a public bathhouse. The walls of the room were covered with small, white tiles. It was very fine, clean work. The floor was covered with orange terra cotta tiles. Nickelplated metal faucets were set into the ceiling.

That was all. A comfortable, neat little bathhouse set in the middle of a wooded area. There was nothing more to see. But as one stood in front of the entrance to this "bathhouse" one could see hills of lime, and beneath them the giant, still-open mass graves where tens, perhaps hundreds, of thousands of "bathers" lay in eternal rest. Later on, I was told that here, too, they had begun to cremate the bodies in the ditches.

The Chest for Gold Teeth. A further technical improvement for destroying the bodies of the dead Jews—and who knows if it was only dead bodies — would no doubt be introduced in the building on whose construction we were working. People said that it would be a crematorium.

Standing next to the "bathhouse" was a large chest. As I later learned, this chest was used for a special kind of *Werterfassung*. When the machine was in operation and batches of corpses at a time were dragged out from the bathhouse, a Jewish "dentist" would stand there with forceps, examine the mouth of each corpse and extract any gold teeth or platinum caps which he might find there. More than one chestful of gold had been accumulated in this manner. The Germans are good housekeepers.

The Open-Air Concert at the Death Camp. As I stood before the door of the Treblinka "bathhouse," I made a new discovery. Earlier, it had seemed to me that I heard sounds of music. I had thought it was a radio loudspeaker which the Germans had installed in order not to be isolated, God forbid, from their Fatherland's *Kultur* out here in the sticks. I was now to learn that their concern for musical culture went even further. Under a tree, about 40 meters from the bathhouse, not far from the path on which the Jews were driven into the "bath," there was a small orchestra consisting of three Jews with yellow patches and three Jewish musicians from Stoczek (who were later joined by another, better musician from Warsaw). There they stood, playing their instruments. I don't know why, but I was particularly impressed by a long reed instrument, a sort of fife or flute. In addition, there was a violin and, I believe, a mandolin. The musicians were standing there and raising a ruckus for all they were worth. They were probably playing the latest hits which were popular with the Germans and Ukrainians, for whom they also used to play at shindigs in the guard stations. The Jews would play while the Gentiles danced.

A musical people, these Ukrainians. On the eve of the anniversary of the outbreak of the war—the night between August 31 and September 1—the SS men arranged a musical entertainment for the Jews. The musicians were taken to the roll call square and ordered to play Jewish tunes. Several young Jews were ordered to come forward and start to dance. An elderly Ukrainian corporal directed the show. The Germans thoroughly enjoyed the show; they were clapping and rolling with laughter . . .

Later on, when I made more detailed inquiries, I found out that this sort of Jewish open-air concert was held also whenever new transports arrived. No doubt the Jewish tunes merged with the shouts and screams of the Jewish men, women, and children who were being driven into the death bath.

There they would stand and play all the time, the Jewish musicians, near the narrow path along which other Jews ran their last race, opposite the open ditches where tens of thousands of Jews lay in their last sleep. There, they stood and played. They were playing for the right to remain alive a few more weeks.

I returned to my group and continued to work, my mind bent on getting out of the death camp as soon as possible. An opportunity to do this soon materialized. Early one afternoon, I noticed a group of people coming in from the woods, carrying on their shoulders saplings which they had cut down.

These little trees were supposed to be planted in front of the big mass graves on the Death Camp, near the railroad tracks, in order to conceal the graves from the eyes of outsiders. The sadists of Treblinka, with their heavy-handed humor, referred to them as the "kindergarten." Seeing the people carrying the saplings, I picked up a branch from the ground and yelled, "Hello there!" as if I had lagged behind and was now running to catch up with them.

As I ran, I kept looking behind me to see whether by chance there was a bullet flying after me. But I got out all right and after I had made my way through the fence of the Death Camp I threw away the branch and rejoined my "rag detail," which happened to be working that day along the railroad tracks preparing the bundles of rags for transportation.

New Transports. Late that afternoon, preparations were begun for the reception of new transports, which were to start arriving again the next day. During the roll call 40 people who could speak German were taken out of line. I, too, reported for duty. We thought we would be assigned as interpreters in the penal camp [Treblinka No. 1]. One of the SS men even gave us a speech with the usual sweet talk, telling us that we were among the chosen few, that nothing would happen to us, and so forth. We had nothing to lose, so we easily let ourselves be gulled into believing that something good was about to happen. We were glad that we were the most fortunate prisoners in the whole camp, because we had hopes of getting out alive. Why, we would be able to leave the camp the very next morning! We listened until the end of the speech and then went to sleep. At roll call the next morning, our group was called out and told to line up separately from the others. "The Doll" then performed a special small-scale selection with us. He asked each of us our names. If the person asked gave his name in a firm, loud voice, that was good. But if, by chance, he hesitated for a second and called out his name in a somewhat less hearty fashion, he was rejected and sent back to the rest of the group. In this way only about 35 remained of the original 40, and now it turned out that we weren't being sent out anywhere, but that we would remain in camp to help receive and process the new transports. We were given assignments, some to open the boxcars, some to separate the new arrivals—men to the right, women to the left—and so forth. I was assigned to take away the shoes taken off by the new arrivals as they undressed before going to the "showers."

We expected the new transport from Warsaw to arrive any minute.

Chapter Five

New Transports. What would the new transport bring us? Already we had been in Treblinka more than a week, living in terror of the selections all the while. We knew well that the execution of our death sentences had been put off only for a short time. "Perhaps it'll be our turn today" we would think to ourselves as we got into our clothes in the morning. And we groomed ourselves and shaved as thoroughly as we could in order to look sufficiently young and vigorous to pass the selection.

After roll call, our group of 35 men was placed in our new work stations, ready to meet the incoming transport. In the meantime, the rest of the workers had gone back to their old jobs.

About 8 a.m., the train arrived from Warsaw. We saw the camp gates open and close, and in a minute or so the sinister drama was played out with gusto.

All the doors of the cars were thrown open at once. The Ukrainians and SS men leaped into action with their whips and the hot pursuit of the new arrivals was under way. Whoever had the strength to do so raced out of the dark cars into the bright light of the day. The people felt like stretching their legs, restoring circulation to limbs that had gone to sleep from sitting or lying down so long in cramped positions, but this was not the place where they would be allowed to recover from the ordeal they had endured. "Faster! Faster!" the tormentors shouted. We, the "old-timers," who had gone through the death gauntlet only a week earlier, looked into the frightened faces of the Jews and understood their feelings.

As they ran past, they tried to communicate with us. "What's going to happen to us? What should we do? Tell us, Jews, what should we do?" Some of them recognized among us relatives or neighbors who waved or gestured to them, trying to make them understand that it was impossible to talk now because the Germans were watching. Some tried to signal the newcomers to mingle with us, the workers. A few young people did indeed try to get lost in our crowd of "old-timers," acting as if they were helping receive the new transport. In this way they saved themselves for the time being. But the question was, for how long?

This time, the leader of the killers, the commandant of Treblinka, had also turned out to welcome the new transport. He was a captain, 50 years old, stout and of medium height. He had puffed-up red cheeks, and a black mustache; he was the very image of the active soldier. He was always full of anger; it is hard to tell whether it was only towards Jews. He used to carry a rubber truncheon in his hand, and he never failed to vent his anger when he passed some Jews. "Idiots!" was his favorite term of insult, and he used to utter it in a squeaking voice. Whenever you heard that squeak, you could be sure that someone had received his portion, because he let out the squeak at the same moment that he started hitting his victim with all the strength and rage of a well-fed man of action. "*Verdammtes Volk!*" he used to scream, "*Verfluchte Judenbande! Verflucht! Gewitter nocheinmal!*" After each blow, he would almost bend down to the ground, like a man cutting grain. And again and again he would squeak, "*Ihr Idioten! Idio-o-o-ten!!!!*"

On that particular day, the captain was dressed all in white—a white uniform and a white cap, and his adjutant, a tall, fair-haired lieutenant of about his age, was wearing a brand-new white jacket. As I looked at them, I thought to myself that they ought to be wearing gloves, too, because hangmen always used to wear white gloves when they performed their duties.

These two fat old Germans always went about together, strolling around the camp and beating up Jews.

This particular day seemed to be for them a sort of holiday. The death carnival had begun again.

Not all the Jews had left the boxcars. Just as in all the other transports, the new arrivals included many who had passed out or died during the journey due to the terrible crowding, filth and lack of air. We had to drag both kinds directly over to the open, always-ready, mass graves and throw them in. Frequently those who had

109

only fainted woke up along the way and begged for water and help, but there was nothing we could do for them. The only help we could give them so they wouldn't be tossed into the grave alive was to call over one of the Ukrainians and ask him to put an end to their misery with a well-aimed bullet.

Now the mob of Jews was standing at the second gate of this hell and they were separated: men to the right, women and children to the left. Families tried to say goodbye to each other, but the tormentors had no time. "Faster! faster!" Wives were torn away from their husbands, children from their fathers, mothers from their sons, and most of them had no chance even for one last hug, look, or kiss. "Faster! faster!"—Because time didn't stand still, the busy season was underway, and more trains were on their way, waiting their turn . . .

The women and children were chased into the barracks on the left to undress. I had been assigned to gather and remove the shoes of those who undressed and I stationed myself at the open side entrance of the barrack.

"Yehudi, What Are They Going To Do With Us?" It is difficult to describe the scene inside the barrack—the confusion of the women, the terror of the children, the tumult, the weeping. I began to think that perhaps it was better that the murder operations at Treblinka were performed with such haste. Perhaps, if the processing of these doomed people, who already sensed the sinister character of this place from whose terrible grip there would be no escape, would have been allowed to proceed at a slower pace, their pain, anxiety and misery would have been even worse. But as things were, the people had no time even to consider what was happening to them, or to catch their breath. But I doubt that the hangmen were motivated by a desire to cut short the pain of the Jews. They proceeded in this manner primarily because they were afraid to have too large masses of Jews assembled at any one time, lest the Jews have a chance to talk, plan or act. The Jews were not to be given a chance to realize in full what was going to be done with them.

It was, therefore, better to confuse and befuddle the new arrivals as much as possible.

As I stood by the open door and watched the wild scene before me, a blond girl as pretty as a blossom came running over to me and asked me in great haste, "Yehudi [Mr. Jew], what are they going to do with us?"

It was hard for me to tell her the truth. I gave a little shrug and

110

tried to answer her with a look, to calm her fears. But my bearing filled the girl with even more terror and she cried out: "So tell me right now, what are they going to do with us? Maybe I can still get out of here!"

I had no choice but to say something, and so I answered her with one brief word. "Scrap!"

The girl left me and started running all over the barrack like a mouse caught in a trap. She was looking for loose boards, doors and windows. Back and forth she ran, until her turn came to hand in her clothes and an SS man began to hit her with his whip so she should strip naked.

The older women were calmer. Some tried to find consolation with God and prepared to die with the name of God on their lips. Others prayed for a miracle, for a last minute rescue, while others had given up all hope. I saw one tall woman, wearing a ritual wig, standing with arms raised like a cantor at his lectern. Behind her, a group of women had gathered, raising their arms and repeating after her, word for word:

"*Shema Yisroel, Adonai Eloheinu!*"[10] "O God, my one and only God!" the woman cried to a Yom Kippur melody, and stretching out her arms as if toward some sort of heaven which Jews never look upon when they say their prayers. "God, You One and Only God, take revenge on our enemies for their crimes! We are going to die to sanctify Your name. Let our sacrifice not be in vain! Avenge our blood and the blood of our children, and let us say, Amen!"

Thus, or approximately thus, did this Jewish woman cry in a loud voice, and the other women repeated it after her. They took a few steps back, as one does on concluding the recitation of the Eighteen Blessings,[11] and it so happened that the soldiers did not pay any attention to these women until they had fallen silent and had gotten lost in the rest of the crowd.

Some children had come here with their mothers; others had arrived without their mothers, and it's hard to say which of the two represented the greater tragedy. Mothers had to lead their grown daughters to their death, much as in normal times they would have led them to the marriage canopy, and they sent them off with words of love, as one would bid farewell to someone who had already died. The moans of the Jewish women in the barrack sounded like the moans you get to hear at funerals. Here, the people were the mourners at their own funeral.

"*Ja chcę się pożegnać z tatusiem!*"[I want to say good-bye to Daddy!]

111

a little boy of about eight cried. He had come here with his father, and he didn't want to undress before saying good-bye to him. The father was standing at the other side of the door and could not go to him anymore. He was being watched by one guard and his son by another. But a miracle happened. A Ukrainian corporal who was on duty in the barrack was somehow moved. He understood the Polish words and he complied with the child's request. He took the boy outside to his father, who picked him up in his arms, kissed his downy cheeks and then set him back down on the ground. Pacified, the little "delinquent" returned to the barrack with the Ukrainian and got undressed. His last wish had been carried out.

Actually, I did not observe things closely. I had neither the time nor the heart for it; I did not want it to affect me too deeply. Something inside kept telling me, "Spare your nerves! You mustn't break down!"

I heeded this warning. As I watched the scene in the barrack and heard the words and the cries, I suffered greatly. I saw beautiful children who looked like little angels, young girls in their first bloom, and my heart almost burst with pain and anger at how such beauty could be turned into ashes, but this also taught me one lesson: "Get out, get out of here, so you'll live to see revenge, to see something else with those eyes which had to look upon scenes like these!"

I took away the women's shoes, tied them in pairs and put them down outside on a pile, to be carried away to the assembly point.

"*Idioten!*" I suddenly heard the familiar squeak right next to me and that very minute I felt a sharp pain in my face. At first I thought that one of my eyes had been knocked out. The commandant himself was honoring me with his attentions; he started to belabor my head with his rubber truncheon. My offense was that I had been losing too much time from my work. I wasn't supposed to be tying the shoes together; this was the job of the victims themselves, as they got ready for their "showers." They were supposed to tie their own shoes neatly together and hand them over in perfect order. The women at the barrack door looked on in fear and sorrow as this bastard tortured me, and they quickly started tying their shoes together, just to get rid of the mad German dog.

Someone said very correctly that the Jews were more afraid of the Germans than they were of death. They ran right into the arms of the Angel of Death just so they did not have to look into the faces of any more Germans.

When the captain finally got tired of beating me and, exhausted, left me alone, I had to start shouting at the women to hand me their shoes. A few minutes later, after the captain had rested, he again felt like beating up somebody, and so he started "helping me out" in teaching the women how to hand in their shoes. With the same strength that he had used on me, and with the same squeak, "*Idioten!*" he burst into the barrack, fell upon the women and children like a hawk upon a chicken coop and started to beat them all mercilessly with his truncheon. There was a lot of pushing as everyone tried to get as far away as possible from the killer with the red cheeks and the black mustache . . .

Meanwhile, work went on as usual. Somewhere, deep in the woods, the kettles already had been heated and the pipes filled. The Germans and Ukrainians began to chase the first batch of naked women and children along the path to the "showers."

Now there was a new outburst of screams and cries. The last chase had begun and instinctively, perhaps like animals in the slaughterhouse, they sensed what was in store for them. But among the women there was also no lack of naive and the credulous crea- tures who really believed that they were only going to be given a shower, and they took with them a towel and a piece of soap . . .

Before the men were taken to the "showers," they too, were divided into categories. The entire group was inspected and 500 of them were told to move off to the side. The older men were told to move into the barrack which the women had just vacated. They were ordered to undress and to hand over their shoes, and so the whole procedure was set in motion. The only difference was that the men were much calmer than the women, more composed and resigned. If someone wept, he did so quietly, to himself. Some of the more religious people recited the Kaddish or the *Vidduy* [final confession] and told each other that they were dying for *Kiddush Hashem*.[12] When the doors of the barrack were shut behind them, after they had been driven out naked to their last walk, no weeping, no shouts were heard coming from the woods . . .

The first transport from Warsaw had already been taken care of, but what was going to happen to us? We had seen how another group of 500 people had been selected . . .

Suddenly, a rumor spread that a Jew had told the authorities about the inmates plotting an uprising against the German and Ukrainian personnel at the camp. We understood that there would be real trouble now. And before we knew it we realized that we, the

old-timers, were now beyond the barbed wire fence that surrounded the two barracks and the roll call square. It was noon but
we had not been given any soup from the field kitchen. Our soup
had been given to the newly-selected crew. We all grew tired and
weak: how could we be able to save ourselves? There seemed to be
no way out.

Goaded on by my constant, stubborn idea that I had to get out of
there alive, I began to explore every possibility, determined not to
give up hope. First of all, I went over to the Scharführer who was
hanging around our area, and told him that I had accidentally been
left behind outside the fence and I really belonged to the group
that was inside. The answer was a flick of the whip: "*Halt die
Schnauze, Jude!*" [Shut your trap, Jew!]. There was nothing I could
do. But a few minutes later, when the Scharführer had wandered
off, I tried again. I went over to the Ukrainian guard at the entrance to the enclosure. I picked up a gold twenty-dollar coin from
the sand and pressed it into his hand so that he should let me
through. "*Na chto mnye dyengi?* [What do I need money for?]" he
growled, but I was in luck anyway. I don't know whether it was on
account of the bribe or not, but he let me through. I went into the
area farthest inside and joined the group of workers with red
patches who had separate quarters in our barrack. Reluctantly,
they allowed me to join them. I found a piece of red rag, cut out a
red triangle patch for myself, and acted as though I was doing the
same work as they were. I was already glad that I had managed to
save myself for the time being.

It wasn't long before we heard heavy gunfire over to the right,
from the big field of mass graves. The shooting continued for
about half an hour. We knew very well what it meant. They were
finishing off the 500 men from the previous shift. I had been able
to slip away from them.

"*Was machst du hier, du verfluchter Sauhund?* [What are you doing
here, you filthy dog?]" I suddenly heard the familiar squeak beside
me, and felt his whip coming down on my head. I was still hurting
badly from the whipping I had received that morning from the
commandant; now this new heavy blow almost knocked me unconscious. But my will, my determination to remain alive, constantly
gave me new strength. This was the same Scharführer whom I had
previously told that I belonged to the group working inside the
fence. He had recognized me and remembered that he had forbid-

den me to come here. Now I could already feel his paw dragging me away by the collar to be shot.

Mustering my very best German, I answered him. "All I did was join my own group. I'm supposed to be working with these people. Just ask the kapo."

The trick with the kapo worked. A few days earlier, I had had a little chat with the Jewish leader of the group with the red patches. It turned out that, like myself, he had relatives in Mauritius,[13] and he knew me.

"Kapo, come over here!" The Scharführer barked at him, without relinquishing his grip on my collar. "Is this man working with you?"

"*Jawohl, Herr Scharführer*, and he's a very good worker, too," the kapo replied. Once again, I was saved.

As we cleaned up the roll call square we were in a deep depression. The new setup wasn't clear as yet. The new group of workers selected from the Warsaw transport was also in the roll call square, but they hadn't received any assignments yet. A little later, the lieutenant showed up in the yard, called over the Jewish kapo, and officially notified him that the 500 people had been shot because they had been plotting a revolt.

Clearly, this notification was no accident. It was only another link in the chain of lies and terror in which the bosses of the camp kept us enmeshed. The fact is that the Germans really were afraid that the Jews might commit some act of revenge or make attempts at self-defense, and so their entire policy was designed to forestall any possible chance of danger to their own people, no matter how remote. That was why they didn't allow those who had become familiar with the camp to remain alive too long. But at the same time they kept these people captive with false hopes that they would remain alive if only they would do their work, keep quiet and wouldn't try to plot anything. This strategy did indeed sow defeatism and demoralization among the young workers, who in their desperation might otherwise have been able to unite for some concerted action. Actually, this was just a continuation of the strategy which had been employed during the *Aktionen* in the larger cities. The people were led by the nose so that each one of them would be fully occupied with his own problem and cherish the illusion that he could be able to avoid the worst as long as he conformed to each day's new demands. And, just as in the workshops in Warsaw, everyone saw the specter of a selection before his eyes.

As far as I know, there was no effort at collective action by the Jews in Treblinka.[14] There were only some individual attempts, as I will have occasion to tell later on. Perhaps the plotters had been given away by an informer. It was rumored that a young man from the provinces—he was even pointed out to me among the workers—had wanted to get into the good graces of the Germans and had run to them with the tale that the Jews were plotting an uprising. This is the sad truth.

I spent that night in the barrack with the red-patch workers, who occupied a separate section there. Not a trace had remained of my former comrades. They were already sleeping that night on the other side of the wall, on the other side of the fence, in the mass graves. I was to meet only one of them the next day—but what a meeting it was! This was quite a young man, perhaps 17 or 18 years old; I think he hailed from the Kielce district. This is what had happened to him: The execution of the 500 had been begun with 10 men at a time being taken, ordered to strip naked, stationed next to the open ditch and getting a bullet in the neck. After a while, the hangmen saw that this was taking too long; so they finished off the slaughter with the aid of a machine gun. This young man had been part of the first group and it just so happened that in his case the bullet had missed its mark. It had only grazed his cheek. But the young man had enough sense to pretend that he had been shot. He remained lying in the ditch until that evening. He then crawled out, found something to wear among the rags [left there by earlier arrivals] and remained there in the pile of rags until the next morning. That's where we found him—I, and a young man from the red-patch group. He had developed a fever from his wound, but otherwise he was ready to fight for his life no matter what he felt. As soon as he saw us he started to beg us pitifully for a little water to wash the blood from his cheek so nobody would see he had been hit. His cheek was quite swollen. I can still see his face before me and his plea still rings in my ears. "Have pity on me, dear Jews . . . Water . . . Some water!"

There could be no question of getting any water. It was impossible to go to the well for water, and we had no cologne or any other liquid on hand. We tried to look through the packages and bags, but before we could find anything there, one of the chief sadists in the camp, the Scharführer whom I had encountered on my first day there, noticed that something unusual was going on. He came over to us, led the youth to the ditch, and ordered him to undress once again. This time the bullet did not miss its mark. . . .

Meanwhile, on that day, the fun really began at the camp. Transport after transport arrived. So as not to have too many people at a time in one place, some of the cars were detained at Malkinia, and whenever one batch had been finished off, the next one was brought on.

I am neither able nor willing to dwell on the horrible scenes I watched. The yellowed faces, the eyes, the bent backs of children who looked like little old people . . . I don't want to dredge up the nightmare. The wound will never heal, anyway . . . All I want to tell is how one young girl tried to save herself.

Women were much worse off in Treblinka than men. Some of the men, young people, were allowed to remain alive, and in a few isolated cases even managed to escape from this murder establishment, but I believe that not one woman has survived here for more than one day.

One young girl from Warsaw had a bright idea. She would put on men's clothes and mingle with the men working here. Somehow, she got hold of a suit and had actually managed to leave the barrack, but the game was over soon. She was found out, beaten, and forced to strip naked once again. And so she vanished along with the others. . . .

I avoided the barrack that day. I was still sick from the blows I had received from the commandant the day before, in the incident with the shoes. I tried to keep away as far as possible from the commotion. I spent my time baling rags; I could not bear to watch all that suffering. I became more determined than ever and strained every nerve to find a way of getting out of there.

That same evening, I had a pleasant meeting—if meeting a friend in Treblinka can be called pleasant. As I stood in the ranks at roll call, I heard a familiar voice behind me whispering. I turned around as soon as I could, and there, to my joy and sorrow, I saw Żelichower, an old acquaintance from my home town, Danzig. He had arrived the day before, had joined the new labor crew, and now he was in the woodcutters' group which was working in the woods. This group consisted of 30 men. Half of them were cutting down saplings in the woods, and the other half were carrying the saplings to the railroad tracks, where they were used to make a hedge around the barbed wire fence, to camouflage the camp from the eyes of outsiders traveling past. I asked Żelichower what the work in the woods was like, and I learned from him that they were guarded only by a few Ukrainians and one SS man who was not very strict. The only problem was food, because they received nothing except their daily ration of soup, and they couldn't find anything on their own because, naturally, there were no packages left there by Jewish deportees where additional food could have been found. I gave Żelichower some bread and sugar which I happened to have on me, and we got to talking about how to find a way of getting out of Treblinka. He tried to persuade me to join the workers in the woods; it might be easier to think up something if we were together.

Żelichower told me that Warsaw had been heavily bombed the week before and how weak the German defenses were, and we told each other that deliverance might be closer than we had thought.

I let Żelichower persuade me to go into the woods. But it took a few days before I was able to join his group.

The next day, the following incident occurred: several hundred men from a transport had been selected and sent somewhere outside the camp. As I watched the people being selected, I didn't know whether this would be good or bad, for us, and so I passed up the opportunity to mingle with them. About an hour later, a horde of tattered, worn-out, starving and beaten young men arrived at the camp on foot. They were immediately taken to the "showers" with the next shift of men. This had been a sort of exchange between Treblinka 1 and Treblinka 2. The Jews over there also were put through selection. New human material was taken from our group and we received the rejects from the penal camp, who were ready to be turned into "scrap," as the saying went.

That night, I had another meeting with my friend from Danzig. He could speak German well and from time to time had a chance to talk with one of the SS men. He told me that in his opinion neither the Germans nor the Ukrainians in the woods were as wild and dangerous as those inside the camp. One of the SS men had confided to Żelichower that he was sick and tired of this work and that he would have run away long ago if only he could speak Polish. He would have changed into civilian clothes and fled.

I now wanted to get into the woods as soon as possible. But no opportunity offered itself the next day, either. I was still working among the rags at the very hub of the murder orgy. Dozens of times a day I almost collapsed at the sight of so much human

118

suffering and fear. My heart burned with pain and anger when I saw the confusion, the terror, the disarray of these thousands, the helplessness of weak souls quivering in the clutches of the devil— the women, the little children, men who were as strong as oak trees and yet as helpless as little children. They were not able to use their brains, their experience, their strength. They felt abandoned by God and man alike.

"Verdammtes Volk!" squeaked the commandant and sent his club down on the heads nearest him. Damned people, indeed, pushed down in the caverns of hell, and this was one of the devils, a minion of hell with red cheeks and a black mustache. This SS man had no horns, he merely used fire and brimstone, heat and steam . . .

"Away! Away! Let me out of here before I go crazy! I'm getting into a state where I'd be ready to jump into the death cauldron on my own!" I thought. I tried to calm my nerves and to allow myself not to become so upset. Just one more time in my life I wanted to see people with calm faces, with other things to do than running beneath the whip in a death chase. Herds of human beings like herds of oxen, herds of sheep, driven to the slaughter, with the only difference that oxen and sheep don't know what will happen to them until the last minute, while in the case of humans, even the youngest children understand the situation sooner and can see and sense what's coming. Even animals sometimes have feelings, and a human being who sees their suffering will sympathize with them. But many, many Germans have hard, cold nerves; they are capable of looking at men just like themselves without noticing or feeling anything. They don't feel the pain of others; they have never felt pity or sympathy, although the German language has words for such emotions. They are born material for murderers and hangmen.

They are only capable of fear for their own lives. It's really a pleasure to see how good these hangmen are at looking out for themselves.

Before I left the German murder factory in Treblinka, I was rated to see how much afraid Germans can be, how the murderers of millions can tremble when danger comes too close to their own vile skins. If only I could see many more such pictures, they might blur the memory of other scenes.

Twice in Treblinka did I have occasion to see how frightened Germans can get, but I'll talk about that later.

Meanwhile, I was still working at sorting clothes. Every day I would march through the German camp to the barracks of the *Werterfassung*. When transports arrived, they would take us away from the work we were doing and draft us for the extra duty of taking away the clothes of the new arrivals. Something new was now introduced when the men got undressed. To prevent them from getting lost among the workers in the confusion of arrival, the new arrivals were ordered to take off their shoes as soon as they were separated from the women and to stand in line, holding their shoes, tied together, in their hands. Nevertheless, a few young people managed to sneak in among us from each transport and, at roll call a few days later, a curious thing would happen. Five hundred had grown to five hundred fifty-six. When this total was sounded off, it became unnaturally quiet in the square. About a minute later, the Scharführer's voice was heard: "All new arrivals, fall out! Don't be afraid; nothing will happen to you."

We knew from experience that German promises were never to be believed. The Scharführer did not threaten to punish us if his orders were not obeyed, but it would have been impossible to hide because the Germans knew the faces of the previous group of workers and would have recognized the new people anyway. The young men stepped out of our ranks and stood off to one side. We watched these youngsters with sorrow and our hearts froze at the thought of what was about to happen to them. We thought that these people were as good as dead. After all, they had taken unto themselves the right to live a few days longer without permission from the Germans. Every moment we expected to hear the command: "Fall out! Turn around!" and then, bullet after bullet in the back of the head.

But then, wonder of wonders! The Scharführer counted them, 56 individuals, and divided them among the various groups of workers.

"Humph!" he said. "So you want to work? Well, now there's work for you to do!"

The way he handled the situation was so unexpected that everyone wanted to know who he was.

"What's his name? What's his name?" we all asked each other, and eventually we learned the name of this saint among Gentiles: he was Max Bieler [Bielas].[15]

I made a mental note of this name. I had already observed previously that this particular SS man was not the worst in the lot; that is, he didn't shoot or beat anyone on his own initiative. He only did what he was ordered to do.

Additional transports from Warsaw brought in some more people that I had known from before. Together with other workers, I stood near the railroad tracks sorting out clothing and looking at the people who were getting up out of the boxcars. In the line which was chased to the entrance of the square between the two barracks, I suddenly recognized a friend of mine from my kibbutz of *halutzim*[16] and I shouted: "Moshe Blanket!"

Pale, worn out, parched from heat and thirst, the young man gave a glance in my direction and joy suddenly flickered in his eyes. He almost leaped up in surprise.

"Ah! Krzepicki is here!" he called out in a voice full of hope.

Alas, he was happy to see me for the wrong reason. Seeing that I had been given work, and aware that I had arrived here from Warsaw a good two weeks earlier [and was still around], he probably thought that this was really just a labor camp. Secondly, he no doubt thought that since I was an old-timer by now, I would be able to help him in some way. But I couldn't even get closer to him because that would have meant joining the new crowd and going along with them into the "showers." In the midst of this commotion no argument would have swayed the Germans or Ukrainians. I thought that I would be able to see him once more while they were taking off their shoes. But our group was not drafted for this work today and so I never had a chance to say good-bye to this friend.

Another one of my encounters was with Samuel Kaplan, the well-known youth leader, who had been the head of the halutzim organization in Poland. When I caught sight of him, he was in a very bad way. He was already barefoot, holding his shoes in his hands not far from the well near the Ukrainian guard. Bent all the way over the well with his head hanging down, with eyes half-closed and lips parted, he looked as if he were trying to breathe in the very smell of the water. It was a picture of horrible thirst and prostration. The Jewish workers were ordered at that time to form a cordon along the length of the disrobing barrack so that men from the new transport would not be able to mingle with the workers who had arrived earlier. I was then in the yard, with some Ukrainians and SS men standing behind me guarding us. I very much wanted to walk over to Kaplan, to give him something to drink, but it was the same story all over again: to go to him would have meant to join those who were going into the "showers." As I later learned, they had taken away Kaplan's wife and his wonderful little boy, who had been the pet of the whole organization, and he had gone to the *Umschlagplatz* of his own accord in the hope of joining them. Maybe I should have sacrificed myself to help my comrade and leader in his last hour; or perhaps I should have died with him. But I admit that I was too weak to do that. Or maybe the voice within me which said I must get out alive was too strong.

On the last day I was at work sorting clothes, I discovered something odd in the German camp.

I had gone with one of the Ukrainians to get a bucket of water for our "rag detail," which was working that day at the *Werterfassungsstelle*. The well was located inside the German camp. Next to the well, there was a tiny trap door with a glass window sunk into the ground. I had never noticed the tiny door when I had passed by before. Imagine my amazement now, when I looked through the window and saw a Ukrainian sitting beneath it. It turned out to be a kind of dungeon for Ukrainians who had been found guilty of some offense. While I was at Treblinka, it happened once that a Ukrainian had escaped; another one was shot. In general, the Germans treated the Ukrainians as second-class citizens. When they thought the Germans weren't looking, some of them would start conversations with us. They spoke Russian, and some of them knew some Polish; but actually, they were Soviet prisoners of war who, if they did not want to die of starvation, had no alternative but to join the special Ukrainian formations which the Germans had set up for political reasons. The Ukrainians felt just as much a part of these formations as they felt part of the Soviet army. One of the "Ukrainians" with whom I had a conversation was the son of a woman who taught school in Moscow. These "Ukrainians" had the feeling that, one way or another, they would come to a bad end, and that they would be spared from ever having to give an account for their treason [to the Russians] because the Germans would shoot them all as soon as they no longer needed them to do their dirty work. I hope that they are right.

That same evening, at roll call, the following scene took place. As usual, the Jewish kapo, Engineer G[alewski], stepped forward in front of the assembled ranks and reported the numbers of the day's roll call to "The Doll." "Report 525 Jews present, including 10 sick." He had the 10 sick men move off to one side.

"The Doll" and another Scharführer strolled between the ranks with notebook and pencil in hand. "The Doll" quickly and neatly counted off the ranks with a gesture of his outstretched hand, like sticking roasted meat on a long spit, counting, noting down numbers, counting, noting down numbers, and when they got through counting, and as they were about to leave the roll call square, they pointed — as if by way of parentheses — to the group of sick inmates who were standing on one side, and they said: "Hans, take them with you!"

Hans took them along. Their destination was clear. The path led through the opening in our fence leading to the large field of open mass graves. Before long, we heard a volley of pistol shots coming from that direction.

Chapter Six
Working in the Woods

That evening, I spoke again with Żelichower about moving to the woods. I was anxious to get to the new place of work, because there I would have hopes of finding a way to escape. We waited for an opening to appear in the group of men working in the woods. They were 30 men, but constant selections and incidents like these which had occurred at the last roll call often created openings for new workers. And that is exactly what happened. At the next day's roll call Żelichower gave me a signal that the moment had come and that now I could join his group. When Scharführer Biel[as] (it was he or "The Doll" who always conducted our roll calls now) called out, "Woods detail, fall out!" I slipped to the side and a moment later I was standing among the 30 as if I had always been one of them. "Extend arms!" came the next command, and I turned sideways and placed my hands on the shoulders of the man in front of me. This was the Germans' latest device, making the workers stand in line with each man's hands on the shoulders of the man in front of him. It made it easier for them to count us.

A few blows were struck right and left because our line was not straight enough and we had been too slow forming it. We were counted once again, the command "March off!" was given and off we marched, four abreast, into the woods. I was in the second row.

We left barbed wire enclosures behind us, entered new enclosures, marched through the German camp, away near the barracks, where only the day before I had been working at sorting the rags. And then, lo and behold, I found myself beyond all the wires and fences, on a sandy wooded path. I allowed myself a look at the clear

123

sky above and the green, rustling foliage around me. Would this be my way to freedom?

One-half of our group of 30 had the job of cutting down trees—the other half carried the trees into the camp to the railroad tracks, where German Jews of the *Zaunkommando* [fence detail] were employed at reinforcing and increasing the height of the wooden fence along the tracks, to make it harder for the passengers on the passing trains to look into the camp and become unduly curious about what was going on at Treblinka No. 2. The group which cut down the trees was given three saws and several axes to do their job. I walked along with a saw over my shoulder and felt as if something were breathing down my neck. We were escorted by four or five Ukrainians and one SS man. But then the SS man went off and stayed behind, and we were left alone — just Jews and Ukrainians.

We marched about a kilometer from the camp and arrived at a clearing, where we stopped. I quickly observed that there was a close understanding between the Ukrainians and the Jews who were working here. The days when the workers in the woods were hungry and I had to get Żelichower something to eat were a thing of the past. Now they were dining like kings in the woods. A Ukrainian went around whispering to the workers, and money was counted out. Then the Ukrainian went deeper into the woods and there was still more whispering. It seemed to me that there was a peasant couple somewhere off in the distance, passing among the trees, and then another peasant. By and by, the Ukrainian came back with two heavy baskets in his hands. Somebody gave us a sign that the German guard was coming our way and that we should hide the baskets. The baskets promptly vanished beneath a pile of moss, the workers smoothly went into action and started working. The German disappeared; now the baskets came out into the open again, and the crowd took the food they had ordered.

A meal in Treblinka was always like the meal Jews are supposed to eat after a funeral. Its purpose was to keep up our strength and, above all, to keep up our spirits. And if there was a shot of brandy, too, so much the better. I myself have shared meals like that in Treblinka. When two or three relatively peaceful days had gone by, our appetites would get better and when the people returned to the barrack to go to sleep, a lively barter trade would begin among the workers. "I'll trade you your sausage for some sugar," or, "I'll give you some cocoa for your sugar and ham." Cognac, rum, and good wines, sardines, rice, chocolate, and raisins—whatever anyone had in his possession, whatever he had saved up from before the war, whatever anyone had received in packages from relatives and friends overseas—the finest, the best, the nicest—he had packed it into his knapsack and taken it along to Treblinka. Even the poorest pack contained something which had been put away for an hour of need, but when the hour of need arrived, the people had to strip naked and nobody had a mind to reach into their packs. Most of the people threw away their packs as soon as they set foot on the soil of Treblinka. There was more sugar and tea in Treblinka than there is in the Warsaw ghetto today. There was no barter trade in the woods, no regular cash transactions, although these, too, were done with goods left behind by those who had perished. Each of the Jewish workers had money to burn; they had picked up the money that could be found underfoot wherever you went in the camp. The peasants in the district knew this well and they understood that nowhere else in the world would they be able to beat the prices for their products that they could obtain in Treblinka. They had learned about the workers in the woods and very quickly perceived the opportunities for doing business. They made arrangements with the Ukrainians, who acted as middlemen here. And so it came to pass that baskets filled with white rolls, roasted chickens, cheese, butter, cream, and so forth began to arrive each day at Treblinka. The young men gave money to one of the Ukrainians and afterwards he brought back the food that the workers had ordered. The Ukrainians' profits also included foodstuffs. The Ukrainians were quite ready to have friendly chats with the Jewish workers, but they ate separately from them because they were afraid of the Germans. They didn't rush us too much at our work, and so, gradually, we were able to rest up in the woods, catch our breath, and even talk to each other.

But what was there to chat about in Treblinka during lunch, when the wind now and then brought us echoes of screams just like from a slaughterhouse, from that little "bathhouse" in the middle of the woods. . . .?

"How do we get out of here, fellows?" Most of the young men were strangely dependent and passive when it came to discussing that question, as if there were some other way to escape the sure death which lay in wait for everyone, if not today, then certainly tomorrow. It was amazing how people could become accustomed so quickly to living not just from day to day, but from hour to hour and literally from minute to minute, and how skillfully they could blank out the thoughts of certain death. Others earnestly looked out for deliverance, which they expected to come from the air, from the fields, or with an early end to the war. . . . It was really heartbreaking to see how the urge to survive had made men childish, feeding on hopes which weren't worth an empty eggshell. The conditions which the Germans had so ingeniously created at the camp resulted in most of the healthy young people walking around in a sort of daze, incapable of any action or decision . . .

"Maybe we could attack the Ukrainians in the woods? They often put down their guns. We could grab a few of their guns and run off into the woods."

"All right, supposing that this could be done—where would we go? The *Aktionen* are still going on in Warsaw and in all the other cities and towns. The woods are surrounded, the Poles are against us. We can't do a thing."

Such discussions always left me with a very heavy heart. I could never resign myself to the idea that I would have to die here. The conviction that we must do something, that at any moment it might become too late to act, gave me no rest day and night. Am I really made of different stuff than these young men? I wondered. What are they fooling themselves with? What are they waiting for?

But later it became clear that I was far from alone in my planning. On the third day after my arrival in the woods, two of the workers suddenly disappeared at noon, our Scharführer discovered that two men were missing and he began to scream bloody murder. Our kapo, whose name was Posner, had a bright idea. He said that the men were sleeping in their barracks. He figured that there were always some reserves around, the figures would get confused and everything would turn out all right. Meanwhile, several Ukrainians went searching deeper in the woods and an hour later they returned with the two missing men. They had found them sitting high up in the branches of a tree. Probably they had figured on sitting in the branches until nightfall and then continuing on their way. But alas, they had been out of luck. They were ordered to undress and got their punishment on the spot. Posner, the kapo, received 25 lashes in front of all of us, because he had "lied."

But inside me, a voice kept crying, "I must get out! I must!"

We would return from work in the woods at about 5 p.m., when it was still daylight and we'd find the rigmarole going on full steam.

Transport followed upon transport. Boxcars stood waiting, not yet opened. A crowd of people would be standing in the large reception area. Meanwhile, in the smaller enclosure inside, an earlier transport of women, men and children was being finished off. Other trains were being detained at the Malkinia station, waiting their turn to enter Treblinka.

We would be ordered to put down our axes and saws and to help out in the work, taking away the shoes and clothing of the newcomers, forming a cordon, dragging the dead and unconscious to the mass graves, running here and there, joining in the demons' dance which was in full swing.

September 6 had already passed.[17] The great slaughter had already begun in Warsaw, and the number of victims was growing day by day. Jews from the newly arrived transports told us about the giant "cauldron of death" which had been set up in an area of four square blocks in Warsaw. The wholesale business of murder and death was operating full steam. The air was filled with shouts and smells. A heavy stench of rotting bodies and burning flesh spread for miles around. The workers in the woods could hear the cries of the women and children, like the squeaking of chickens or of pigs in a slaughterhouse. At times we thought we could hear deeper voices, the voices of men bellowing like oxen in a slaughterhouse. Was this, perhaps, because the doors of the "bathhouse" in the woods had been unsealed a minute too soon?

Nor were we ourselves forgotten in the great rat race. The Germans knew how to organize each job perfectly. Every man did his duty to perfection. The workers must not be given a chance to rest too long from their terror and fear. Not a day passed when they didn't lay out a few boys at their work with bullets in the back of the head. Not a day passed when the dreaded selection wasn't carried out while everyone else watched.

If not today, then certainly tomorrow, it'll be your turn.

While we had our little snacks and talked to each other in the woods, I made the acquaintance of a Jew from Warsaw named Berliner.

Berliner was about 45 years old and had lived in Argentina for years. He had served in the Argentinean army and was an Argentinean citizen. It would take us too far afield to relate how he had happened to be stranded in Poland, unable to enjoy the protection of his foreign citizenship, and how he, his wife and his daughter had come to Treblinka.

By the time I met him his family was no longer alive. They had entered the showers a week earlier, as soon as they had gotten out of the boxcar. He, a dark-complexioned, broad-shouldered, healthy man, happened to be among the lucky ones; he was one of the workers who had had their death sentences postponed for a week or two—perhaps even three. Berliner was a man of real integrity, a true friend. At every opportunity, he would share a bite to eat, a cigarette or a drink of water; if there was any chance to help somebody out, he would come running. As a result, he had become well-known and well-liked.

But in our talks in the woods about finding a way to escape, Berliner would not go along with us. "We'd be killed! We'd be killed!" he would say. "But there is one thing I want: revenge." He did like the idea of jumping the Ukrainians and disarming them, but since most of the workers were opposed to this plan and no consensus could be reached, nothing came of it.

As we passed through the enclosed area into the woods, we would often see from a distance peasants working their fields. I looked at them, and I would feel a furious jealousy eating away at my heart. These were human beings, and I was a human being too. But they were free and I was under guard all the time. The sky and trees were beautiful, this world was not big enough for me. However, as I went to work one day, I realized that no one could be free under Nazi rule—not even Poles. We met up with a group of about 60 Poles who were being led through the woods with their hands up. They were followed by several gendarmes with rifles on their shoulders and canes in their hands, driving them on like a herd of cattle. They looked like intellectual types, who probably had been arrested because they had been betrayed by informers. There were also some women in the group. As they passed by, we exchanged glances, Jews doomed to death giving a last salute to Poles condemned to a similar fate. When we got back to the camp that evening, we learned that the 60 Poles had been shot in our own field of corpses, next to the open graves.

As we marched back to camp each night, our hearts grew heavy on the way. Would we be able to sleep through the night? Would we still have our eyes open at this time tomorrow? Would we still be among the living? I was even more nervous than the others, because I had been in Treblinka more than two weeks now and I constantly felt that my turn would soon come.

We arrived at the guard station. The gate closed behind us. In the woods we felt a little more free than in the camp. We didn't have the dog-catchers before our eyes all the time. But as soon as we passed through the camp fence, we felt as if our world had come to an end. Once again we were on the territory of the Treblinka murder factory.

And so September 11 arrived.

That day, as usual, we bought food in the woods from the peasants. The Ukrainians came dragging two big baskets and everything was divided up according to the orders placed by the workers. Some of the young men brought brandy. Berliner, too, bought a bottle of brandy that day.

When we got back to camp at about 6 o'clock that evening, our whole world turned black. Even from some distance away, we could see something new going on in the roll call square.

This was the selection which we had been expecting for so long and with such great fear.

The groups of workers were standing in rows, as usual, but the Scharführer was counting them in a way different from the usual procedure. They were ready to do anything, any kind of work, to submit to any kind of degradation, but the hangman no longer needed their work. They were cheap and worn out, their whole lives and their skins weren't worth a broken penny. They were nothing but human junk—scrap.

"Boys, this is trouble! This is it!" I felt a big void opening up inside my heart: Why, oh why, had I waited so long? Why had I dithered so long about escaping; now probably all was lost. "Oh, God, my God!" I prayed silently, "Let me come out of this mess in one piece just this one more time, and I won't wait another day!"

A few individuals, and then the whole group, tried to pull a fast one and slip away into the barracks, to crawl into some hole, but it was impossible. The earth refused to open up beneath our feet and there was no other hiding place. "Line up! Fall in!" We were driven forward, and here we were, like little lambs ready to let themselves be chewed up by the wild wolf. Several hundred healthy young Jewish men stood there, as meek as little children, and two Germans plus several Ukrainians, arrogant and insolent, had their way with us. A finger pointed at this one, then at that one. A couple of bums, a few spoiled Gentile youths were the masters of life and death, ready to finish off a man with just a wink, to finish off a whole world represented by the soul of one human being.

Sometimes we didn't even know where danger or death was lurking. The Scharführer divided us with his whip—this one to the right, that one to the left. I was put with those who were sent to the left—to the "showers."

Terror shackled our hands and legs. We stood like statues and, though we had nothing left to lose, meekly obeyed, still trembling before the anger of the hangman, as if a man had more than one life to lose and the hangman could do more than take away that one life. Would it really have made such a big difference whether we would die from a bullet in the back of the head or whether we would be asphyxiated in hot steam a few minutes later?

"Who will avenge all these lives that have been cut off?" something cried out within me. "Why aren't these shameless murderers afraid of us? How did they manage to break our spirits, so that there was not even so much as one shout, one scream of protest, no resistance worth the bite of a drowning cat?

No! No! It couldn't be. Not all of us were such cowards. What had gone wrong? What had gone wrong?"

I was standing right next to Berliner. I didn't notice anything. I never saw when, or from where, he pulled his knife. I looked at him only after he had leaped out of our line and with all his strength had plunged his knife into the back of the Scharführer who was doing the selection.

The German groaned and turned deathly pale. Two men rushed to the scene and carried him away half-unconscious.

It would be hard to describe the turmoil which ensued in the roll call square. Jews, Germans and Ukrainians alike were plunged into utter confusion.

SS men came running. *Was ist los, was ist los?* [What's the matter? What's the matter?]. They seemed to be terrified. They drew their revolvers from their holsters and didn't know in what direction to shoot, upon whom to throw themselves like wild animals, or from whom to defend themselves. It was a real pleasure to see how they lost their heads.

Berliner made no attempt to flee or to hide. He just stood there, cold-blooded and calm, with a strange little smile on his lips, his hands opening the flaps of his jacket, leaving his chest bare.

"Please," he said, "I'm not afraid. You can kill me."

His death was terrible. I don't know from where the shovels with which the Ukrainians and SS men attacked Berliner had come to the roll call square, or whose order it had been to kill him with these tools. But minutes later, he was stretched out on the ground, his face terribly mutilated and blood gushing from his mouth. The SS man whom Berliner had stabbed was perhaps the nicest—if such an adjective can be used—of the Treblinka Germans: Scharführer Max Bieler [Bielas] . . .

Biel[as] died of the stab wound only a few days later. But by that time I was no longer in Treblinka.

Two other Jews fell beneath the shovels along with Berliner. The Ukrainians and SS men struck out to the left and right without knowing what they were doing. They drove us up against the fences with their whips and the fences were flattened.

We who had been destined for the "showers" immediately wanted to take advantage of the confusion and mingle among the remaining crowd. But the other Jews were afraid to have us mingle with them. Only after the chaos had spread did everybody else break ranks so that it all became one tangle of terrified people, like a herd of frightened cattle during a fire. The commandant was shouting at the SS men for having remained idle in their barracks; then he started whipping the kapo, the engineer Galewski, in the face with all his might. "The Doll" started choking a Jew from Prague, who had served as a captain in the Czech army before the war, and who was now the kapo's deputy. In short, everybody was having a merry old time. After the two Germans had finally blown off some steam, they apparently decided to act with "moderation" for the time being, and the captain ordered "The Doll" to shoot 10 men. Naturally, the latter carried out this order with pleasure; together with another SS man he took his victims out of the ranks, lined them up and, after keeping them on the rack for a while by pulling the trigger without the gun going off, he gunned them all down. Actually, the two Germans divided the job between themselves: the first one shot the first, third, and fifth Jew, while the second one shot the second, fourth, sixth, and so on.

I was standing right there; however, fate so willed it that the two Germans took out one man at my right and one man at my left, but I was left behind. For the moment, we did not think about the selectees' being sent to the "showers," but we asked ourselves what the consequences would be for us. "The Doll" gave a speech, in which he said, *"Es wird euch teuer kosten!* [You'll pay the price!]." We got no supper that night.

It was another execution eve: we recited the Kaddish, there were calls for repentance, and all the rest. The next morning there was no roll call. Six o'clock went by, then seven and half past seven. At

half past seven, we were driven outside and another selection began. But at the moment they took only 60 men. It seemed as if the
hangmen were continuing their policy of circumspection.

I remained rooted to the spot, stupefied; Zelichower was standing on my left in my row. The killer-prizefighter pointed his finger
at the man on my right and the one on my left. Before long, 60 men
had been set aside in a separate group, and I remained standing,
wondering what to do with myself. Were they selecting people to
remain behind, or were they selecting people to be shot? Both cases
had occurred also in the past. Should I, then, try to join the group
in which Zelichower was? In the end, I remained in my place; to
this day, I don't know what held me back. Perhaps it was a feeling
of paralysis, or maybe it was instinct that told me not to mingle
anywhere this time. Be that as it may, I remained alive for the time
being, while Zelichower and the others were all gunned down
within 20 minutes.

Berliner, too, was dead. His body was thrown along with the
others into one of the huge mass graves at the edge of the great
field of corpses. But Berliner did not die like a mouse caught in a
trap, or like a lamb slaughtered for meat, for skins, for some old
rags or a gold tooth. He had died only half a day before Żelichower,
but he died like a hero. He told the hangmen that the day would
come when they would have to pay for their crimes, that some day
they would be called to a strict accounting for their mass murder
and mass robbery and on that day their heads and their lives would
not be worth any more than the life of the most humble among
their victims, of the Jewish paupers and beggars whom they had
cleared from the streets of the Jewish ghettos.

The hangmen and murderers sensed this. Somehow, the terror,
no less great than their crime, had settled in their bones. They
trembled before the hands of the Jews. I still spent an entire day in
Treblinka after Berliner's act, and until I left I saw Jews passing
near Germans with their hands up. That's what the Germans had
commanded: "*Hände hoch!* [Hands up!]." And whenever the Germans came near a Jew they looked closely at his hands. They were
afraid of what the Jews might do to them with those hands.

Night came to the newly-cleared barracks—execution night. No
air, no food. At 5 the next morning—5:30—7:30—there was still no
roll call. Everyone was sure we'd be going to the "showers." Meanwhile, people called out, "Line up five abreast! Selection! Control
yourselves! Don't give in!" Commands were called out. I went along

with the woods detail. Today, I must get out of here, no matter what befalls, to clear my conscience. Then, even if I'm killed, I'll know why. I decided that when it got dark, I would move away from my group. I was restless at my work. This went on until 4 p.m. The cries from the murder site continued that day as usual. I was happy to be here in the woods, away from the noise.

At about 4 o'clock in the afternoon, we learned that boxcars had arrived to take away the rags from the camp. I wanted to flee, climbing into one of those cars as quickly as I could to try my luck, but unfortunately it wasn't up to me. We continued working until 7 and I became very impatient. By the time we went back to the camp I was very nervous and determined to run away.

Near the railroad tracks I met another old acquaintance, Jacob Lichtenstern of the Ha-Teḥiyah [Zionist youth] movement. He cried bitterly and told me that he was hungry. I ran over to the pile of rags and got him some bread and honey. The Germans ordered us to join in and help load the rags onto the cars. But most of the boxcars were already loaded to capacity and I was sorry I had not come here from the woods any sooner. Now it was too late. The Germans were urging us on—"Faster! Faster!"—and dealing out blows with their whips. They ordered us to place packs of the rags along the tracks. A little later 12 additional boxcars arrived. I went through all the cars, looking for a place to hide, and when I saw the kapo I went over to him and begged him to save me by letting me into one of the cars. He categorically refused to do that. I tried gentle persuasion, but I could see that it was a waste of time. I went to one of the other cars and started to talk to Lichtenstern—"Do you have any money on you?" I asked him. He had 600 dollars, and also some Polish currency. I tried hard to persuade him to run away, but at the last moment he disappeared. I got hold of a bottle of water—money didn't interest me. I only took a bottle of water and some foreign currency. I noticed a whole suitcase full of money, and valuables, but I didn't have the mind to take any of the stuff, although all I would have needed to do was cover it with a blanket and pick it up.

The Herschkowitzes, father and son, helped me and wanted to come along with me into the boxcar. I saw a little later that someone had thrown a coat into the car. It turned out to be my own coat and I took this as a good omen. But I didn't take it along with me. Instead, I grabbed a long Ḥasidic coat in the dark. There was a fourth person in the car who was covered up by the others. We sat in fear and trembling as we waited for the train to start moving. Perhaps, God forbid, it would not leave until the morning. About 15 minutes later a German came by to do an inspection. He passed us by without incident. Then we heard somebody running beneath the wheels of our car, and German and Ukrainian voices. Again, we got by all right. The train started to move. We were riding along. We passed the first station about two kilometers away. We wanted to jump off the train after that station, but we heard Ukrainian voices and agreed to wait for another three kilometers. We agreed that the last to jump would wait for the others. Only three jumped out. I don't know until this day what became of the fourth one. Perhaps he was smothered by the rags.

1 a.m. My first feeling—I had freed myself from Treblinka. The others were with me. Where should we go? I led them to the left, towards Warsaw. We walked along a few kilometers through gardens . . . Terror . . . We turned to the right. Until morning. Along the way, we refreshed ourselves with a can of sprats. At 6 a.m. we reached a small village 12 kilometers from Kosów. We knocked on the door of a house and offered to pay 300 zlotys for a place to sleep and some food. The peasant didn't want to take us in; this was a border point, he said, and there were German guards. We knocked on a second door and got the same answer. I suggested that we leave the village. We ought to hide out in the bushes and wait out the day. We should proceed only at night. That's what we did, and we lay down on the ground. Two peasant women came by and we bought bread from them for 20 zlotys a loaf. Later in the day another peasant came along and agreed to take us in, but said he would have to talk it over first with his wife. Herschkowitz gave him a watch. After a while, he came back with another man and said he would take us to his house one by one; I would be the first to go. . . . They took 5,000 zlotys, other valuables and a watch. Then, they left me by myself. I asked them to tell me where I was, but they didn't want to say. Now I was all alone, you may determine for yourself whether happily or unhappily. I went back to the bushes, but there was no one there.

A beautiful sky, a big world, but there seemed to be no room in it for me. I gathered all my strength, reminded myself of the motto "Revenge!" and marched off on my own. In another village, I saw a cottage, knocked on the door and tried to buy bread, but they didn't want to sell me any. I was thirsty and went to a well to drink my fill. I went on. More fields. Late that afternoon, I came upon a peasant pasturing horses in a meadow. I struck a bargain with him for 2,000 zlotys. He asked where I had come from. I replied that I had been resettled from Jędrzejów. The peasant said that if he were not afraid of the Germans he would help me free of charge, but it just couldn't be done; the risk was too great. The peasant took me with him, he was on horseback and I ran behind his horse. He asked me to stay outside his house so his large family wouldn't know anything about this. He said that after they all had gone to bed he would take me into his barn, spread some hay, and bring me some bread and milk. He kept his promise. At about 3 a.m., the peasant awakened me to drive me to Stoczek. When I learned that we would have to pass by Treblinka, I didn't want to do it, but I had no other choice. And so I got to see the original village of Treblinka, where there was not a trace of the murder factory. It was a village just like any other.

We arrived at Stoczek on market day, at 7 a.m. Life here was normal; there were Jews doing business. When the people learned that someone from Treblinka had come to town, they started bringing me photographs and asking whether I recognized any of their loved ones. I did indeed see some carpenters. There were also other people from Treblinka in town. I talked with them. "What should I do? Where should I go?" They answered, "Don't rush to Warsaw because it's dangerous there." Two men had returned from there and told that you could get neither into the ghetto nor out of it. They had run afoul of a Polish policeman, who called them over and said that he also wanted to live, and asked them for 100 zlotys. They had given him only 50. They told about labor service in the ghetto and selections. They had returned to Stoczek on the day when 800 had been killed in the ghetto. They had traveled on the train passing as Gentiles. I made arrangements for myself in the ghetto; I rented a place to sleep from a woman called Freyde-Dvoyre, a butcher's daughter. She treated me well and asked plenty of money for everything. It really would be proper to stop here and describe the little town and the troubles one had there from the local Judenrat and ghetto police, who were afraid that if they would help any of the escapees from Treblinka they would be deported themselves. I was dying of thirst for water, but the water there was disgustingly bitter. In the synagogue that Sabbath, I was called upon to recite the prayer said in public by one who has narrowly escaped a great danger. The Jewish population there actually did want to become acquainted with escapees from

Treblinka, because they knew that Treblinka people had a lot of money, and so they could charge them prices ten times what they charged normally. From time to time a certain gendarme would come to that town from the countryside and kill a few Jews each time. They used to call him the "Little Black Head." The terror in the town was very great. Nevertheless, they actually believed the women's and children's prattle that nobody would harm them; the commandant of Treblinka, they insisted, had said so because the Jews from Stoczek had built the camp. Wherever I went in that town, I blamed them for having known about the camp but not telling the Jewish community of Warsaw what was really going on. Some of them claimed that they had in fact written letters to Warsaw [on this subject].

The population tried to milk Treblinka for all it was worth and some brisk trading was done. They bought everything from the Treblinka people: gold and securities.

I tried to get out of that town as soon as I could because there were more and more rumors about an impending "resettlement" and I did not want to take any chances. Some people didn't want to face this possibility, but I didn't want to let myself be fooled. On Yom Kippur eve, I heard a commotion some distance away. When I came closer, I saw a Gentile beating up a Jew in the street where the Jews lived. People were so scared that at first they did not want to attend Yom Kippur Eve services at the synagogue. But things quieted down and everybody flocked to the synagogue. They returned home and weather was so nice that people were not eager to go to bed with the fleas. I was standing with a certain Dr. Halpern from Lwów and another man named Heniek and we discussed ways of saving ourselves. Suddenly, we heard footsteps. A fireman opened the door and called us to the Police Precinct to present our documents. We bought our way out with 50 zlotys. This whetted the fireman's appetite and he grabbed a young man in the street and asked him to point out Treblinka escapees. The young man, frightened, pointed us out and the fireman used the opportunity to squeeze more money out of us. I thought of going back to Warsaw but I was afraid and decided to put it off until after Yom Kippur. There was a commotion at the Yom Kippur services: "Little Black Head" had arrived and all the Jews ran home from the synagogue.

The day after Yom Kippur, I got up as usual; and at about 10 or 11 a.m. a panic broke out. It was reported that Węgrów was surrounded. One person telephoned here, another person telephoned there, but none of the calls went through. A little later, extreme panic set in and everyone started running. I was running together with a young man from Stoczek. We wanted to go to Ostrowiec, because from there you could take a train to Warsaw. On the way we met a Gentile woman who told us that a big manhunt was going on because a gendarme had been killed. It was said that this had been done by partisans, who were supposedly operating out of the Sadowna woods. I had already thought on several occasions about joining them, but I heard that they didn't take in Jews.

* * *

Stoczek. People brought me photographs to see whether the people in the pictures were still in Treblinka. I did recognize several men from the group with the yellow patches.

I was robbed of 50,000 zlotys in Polish currency and foreign currency. One of the robbers pinned back my arms while the other one searched me and also took a gold watch. Since I saw that it would do no good to resist them, I let them take what they wanted.

As I traveled through the villages, people stared after me. I tried to hide in some hay; the peasant didn't let me, it would be just plain theft, he said. As we walked along, I saw that he took off his cap before a wayside cross. I was afraid to ride into Stoczek and got off a kilometer outside of town. I asked a peasant whether there were Jews in Stoczek. He answered, "Yes, they are all in one neighborhood."

The Woods

The first night I slept with the Hasid, at 4 a.m. I heard shooting and screams. I realized that the *Aktion* in Stoczek had begun. So I went deeper into the woods. Soon we began to see groups of people, mainly young people, who had fled from the town and were looking for a place to hide. We also heard screams and pitiful weeping. Children who had lost their parents in the turmoil ran around crying, "Mama!" The two of us were joined by a third person, a boy from Warsaw who was working as a shepherd for a peasant. He was from the Warsaw kibbutz [group of young Zionists] on Dzielna Street. We stayed together that day. As we moved through the woods, we met some shepherds from whom we bought food, bread, milk and potatoes. The shepherds charged us

137

a lot of money. We made a fire and roasted the potatoes. That's how we got through the day. Looking out from among the bushes along the highway leading to the Sadowna station, we saw groups of Jews a few hundred meters from us being chased to the station; from there, they probably would be taken to Treblinka. The Jews were walking four abreast, tied to each other by the hands.

The cries in the woods didn't cease. We kept on hearing the echoes of children's voices; the children were still searching and crying for their parents, who were now, perhaps, marching in the columns we had seen from a distance.

Thus the day passed. Towards evening, we waited until the peasants had left the fields and then we went into a meadow where there were haystacks. We burrowed into the hay and slept until 4 the next morning. We got up at 4 a.m. I decided to go to the Ostrówek station in order to get closer to Warsaw. The third member of our group, the *halutz*,[18] said that we shouldn't go. We should rather wait in the woods until the *Aktion* was over and then go back to town. I refused to allow myself to be persuaded, and so we separated. The *halutz* remained on the spot, and the two of us (the Hasid and I) proceeded to the station. We walked through fields and meadows. On our way, we came to a little stream. So we took off our shoes and waded to the other side. It was worse when we had to cut across a highway that had continuous automobile traffic. We decided to crawl up to the highway, lie down in a ditch and wait for a quiet moment to run over to the other side. In addition to everything else, the behavior of my companion, the Hasid, made me very nervous. Instead of watching whether there were any Germans around, he prayed all the time and didn't seem to care about his own safety.

After crossing the highway, we went to a cottage to buy some bread. The peasant would not sell us any. We went on to another cottage. I saw that we wouldn't be able to buy anything, so we tried begging. Somebody told us that there was no bread around, but that he could spare some potatoes. I didn't want to take any, and we resumed our journey towards Ostrowek. Along the way, we met a very decent Gentile, who told us what had happened at the "evacuation" in Stoczek. A great number of Jews had been killed right on the spot and the rest had been sent via Sadowna station to Treblinka. He told us that we should try to save ourselves; we should never use highways but only fields, because we could run afoul of gendarmes. We had earlier talked to a Gentile woman at this place who had told us that we had no place to run to. The Jews had been expelled from everywhere; besides, the Germans would kill us anyway.

We went on and came to a thick stretch of woodland. Suddenly, I saw something moving in the woods. As we came closer, we noticed a group of ten people and saw that these were Jews from Stoczek with a few Treblinka escapees included. They started to question us about Stoczek and in fact we did know a little more than they did. We described for them what the "evacuation" of Stoczek had been like.

It was now 7 a.m. We had remained together with the Stoczek people. We were very hungry, so they gave us something to eat from the supplies which they had bought and which had already cost them 800 zlotys, because, as always, the peasants charged the escapees very high prices for food. We remained stretched out in the thicket, where it was extremely still. We became very thirsty, but we were afraid to go out and look for water. At about 6 p.m., we saw a Gentile pass by, and soon someone began to throw rocks at our little hideout. We were terror-stricken because we were expecting the Germans, helped by Poles, to carry out manhunts in the woods for Jews who were hiding out there. We decided to leave the place and waited only until it got dark. When night fell, we started off for another wooded area. Some of these Stoczek Jews knew the area well.

At night, we walked single file, cautiously and in great terror lest someone might hear us. Everything was still. The calm in the fields was almost unnatural, as if a herd of homeless, frightened, hounded souls had never blundered by. And then we arrived in another forest, crawled into a thicket and lay down to sleep. It was the [holiday] season, toward the end of September, and the nights were already quite cold. We really couldn't find a good place to bed down because of the cold. There was nothing to lie down on and nothing to cover ourselves with, and we couldn't even fall asleep because of the cold. Some of those among us were ready to give up. "Look, fellows," they argued, "there's no way out. The world had no room for us. It's no good. We'll all get killed!" Two of us went away to search for provisions, and towards 1 a.m. they came back carrying 12 kilos of bread, some small pears and several bottles of water. They had spent several hundred zlotys.

At last the night was over. We became a little more lively and enterprising. Since it had become a little warmer, we gradually

139

dropped off to sleep and slept until noon. At around noon, some more Jews appeared. They told us that there were manhunts in the woods. Several men who had been found in the woods had already been shot. We lay in great fear until nightfall. We decided to prepare hideouts for ourselves. We borrowed a spade from the Gentile who had sold us provisions and we dug two ditches, each one of them big enough to accommodate six men. They were one and a half meters in depth and width and about two meters long. We worked very hard and with great care to leave no visible traces. We gathered the dirt we had dug up, wrapped it in our coats and carried it some distance away. In order to camouflage the ditches, we cut down some saplings with a couple of butcher knives which the Stoczek people had with them. We laid the saplings across the ditches and covered them with squares of turf which we had brought from some distance away. But as we worked, we literally dropped like flies because lack of food and sleep had left us too weak for hard work. We left a small hole in the top of the ditch for getting in and out, and camouflaged it with another sapling. And so our difficult job was done. Late that night, we got through and dropped off to sleep. Some of us crawled into the ditches to sleep. We were too exhausted even to feel the cold, and we slept until the next morning.

I had more trouble with my Hasid. While everybody was hard at work digging the ditches, I asked him, "How come you're not doing anything?" He answered that this was the Sabbath, so he wouldn't work. This was on Friday night.

We spent quite a few days in the ditches in the thicket. Our lives became very tedious and boring. We had nothing to wash with, so we became filthy and unkempt. Some of us, having nothing to do, sat in the sun and searched our bodies for lice. Fortunately, there was never any need for us to take cover in the ditches. The days and nights passed quietly, except for the fear which made us gasp for breath every time we heard the noise of a bird or a squirrel in the branches. Every night, two men went out for provisions, but our cash was getting low because of the high prices which we had to pay for even the smallest bit of bread.

We stayed where we were until our hiding place was discovered by a Pole. Early one morning, a Gentile youth suddenly appeared before us. He gave us some sweet talk, telling us not to be afraid of him, and when we asked him to get us some bread and water, he promised to do it. We gave him a few dozen zlotys; he was supposed to be back in about an hour. The Gentile boy did return an hour later with a bucket of water; he said he'd get the bread later, when he would go into town. That town was our own Stoczek.

I and another Treblinka man asked the Gentile how to get to Warsaw. By now the life here was grating on our nerves and we wanted to move on to Warsaw no matter what befell. Our friend quickly agreed to help us. He said he would take us into his house at night, buy us train tickets and see us off to Warsaw.

After he had left, other Gentiles appeared, including the peasant Klimek, from whom we used to buy food. He had never visited us before and hadn't known where we were holding out. We could see now that our hideout had been discovered and was no good to us anymore. We discussed what to do next; we decided not to remain together as a group, but to split up and let each man look out for himself. I decided to part from my Hasid (he had fled naked through the barbed wire on the path to the gas chamber; there were wounds all over his skin and he didn't have a penny to his name). I had been glad to help him out but his fanaticism had repelled me and I decided to pick another friend. I asked him how much money he needed and he answered four zlotys. I gave him ten zlotys and we parted. His name was Wiener. The name of my new friend was Anshel Mędrzycki, a bigshot and a loudmouth. He turned out to be a nicer guy than the Hasid and we decided to stay together. He, too, had run away naked from Treblinka, and I undertook to finance his trip. In order to get some cash, I proposed that I should sell a gold watch to the peasant Klimek. Mędrzycki agreed to come along, and we struck a bargain for 500 zlotys and 5 kilos of corn which I wanted to take along so I could create the impression that I was a smuggler. I went with Klimek to get the corn, so we would be ready when the boy came back.

I returned with Klimek at about 4 p.m. Just then I heard shouts from the woods and I recognized Mędrzycki's voice. As I approached, the shouting stopped. I found Mędrzycki confused and bewildered. He had been robbed. The Gentile boy, our supposed benefactor, had returned with a friend, held up my traveling companion and robbed him of 200 zlotys which he had on him. Other Jews had come running up, and it was my luck to arrive five minutes after this thing had happened. My partner was in despair and kept asking me and the other Jews whom we met to chip in 50 zlotys each to make up for his loss. I later learned he still had some money hidden away, but he was an exploiter, a creature without a

141

moral sense, who had come from the Warsaw underworld, and he tried to take advantage of me as much as he could.

After the incident with the Gentile, we went back to Klimek to spend the night at his place, but he asked 100 zlotys from each of us. So we only ate supper with him and went off to sleep in bushes which the money grubber pointed out to us after charging us 20 zlotys for lending us an old rag quilt to cover ourselves with.

The next morning we went to other bushes to hide out for the day and wait for a chance to set out for Warsaw. At about 10 a.m. Klimek came to us and we talked about getting a ride to the station. He wanted 500 zlotys for each of us, in addition to 100 zlotys for buying railroad tickets. He suspected that I still had some money on me, so he tried to persuade us not to go to Warsaw, telling us that the trip was dangerous and that some men had just been shot. Manhunts for Jews were going on everywhere. But I refused to give up the idea of going to Warsaw. Since we couldn't come to terms with Klimek, we remained in the bushes.

At about 1 p.m. I saw an older Gentile woman passing by. My partner didn't want to let me make a move, but my heart told me that I must get hold of this woman, that she might be the one sent by fate to save us. With utter disregard for possible consequences, I ran over to the Gentile woman.

As I came near, I saw before me a friendly face with kind eyes. I briefly told her who we were and what we wanted, and I must say I was amazed when the woman told us without hesitation to come along with her. She didn't ask us for any money; on the contrary, when I handed her 50 zlotys, she replied that one doesn't take money for doing a thing like this. This was the first time since my escape from Treblinka that anyone, Jew or Gentile, helped me get to safety without trying to extort money from me. I called Mędrzycki and the next thing we knew we were walking along as a threesome, with the Gentile woman in the lead, toward her village. Klimek lived in the village of Mała Wielga, and the peasant woman lived a few kilometers further on, in Duża Wielga, which was only three kilometers from the Ostrowek station.

After we had walked some distance we were overtaken by a man in a jeep. We both heard him coming and hid on the side of the road. The man in the jeep turned out to be the bailiff of the village of Wielga. Our peasant woman chatted with him for over half an hour while we waited very impatiently for the conversation to end. At long last, they bade each other good-bye. The bailiff in the jeep drove away and we and our Gentile woman continued on our way. Farther along on the highway, we encountered a car full of Germans. Once again, we hid on the side of the road. Afterwards, everything went all right until we got to Wielga. The Gentile woman's house was one of the first as we entered the village. She went on ahead and told us to sneak in a little later. That's how we did it; we walked into her yard and lay down in the garden behind the house so that no one would see us. It wasn't long before the Gentile woman came out together with her husband. They led us to a potato cellar in the yard. They told us to get into the cellar and stay there until they would come for us. Soon the woman also brought us some food, beans and bread and a pot of boiled warm milk. After I finished eating, I took out 25 zlotys and wanted to pay for the food. The peasant woman said that this was too much, she didn't want to derive profit from us unfortunates. But I refused to take the money back. After we had eaten, the husband came out and advised us not to be in a hurry to get to Warsaw, but to be careful and wait until he got us a guide. Meanwhile, it had become dark outside and he led us from the cellar to the barn, brought us a warm blanket to cover ourselves, and we went to sleep in the barn.

We slept long and quietly, a deep and healthy sleep. Even as we slept, we sensed that we were at the home of good people.

We started a whole new life in that barn. The peasant had instructed us not to show our faces outside the barn. We were supposed to wait until some of his relatives would come visiting from Warsaw; these people would take us back with them. These relatives were smugglers who traveled back and forth all the time with merchandise.

[Our hosts] would bring us food to the barn three times each day—potato soup, dumplings with milk and similar village foods. We were getting bored, but we slept most of the time. We got enough sleep and rest to last us a lifetime. A few days later, a Gentile woman arrived from Warsaw and [our hosts] asked her to take us back with her. She promised to do so, and showed us great compassion. When we told her about Treblinka, she sighed and wept. She had worked for Jews all her life and she was truly upset at what was happening to the Jews. Nevertheless, nothing came of the proposal that we should travel with her. She promised to come back for us, and she remained in the village for several days, but we never saw her again. Our host tried to cheer us up and promised that when his brother-in-law came from Warsaw he would certainly

143

take us back with him. And so it really was. A week later the brother-in-law arrived, a middle-aged Gentile whose business was trading and smuggling. We paid him 450 zlotys to take us to Warsaw. He confirmed the reports we had heard that the *Aktion* in Warsaw was over and that we could go back there.

At 7:30 that evening, the train left Ostrowek station for Warsaw. We said good-bye to our hosts and thanked them for their genuine humanity and goodness. Then we were on our way. I've forgotten to add that not even the children of this peasant were aware that we were in the barn; that's how closely those old folks kept our secret and watched over us.

I had exchanged my package of corn for bread, and had outfitted myself like a smuggler. When I arrived at the railroad station, a German stopped us for an inspection. I pulled the brim of my hat down over my eyes, positioned myself in such a way that the shadows of the early autumn evening covered my Jewish face, and pretended that I didn't understand a word of German. I kept repeating "*Chleb, chleb!* [bread, bread!]" until the Kraut let me move on.

This was my last encounter on the journey from Warsaw to Treblinka and back. They took our tickets, we got on the train and about two hours later we arrived at the central railroad station in Warsaw. Our guide lived on Zlota Street. He took us with him into his house and put us up for three days. On the third day, just before dark, he took us to the corner of Żelazna and Leszno. We joined a group of workers and entered the ghetto.

The Gentiles from Zlota Street were decent people too. They took next to nothing for keeping us for three days and when we parted they promised us that we had a standing invitation at their home if we ever would have to flee from the ghetto and look for a place to hide. After meeting so many exploiters and other mean characters, these fine Gentiles from the village of Wielga and their relatives in Warsaw became our helpers and saviors at the hour of great need and danger. May they in future receive as much goodness as they gave us!

Translated from the Yiddish

1. Toporol (Towarzystwo Popierania Rolnictwa)—Society for the Promotion of Agriculture. This organization utilized every inch of soil in the Warsaw Ghetto to cultivate vegetables.

2. Brandt: head of the Jewish Section of the Warsaw Gestapo.

3. Jakub Lejkin, deputy commandant of the (Warsaw) ghetto police.

4. Shaulis: uniformed Lithuanians in the service of the Nazis.

5. *Smattes*: in Krzepicki's Lithuanian-Yiddish dialect. The proper pronunciation is *shmattes* (rags).

6. Treblinka No. 1 was a penal camp which was intended mostly for delinquent Poles. It was about 3 kilometers away from the extermination camp, which was officially known as Treblinka No. 2.

7. Galewski.

8. This is not correct. *Lalka* (Kurt Franz) was by trade an apprentice cook.

9. Dollar bills.

10. "Hear O Israel, the Lord is our God, the Lord is One."

11. At the conclusion of the Eighteen Blessings, the main prayer at the daily services, the worshippers take three steps backward, then three steps forward, as if leaving the presence of a king after an audience.

12. The sanctification of God's Name; i.e. martyrdom.

13. An island in the Indian Ocean where the British had interned some 2,000 Jewish refugees who had tried to enter Palestine.

14. This was, of course, written prior to the Treblinka revolt.

15. The correct name was Max Bielas. Other prisoners didn't share Krzepicki's favorable opinion about Bielas.

16. Zionist groups which had trained in Europe and America to work as pioneers in what is now the State of Israel.

17. September 6, 1942 was the date of the "cauldron of death" discussed by the author here.

18. Lit., "pioneer." Before the war, this man had trained for emigration to Palestine as a pioneer.

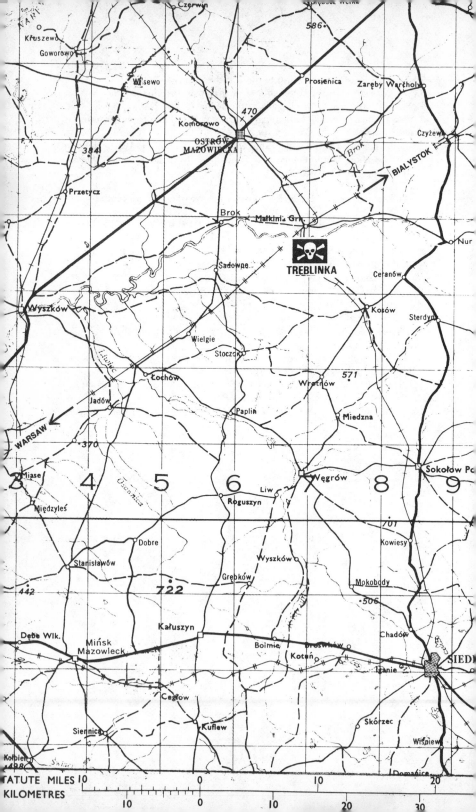

ONE YEAR
IN TREBLINKA

JANKIEL WIERNIK

One day in August, 1943, an emaciated man of middle years, his body covered with vermin, knocked on the door of the apartment of Stefan Krzywoszewski, a Polish newspaper editor, on Smolna Street in Warsaw. He told Krzywoszewski the incredible story of how he had escaped from Treblinka after the successful uprising which had put an end to the notorious death camp.

The name of this man was Jankiel Wiernik. Krzywoszewski found him a place in the countryside where he would be able to hide out, procured for him forged Gentile papers made out under the name of Kowalczyk, and put him in touch with Adolf Berman and Leon Feiner, who were leaders in the Jewish underground. The Jewish Coordination Committee in Warsaw, the representative body of the Jewish underground, commissioned Wiernik to write down his story. The unique document was set in type at a clandestine print shop in Warsaw and published in May, 1944 in an edition of 2,000 copies in the Polish language.

The impact of this report was shattering. A courier from the Polish underground took one copy to Dr. Isaac Schwarzbart and Dr. Emanuel Szerer, Jews who were members of the Polish government-in-exile in London. Later that year, the pamphlet was published in Yiddish and English by the American representatives of the General Jewish Workers' Union of Poland who had settled in the United States.

Jankiel Wiernik was born in Biala Podlaska in 1890. He studied for some time at a heder (children's class in Jewish studies). At the age of 20 he left home. In 1904 he joined the Bund (Socialist Jewish organization in Eastern Europe), was arrested and sent to Siberia. After completing a term of service in the Tsarist army he settled in Warsaw, where he became a building contractor. On August 23, 1942 he was deported to Treblinka.

Wiernik played a crucial role in the Treblinka uprising. Employed as a carpenter at the camp, he was the only inmate able to maintain contacts between the conspirators in Treblinka No. 1 and their counterparts in the "Totenlager" Treblinka No. 2.

He eventually settled in Israel, where he died in 1972.

CHAPTER I

Dear Reader:

IT IS FOR YOUR SAKE that I continue to hang on to my miserable existence, though it has lost all attraction for me. How can I breathe freely and enjoy all that which nature has created?

Time and again I wake up in the middle of the night moaning pitifully. Ghastly nightmares break up the sleep I need so badly. I see thousands of skeletons extending their bony arms towards me, as if begging for mercy and life, but I, drenched with sweat, am unable to help. And then I jump up, rub my eyes and actually rejoice that it was all only a dream. My life is embittered. Phantoms of death haunt me, specters of children, little children, nothing but children.

I sacrificed all those nearest and dearest to me. I myself took them to the execution site. I built their death chambers for them.

Today I am a homeless old man without a roof over my head, without a family, without any next of kin. I keep talking to myself. I answer my own questions. I am a nomad. It is with a sense of fear that I pass through places of human habitation. I have a feeling that all my experiences are etched upon my face. Whenever I look at my reflection in a stream or a pool of water, fear and surprise twist my face into an ugly grimace. Do I look like a human being? No, definitely not. Disheveled, untidy, destroyed. It seems as if I were carrying the load of a hundred centuries on my shoulders. The load is wearisome, very wearisome, but for the time being I must bear it. I want to bear it and bear it I must. I, who witnessed the doom of three generations, must keep on living for the sake of the future. The whole world must be told of the infamy of those barbarians, so that centuries and generations to come may execrate them. And, it is I who shall make it happen. No imagination, no matter how daring, could possibly conceive of anything like what I have seen and experienced. Nor could any pen, no matter how facile, describe it properly. I intend to present everything accurately so that all the world may know what western *Kultur* was like. I suffered as I led millions of human beings to their doom; therefore let many millions of other human beings know about it. That is what I am living for. That is my one aim in life. In quiet loneliness I go over the whole ground once again, and I am presenting it with faithful accuracy. Quiet and loneliness are my trusted friends and nothing but the chirping of birds accompanies my labors and meditations. Those dear birds! They still love me; otherwise they would not chirp away so cheerfully and would not become accustomed to me so easily. I love them as I love all of God's creatures. Perhaps the birds will restore my peace of mind. Perhaps some day I shall know how to laugh again.

Perhaps this will happen once I have accomplished my work and after the fetters which now bind us have fallen away.

CHAPTER II

It happened in Warsaw on August 23, 1942, at the time of the ghetto blockade. I had been visiting my neighbors and was never able to return to my own home. We heard the crack of rifle fire from every direction, but had no inkling of the whole truth. Our terror was intensified by the entry of German Scharführers and of Ukrainian militiamen who shouted in menacing tones: "Everybody out!"

In the street one of the leaders arranged the people in ranks, without any distinction as to age or sex, performing his task with glee, a satisfied smile on his face. Agile and quick of movement, he was here, there and everywhere. He looked us over appraisingly, his eyes darting up and down the ranks. With a sadistic sneer he contemplated the great accomplishment of his mighty Fatherland which, at one stroke, would chop off the head of the loathsome serpent.

I looked at him. He was the vilest of them all. Human life meant nothing to him, and to inflict death and untold torture was his supreme delight. Because of his "heroic deeds," he subsequently was promoted to the rank of Untersturmführer. His name was Franz. He had a dog named Barry, about which I shall speak later.

I was standing on line directly opposite the house on Wolynska Street where I lived. From there, we were taken to Zamenhof Street. The Ukrainians divided our possessions among themselves before our very eyes. They fought over our things, opened up all bundles and assorted their contents.

Despite the large number of people in the street, a dead silence hung like a pall over the crowd. We had been seized with mute despair—or was it resignation? And still we did not know the whole truth. They photographed us as if we were prehistoric animals.

Part of the crowd seemed pleased, and I myself hoped to be able to return home, thinking that we were merely being put through some identification procedure.

At a word of command we got under way. And then, to our dismay, we came face to face with stark reality. There were railroad cars, empty railroad cars, waiting to receive us. It was a bright, hot summer day. It seemed to us that the sun itself rebelled against this injustice. What had our wives, children and mothers done to deserve this? Why all this? The beautiful, bright, radiant sun disappeared behind the clouds as if loath to look down upon our suffering and degradation.

Next came the command to board the train. As many as 80 persons were crowded into each car, with no way of escape. I was wearing only a pair of pants, a shirt and a pair of slippers. I had left at home a packed knapsack and a pair of boots which I had prepared because of rumors that we would be taken to the Ukraine and put to work there. Our train was shunted from one siding to another. Since I was familiar with this railroad junction I realized that our train was not moving out of the station. We were able to hear their shouts and raucous laughter.

The air in the cars was becoming stiflingly hot and oppressive. It was difficult for us to breathe. Despair descended on us like a pall. I saw all of my companions in misery, but my mind was still unable to grasp the fate that lay in store for us. I had thought in terms of suffering, homelessness and hunger, but I still did not realize that the hangman's ruthless arm was threatening all of us, our children, our very existence.

Amidst untold agonies, we finally reached Malkinia, where our train stopped for the night. Ukrainian guards came into our car and demanded our valuables. Everyone who had any surrendered them just to gain a little longer lease on life. Unfortunately, I had nothing of value because I had left my home unexpectedly and because I had been unemployed and had gradually sold all my possessions in order to keep going. The next morning our train started to move again. We saw a train passing by filled with tattered, half-naked, starved people. They were trying to say something to us, but we could not understand what they were saying.

As the day was unusually hot and sultry, we suffered greatly from thirst. Looking out of the window, I saw peasants peddling bottles of water at 100 zlotys apiece. I had only 10 zlotys on me plus two, five and ten-zloty coins in silver, with Marshal Pilsudski's effigy on them, which I had saved as souvenirs. And so I had to do without the water. But others bought the water and bread too, at the price of 500 zlotys for one kilogram of dark bread.

Until noon I suffered greatly from thirst. Then a German, who subsequently became a Hauptsturmführer, entered our car and picked out ten men to get water for us all. At last I was able to quench my thirst to some extent. An order came to remove all dead bodies, if there were any, but there were none.

At 4 p.m. the train started to move again and within a few minutes, we pulled into the Treblinka camp. Only when we arrived there did the full truth dawn on us in all its horror. Ukrainians armed with rifles and machine guns were stationed on the roofs of the barracks. The camp yard was littered with corpses, some still in their clothes and others stark naked, their faces distorted with terror, black and swollen, the eyes wide open, with tongues protruding, skulls crushed, bodies mangled. And blood everywhere—the blood of innocent people, the blood of our children, of our brothers and sisters, our fathers and mothers.

Helpless, we intuitively felt that we would not be able to escape our destiny and would also become victims of our executioners. But what could be done about it? If only all this were just a nightmare! But no, it was stark reality. We were faced with what was termed "resettlement," but actually meant removal into the great beyond under untold tortures. We were ordered to get off the train and leave whatever packages we had in the cars.

CHAPTER III

They took us into the camp yard, which was flanked by barracks on either side. There were two large posters with big signs bearing instructions to surrender all gold, silver, diamonds, cash and other valuables under penalty of death. All the while Ukrainian guards stood on the roofs of the barracks, their machine guns at the ready.

The women and children were ordered to move to the left, and the men were told to line up at the right and squat on the ground. Some distance away from us a group of men was busy piling up our bundles, which they had taken from the trains. I managed to mingle with this group and began to work along with them. It was then that I received the first blow with a whip from a German whom we called Frankenstein. The women and children were

151

ordered to undress, but I never found out what had become of the men. I never saw them again.

Late in the afternoon another train arrived from Miedzyrzec (Mezrich), but 80 per cent of its human cargo consisted of corpses. We had to carry them out of the train, under the whiplashes of the guards. At last we completed our gruesome chore. I asked one of my fellow workers what it meant. He merely replied that whoever you talk to today will not live to see tomorrow.

We waited in fear and suspense. After a while we were ordered to form a semi-circle. The Scharführer Franz walked up to us, accompanied by his dog and a Ukrainian guard armed with a machine gun. We were about 500 persons. We stood in mute suspense. About 100 of us were picked from the group, lined up five abreast, marched away some distance and ordered to kneel. I was one of those picked out. All of a sudden there was a roar of machine guns and the air was rent with the moans and screams of the victims. I never saw any of these people again. Under a rain of blows from whips and rifle butts the rest of us were driven into the barracks, which were dark and had no floors. I sat down on the sandy ground and dropped off to sleep.

The next morning we were awakened by loud shouts to get up. We jumped up at once and went out into the yard amid the yells of our Ukrainian guards. The Scharführer continued to beat us with whips and rifle butts at every step as we were being lined up. We stood for quite some time without receiving any orders, but the beatings continued. Day was just breaking and I thought that nature itself would come to our aid and send down streaks of lightning to strike our tormentors. But the sun merely obeyed the law of nature; it rose in shining splendor and its rays fell on our tortured bodies and aching hearts.

I was jolted from my thoughts by the command: "Attention!" A group of Scharführers and Ukrainian guards, headed by Untersturmführer Franz with his dog Barry stood before us. Franz announced that he was about to give a command. At a signal from him, they began to torture us anew, blows falling thick and fast. Our faces and bodies were cruelly torn, but we all had to keep standing erect, because if one so much as stooped over but a little, he would be shot because he would be considered unfit for work.

When our tormentors had satisfied their thirst for blood, we were divided into groups. I was put with a group that was assigned to handle the corpses. The work was very hard, because we had to drag each corpse, in teams of two, for a distance of approximately 300 meters. Sometimes we tied ropes around the dead bodies to pull them to their graves.

Suddenly, I saw a live woman in the distance. She was entirely nude; she was young and beautiful, but there was a demented look in her eyes. She was saying something to us, but we could not understand what she was saying and could not help her. She had wrapped herself in a bed sheet under which she was hiding a little child, and she was frantically looking for shelter. Just then one of the Germans saw her, ordered her to get into a ditch and shot her and the child. It was the first shooting I had ever seen.

I looked at the ditches around me. The dimensions of each ditch were 50 by 25 by 10 meters. I stood over one of them, intending to throw in one of the corpses, when suddenly a German came up from behind and wanted to shoot me. I turned around and asked him what I had done, whereupon he told me that I had attempted to climb into the ditch without having been told to do so. I explained that I had only wanted to throw the corpse in.

Next to nearly every one of us there was either a German with a whip or a Ukrainian armed with a gun. As we worked, we would be hit over the head. Some distance away there was an excavator which dug out the ditches.

We had to carry or drag the corpses on the run, since the slightest infraction of the rules meant a severe beating. The corpses had been lying around for quite some time and decomposition had already set in, making the air foul with the stench of decay. Already worms were crawling all over the bodies. It often happened that an arm or a leg fell off when we tied straps around them in order to drag the bodies away. Thus we worked from dawn to sunset, without food or water, on what some day would be our own graves. During the day it was very hot and we were tortured by thirst.

When we returned to our barracks at night, each of us looked for the men we had met the day before but, alas, we could not find them because they were no longer among the living. Those who worked at assorting the bundles fell victim far more frequently than the others. Because they were starved, they pilfered food from the packages taken from the trains, and when they were caught, they were marched to the nearest open ditch and their miserable existence was cut short by a quick bullet. The entire yard was littered with parcels, valises, clothing and knapsacks which had been discarded by the victims before they met their doom. As I worked, I noticed that some of the workers had red or yellow patches on their pants. I had no idea what this meant. They occupied a part of our barrack marked off by a partition. They were 50 men and one woman. I spent four days working with the corpses and living under these appalling conditions.

CHAPTER IV

One Friday, I believe it was August 28, 1942, we returned from work. Everything went off in accordance with routine, "Attention! Headgear off! Headgear on!" and a speech by Franz. He appointed a headman from among us and several bosses (kapos), who were to drive us to work. In his talk, Franz told us that if we worked hard, we would get everything we needed. If not, he would find ways and means of dealing with us. A German proved his skill, Franz said, by his ability to master any situation. Thus, the Germans carried out the deportations in such a way that the Jews pushed into the trains of their own free will, without thinking of what might be in store for them. All of Franz's talk was spiced profusely with his usual invective.

On August 29 there was the usual reveille, but this time it was in Polish. We got up quickly and went out into the yard. Since we slept in our clothes, we did not have to get dressed; accordingly, we were able to obey the order quickly and to form ranks. The commands were given in the Polish language, and by and large we were treated politely. Once again, Franz delivered a speech in which he said that from now on everybody was going to be put to work at his own occupation.

The first to be called were specialists in the building trades; I reported as a master construction worker. All those in this group were separated from the others. There were fifteen of us in our construction group, to which three Ukrainians were assigned as guards. One of them, an older soldier by the name of Kostenko, did not look too menacing. The second, Andreyev, a typical "guard," was of medium size, stout, with a round red face, a kind, quiet individual. The third one, Nikolay, was short, skinny, mean, with evil eyes, a sadistic type. There were also two other Ukrainians, armed with rifles, who were to stand guard over us.

We were marched to the woods and were ordered to dismantle the barbed wire fences and cut timber. Kostenko and Andreyev were very gentle. Nikolay, however, used the whip freely. Truth to tell, there were no real specialists among those who had been picked for the construction gang. They had simply reported as "carpenters" because they did not want to be put to work handling corpses. They were continuously whipped and humiliated.

At noon we stopped working and returned to the barracks for our meal, which consisted of soup, groats and some moldy bread. Under normal conditions, a meal like ours would have been considered unfit for human consumption, but, starved and tired as we were, we ate it all. At 1 p.m. our guards came with the Ukrainians to take us back to work, at which we remained until evening, when we returned to the barracks. Then came the usual routine, commands, and so forth.

On that particular day there were many Germans around, and we were about 700. Franz was there, too, with his dog. All of a sudden he asked, with a smile on his face, whether any of us knew German. Approximately 50 men stepped forward. He ordered them all out and form a separate group, smiling all the while to allay our suspicions. The men who admitted knowing German were taken away and never came back. Their names did not appear on the list of survivors and no pen will ever be able to describe the tortures under which they died. Again, a few days went by. We worked at the same assignment and lived under the same conditions. All this time I was working with one of my colleagues and fate was strangely kind to us. Perhaps it was because we were both specialists in our trade, or because we had been destined to witness the sufferings of our brethren, to look at their tortured corpses, and to live to tell the tale. Our bosses gave me and my colleague boxes for lime. Andreyev supervised us. Our guard considered our work satisfactory. He showed us considerable kindness and even gave each one of us a piece of bread, which was quite a treat since we were practically starving to death. Some people who had been spared from another form of death, which I shall discuss later on, would become yellow and swollen from hunger and finally drop dead. Our group of workers grew; additional workers arrived. The foundations were dug for some sort of building. No one knew what kind of a building this would be. There was in the courtyard one wooden building surrounded by a tall fence. The function of this building was a secret.

A few days later a German architect arrived with an assistant and the construction work got under way. There was a shortage of bricklayers, although many pretended to be skilled laborers in order to avoid being ordered to handle corpses. Most of these men, however, had been killed off. Once, while doing some bricklaying, I noticed a man I had known in Warsaw. His name was Razanowicz. He had a black eye from which I inferred that he would be shot by evening. An engineer from Warsaw by the name of Ebert and his son were also working with us, but within a short time they, too, were put to death. Fate spared me nothing. A few days later I learned the purpose of the building behind the fence, and the discovery left me shuddering with terror.

The next job for my colleague and myself was to cut and process lumber. It was hard for the two of us. I had not done such work in 25 years, and my colleague was a cabinetmaker by trade and not very adept with an axe, but, with my help, he managed to hold on to the job. I am a carpenter by trade, but for many years I had functioned only as a member of the examining board of the Warsaw Chamber of Artisans. Meanwhile, eight more indescribable days of hard existence went by. No new transports were arriving. Finally, on the eighth day, a new transport arrived from Warsaw.

CHAPTER V

Camp Treblinka was divided into two sections. In Camp No. 1 there was a railroad siding and a platform for unloading the human cargo, and also a wide open space, where the baggage of the new arrivals was piled up. Jews from foreign countries brought considerable luggage with them. Camp No. 1 also contained what was called the *lazaret* (infirmary), a long building measuring 30 × 2 meters. Two men were working there. They wore white aprons and had red crosses on their sleeves; they posed as doctors. They selected from the transports the elderly and the ill, and made them sit on a long bench facing an open ditch. Behind the bench, Germans and Ukrainians were lined up and they shot the victims in the neck. The corpses toppled right into the ditch. After a number of corpses had accumulated, they were piled up and set on fire.

The barracks housing the Germans and Ukrainians were located some distance away, and so were the camp offices, the barracks of the Jewish workers, workshops, stables, pigsties, a food storage house and an arsenal. The camp cars were parked in the yard. To

156

the casual observer the camp presented a rather innocuous appearance and made the impression of a genuine labor camp.

Camp No. 2 was entirely different. It contained a barrack for the workers, 30 × 10 meters, a laundry, a small laboratory, quarters for 17 women, a guard station and a well. In addition there were 13 chambers in which inmates were gassed. All of these buildings were surrounded by a barbed wire fence. Beyond this enclosure, there was a ditch of 3 × 3 meters and, along the outer rim of the ditch, another barbed wire fence. Both of these enclosures were about 3 meters high, and there were steel wire entanglements between them. Ukrainians stood on guard along the wire enclosure. The entire camp (Camps 1 and 2) was surrounded by a barbed wire fence 4 meters high, camouflaged by saplings. Four watchtowers stood in the camp yard, each of them four stories high; there were also six one-storied observation towers. Fifty meters beyond the last outer enclosure there were tank traps.

When I arrived at the camp, three gas chambers were already in operation; another ten were added while I was there. A gas chamber measured 5 × 5 meters and was about 1.90 meters high. The outlet on the roof had a hermetic cap. The chamber was equipped with a gas pipe inlet and a baked tile floor slanting towards the platform. The brick building which housed the gas chambers was separated from Camp No. 1 by a wooden wall. This wooden wall and the brick wall of the building together formed a corridor which was 80 centimeters taller than the building. The chambers were connected with the corridor by a hermetically fitted iron door leading into each of the chambers. On the side of Camp No. 2 the chambers were connected by a platform four meters wide, which ran alongside all three chambers. The platform was about 80 centimeters above ground level. There was also a hermetically fitted wooden door on this side.

Each chamber had a door facing Camp No. 2 (1.80 by 2.50 meters), which could be opened only from the outside by lifting it with iron supports and was closed by iron hooks set into the sash frames, and by wooden bolts. The victims were led into the chambers through the doors leading from the corridor, while the remains of the gassed victims were dragged out through the doors facing Camp No. 2. The power plant operated alongside these chambers, supplying Camps 1 and 2 with electric current. A motor taken from a dismantled Soviet tank stood in the power plant. This motor was used to pump the gas which was let into the chambers by connecting the motor with the inflow pipes. The speed with which death overcame the helpless victims depended on the quantity of combustion gas admitted into the chamber at one time.

The machinery of the gas chambers was operated by two Ukrainians. One of them, Ivan, was tall, and though his eyes seemed kind and gentle, he was a sadist. He enjoyed torturing his victims. He would often pounce upon us while we were working; he would nail our ears to the walls or make us lie down on the floor and whip us brutally. While he did this, his face showed sadistic satisfaction and he laughed and joked. He finished off the victims according to his mood at the moment. The other Ukrainian was called Nicholas. He had a pale face and the same mentality as Ivan.

The day I first saw men, women and children being led into the house of death I almost went insane. I tore at my hair and shed bitter tears of despair. I suffered most when I looked at the children, accompanied by their mothers or walking alone, entirely ignorant of the fact that within a few minutes their lives would be snuffed out amidst horrible tortures. Their eyes glittered with fear and still more, perhaps, with amazement. It seemed as if the question, "What is this? What's it all about?" was frozen on their lips. But seeing the stony expressions on the faces of their elders, they matched their behavior to the occasion. They either stood motionless or pressed tightly against each other or against their parents, and tensely awaited their horrible end.

Suddenly, the entrance door flew open and out came Ivan, holding a heavy gas pipe, and Nicholas, brandishing a saber. At a given signal, they would begin admitting the victims, beating them savagely as they moved into the chamber. The screams of the women, the weeping of the children, cries of despair and misery, the pleas for mercy, for God's vengeance ring in my ears to this day, making it impossible for me to forget the misery I saw.

Between 450 and 500 persons were crowded into a chamber measuring 25 square meters. Parents carried their children in their arms in the vain hope that this would save their children from death. On the way to their doom, they were pushed and beaten with rifle butts and with Ivan's gas pipe. Dogs were set upon them, barking, biting and tearing at them. To escape the blows and the dogs, the crowd rushed to its death, pushing into the chamber, the stronger ones shoving the weaker ones ahead of them. The bedlam lasted only a short while, for soon the doors were slammed shut. The chamber was filled, the motor turned on and connected with the inflow pipes and, within 25 minutes at the most, all lay stretched out dead or, to be more accurate, were standing up dead. Since there was not an inch of free space, they just leaned against each other.

They no longer shouted, because the thread of their lives had been cut off. They had no more needs or desires. Even in death, mothers held their children tightly in their arms. There were no more friends or foes. There was no more jealousy. All were equal. There was no longer any beauty or ugliness, for they all were yellow from the gas. There were no longer any rich or poor, for they all were equal before God's throne. And why all this? I keep asking myself that question. My life is hard, very hard. But I must live on to tell the world about all this barbarism.

As soon as the gassing was over, Ivan and Nicholas inspected the results, moved over to the other side, opened the door leading to the platform, and proceeded to heave out the corpses. It was our task to carry the corpses to the ditches. We were dead tired from working all day at the construction site, but we had no recourse and had no choice but to obey. We could have refused, but that would have meant a whipping or death in the same manner or even worse; so we obeyed without grumbling.

We worked under the supervision of a *Hauptmann* [captain], a medium-sized, bespectacled man whose name I do not know. He whipped us and shouted at us. He beat me, too, without a stop. When I gave him a questioning look, he stopped beating me for a moment and said, "If you weren't the carpenter around here, you would be killed." I looked around and saw that almost all the other workers were sharing my fate. A pack of dogs, along with Germans and Ukrainians, had been let loose on us. Almost one-fourth of the workers were killed. The rest of us tossed their bodies into the ditches without further ado. Fortunately for me, when the *Hauptmann* left, the Unterscharführer relieved me from this work.

Between ten and twelve thousand people were gassed each day. We built a narrow-gauge track and drove the corpses to the ditches on a rolling platform.

One evening, after a hard day's work, we were marched to Camp No. 2 instead of Camp No. 1. The picture here was entirely different; I shall never forget it. My blood froze in my veins. The yard was littered with thousands of corpses, the bodies of the most recent victims. Germans and Ukrainians were barking orders and brutally beating the workers with rifle butts and canes. The faces of the workers were bloody, their eyes blackened and their clothes had been shredded by dogs. Their overseers stood near them.

A one-storied watchtower stood at the entrance of Camp No. 2. It was ascended by means of ladders, and these ladders were used to torture some of the victims. Legs were placed between the rungs and the overseer held the victim's head down in such a way that the poor devil couldn't move while he was beaten savagely, the minimum punishment being 25 lashes. I saw that scene for the first time in the evening. The moon and the reflector lights shed an eerie light upon that appalling massacre of the living, as well as upon the corpses that were strewn all over the place. The moans of the tortured mingling with the swishing of the whips made an infernal noise.

When I arrived at Camp No. 2 there was only one barrack there. The bunks had not yet been finished, and there was a canteen in the yard. I saw there a number of people I had known in Warsaw, but they had changed so much that it was difficult to recognize them. They had been beaten, starved and mistreated. I did not see them for very long, because new faces and new friends kept arriving on the scene. It was a continuous coming and going, and death without end. I learned to look at every living person as a prospective corpse. I appraised him with my eyes and figured out his weight, who was going to carry him to his grave and how badly his bearer would be beaten while dragging his body to the ditch. It was terrible, but true nonetheless. Would you believe that a human being, living under such conditions, could actually smile and make jokes at times? One can get used to anything.

CHAPTER VI

The German system is one of the most efficient in the world. It has authorities upon authorities. Departments and sub-departments. And, most important, there is always the right man in the right place. Whenever ruthless determination and a complete destruction of "vicious and subversive elements" are needed, good patriots can always be found who will carry out any command. Men can always be found who are ready to destroy and kill their fellow men. I never saw them show any compassion or regret. They never showed any pity for the innocent victims. They were robots who performed their tasks as soon as some higher-up pressed a button.

160

Such human hyenas always find a wide field for activity in times of war and revolution. To them the road of evil is easy and more pleasant than any other. But a firm and just order, aided by education, good examples and wise discipline could check these evil tendencies.

Vicious types lurk in disreputable places where they carry on their subversive activities. Today, all ethics have become superfluous. The more vicious and depraved one is, the higher the position he will occupy. Advancement depends on how much one has destroyed, or how many one has killed. People whose hands drip with the blood of innocent victims receive adulation and there is no need for them to wash their hands. On the contrary, these are held aloft so that the world may pay them honor. The dirtier one's conscience and hands, the higher the glory their owner will achieve.

Another amazing character trait of the Germans is their ability to discover, among the populace of other nations, hundreds of depraved types like themselves, and to use them for their own ends. In camps for Jews, there is a need for Jewish executioners, spies and stool pigeons. The Germans managed to find them, to find such gangrenous creatures as Moyshke from near Sochaczew, Itzik Kobyla from Warsaw, Chaskel the thief, and Kuba, a thief and a pimp, both of them born and bred in Warsaw.

CHAPTER VII

The new construction job between Camp No. 1 and Camp No. 2, on which I had been working, was completed in a very short time. It turned out that we were building ten additional gas chambers, more spacious than the old ones, 7 by 7 meters or about 50 square meters. As many as 1,000 to 1,200 persons could be crowded into one gas chamber. The building was laid out according to the corridor system, with five chambers on each side of the corridor. Each chamber had two doors, one door leading into the corridor through which the victims were admitted; the other door, facing the camp, was used for the removal of the corpses. The construction of both doors was the same as that of the doors in the old chambers. The building, when viewed from Camp No. 1, showed five wide concrete steps with bowls of flowers on either side. Next came a long corridor. There was a Star of David on top of the roof facing the camp, so that the building looked like an old-fashioned synagogue. When the construction was finished, the Hauptsturmführer said to his subordinates, "The Jew-town has been completed at last."

The work on these gas chambers lasted five weeks, which to us seemed like centuries. We had to work from dawn to dusk under the ceaseless threat of beatings from whips and rifle butts. One of the guards, Woronkov, tortured us savagely, killing some of the workers each day. Although our physical suffering surpassed the imagination of normal human beings, our spiritual agonies were far worse. New transports of victims arrived each day. They were immediately ordered to disrobe and were led to the three old gas chambers, passing us on the way. Many of us saw our children, wives and other loved ones among the victims. And when, on the impulse of grief, someone rushed to his loved ones, he would be killed on the spot. It was under these conditions that we constructed death chambers for our brethren and ourselves.

This went on for five weeks. After the work on the gas chambers had been completed, I was transferred back to Camp No. 1, where I had to set up a barber shop. Before killing the women, the Germans cut off their hair and gathered it all up carefully. I never learned for what purpose the hair was used.

My quarters were still in Camp No. 2 but, because of a shortage of craftsmen, I was taken each day to Camp No. 1, with Unterscharführer Hermann as my escort. He was about 50 years old, tall and kind. He understood us and was sorry for us. The first time he came to Camp No. 2 and saw the piles of gassed corpses, he turned pale and looked at them with horror and pity. He left with me at once in order to get away from the gruesome scene. He treated us workers very well. Often, he surreptitiously brought us some food from the German kitchen. There was so much kindness in his eyes that one might have been tempted to pour one's heart out to him, but he never talked to the inmates. He was afraid of his colleagues. But his every move and action showed his forthright character.

While I was working in Camp No. 1 many transports arrived. Each time a new transport came, the women and children were herded into the barracks at once, while the men were kept in the yard. The men were ordered to undress, while the women, naively anticipating a chance to take a shower, unpacked towels and soap. The brutal guards, however, shouted orders for quiet, and kicked and dealt out blows. The children cried, while the grownups moaned and screamed. This made things even worse; the whipping only became more cruel.

The women and girls were then taken to the "barber shop" to have their hair clipped. By now they felt sure that they would be taken to have a shower. Then they were escorted, through another exit, to Camp No. 2 where, in freezing weather, they had to stand in the nude, waiting their turn to enter the gas chamber, which had not yet been cleared of the last batch of victims.

All through that winter, small children, stark naked and barefooted, had to stand out in the open for hours on end, awaiting their turn in the increasingly busy gas chambers. The soles of their feet froze and stuck to the icy ground. They stood and cried; some of them froze to death. In the meantime, Germans and Ukrainians walked up and down the ranks, beating and kicking the victims.

One of the Germans, a man named Sepp, was a vile and savage beast, who took special delight in torturing children. When he pushed women around and they begged him to stop because they had children with them, he would frequently snatch a child from the woman's arms and either tear the child in half or grab it by the legs, smash its head against a wall and throw the body away. Such incidents were by no means isolated. Tragic scenes of this kind occurred all the time.

The men endured tortures far worse than the women. They had to undress in the yard, make a neat bundle of their clothing, carry the bundle to a designated spot and deposit it on the pile. They then had to go into the barrack where the women had undressed, and carry the latter's clothes out and arrange them properly. Afterwards, they were lined up and the healthiest, strongest and best-built among them were beaten until their blood flowed freely.

Next, all the men, and women, old people and children had to fall into line and proceed from Camp No. 1 to the gas chambers in Camp No. 2. Along the path leading to the chambers there stood a shack in which some official sat and ordered the people to turn in all their valuables. The unfortunate victims, in the delusion that they would remain alive, tried to hide whatever they could. But the German fiends managed to find everything, if not on the living, then later on the dead. Everyone approaching the shack had to lift his arms high and so the entire macabre procession passed in silence, with arms raised high, into the gas chambers.

A Jew had been selected by the Germans to function as a supposed "bath attendant." He stood at the entrance of the building

163

housing the chambers and urged everyone to hurry inside before the water got cold. What irony! Amidst shouts and blows, the people were chased into the chambers.

As I have already indicated, there was not much space in the gas chambers. People were smothered simply by overcrowding. The motor which generated the gas in the new chambers was defective, and so the helpless victims had to suffer for hours on end before they died. Satan himself could not have devised a more fiendish torture. When the chambers were opened again, many of the victims were only half dead and had to be finished off with rifle butts, bullets or powerful kicks.

Often people were kept in the gas chambers overnight with the motor not turned on at all. Overcrowding and lack of air killed many of them in a very painful way. However, many survived the ordeal of such nights; particularly the children showed a remarkable degree of resistance. They were still alive when they were dragged out of the chambers in the morning, but revolvers used by the Germans made short work of them. . . .

The German fiends were particularly pleased when transports of victims from foreign countries arrived. Such deportations probably caused great indignation abroad. Lest suspicion arise about what was in store for the deportees, these victims from abroad were transported in passenger trains and permitted to take along whatever they needed. These people were well dressed and brought considerable amounts of food and wearing apparel with them. During the journey they had service and even a dining car in the trains. But on their arrival in Treblinka they were faced with stark reality. They were dragged from the trains and subjected to the same procedure as that described above. The next day they had vanished from the scene; all that remained of them was their clothing, their food supplies, and the macabre task of burying them.

The number of transports grew daily, and there were periods when as many as 30,000 people were gassed in one day, with all 13 gas chambers in operation. All we heard was shouts, cries and moans. Those who were left alive to do the work around the camps could neither eat nor control their tears on days when these transports arrived. The less resistant among us, especially the more intelligent, suffered nervous breakdowns and hanged themselves when they returned to the barracks at night after having handled the corpses all day, their ears still ringing with the cries and moans of the victims. Such suicides occurred at the rate of 15 to 20 a day.

These people were unable to endure the abuse and tortures inflicted upon them by the overseers and the Germans.

One day a transport arrived from Warsaw, from which some men were selected as workers for Camp No. 2. Among them I saw a few people whom I had known from before the war. They were not fit for this kind of work.

That same day one of our own men by the name of Kuszer could not stand the torture and attacked his tormentor, a German Oberscharführer named Matthes from Camp No. 2, who was a fiend and a killer, and wounded him. The Hauptsturmführer, on arriving at the scene, dismissed all the craftsmen, and other inmates of the camp were massacred on the spot with blunt tools.

I happened to be working in the woods in between the two camps, dressing lumber. The processions of nude children, men and old people passed that spot in a silent caravan of death. The only sounds we could hear were the shouts of the killers; the victims walked in silence. Now and then, a child would whimper but then some killer's fingers would grasp its thin neck in a vise-like grip, cutting off the last plaintive sobs. The victims walked to their doom with raised arms, stark naked and helpless.

CHAPTER VIII

Between the two camps there were buildings in which the Ukrainian guards had their quarters. The Ukrainians were constantly drunk, and sold whatever they managed to steal in the camps in order to get more money for brandy. The Germans watched them and frequently took the loot away from them.

When they had eaten and drunk their fill, the Ukrainians looked around for other amusements. They frequently selected the best-looking Jewish girls from the transports of nude women passing their quarters, dragged them into their barracks, raped them and then delivered them to the gas chambers. After being outraged by their executioners, the girls died in the gas chambers with all the rest. It was a martyr's death.

On one occasion a girl fell out of line. Nude as she was, she leaped over a barbed wire fence three meters high, and tried to escape in our direction. The Ukrainians noticed this and started to pursue her. One of them almost reached her but he was too close to her to shoot, and she wrenched the rifle from his hands. It wasn't easy to open fire since there were guards all around and there was the danger that one of the guards might be hit. But as the girl held the gun, it went off and killed one of the Ukrainians. The Ukrainians were furious. In her fury, the girl struggled with his comrades. She managed to fire another shot, which hit another Ukrainian, whose arm subsequently had to be amputated. At last they seized her. She paid dearly for her courage. She was beaten, bruised, spat upon, kicked and finally killed. She was our nameless heroine.

On another occasion a transport arrived from Germany. The new arrivals were put through the usual routine. When the people were ordered to undress, one of the women stepped forward with her two children, both of them boys. She presented identity papers showing that she was of pure German stock and had boarded this train by mistake. All her documents were found to be in order and her two sons had not been circumcised. She was a good-looking woman, but there was terror in her eyes. She clung to her children and tried to soothe them, saying that their troubles would soon be cleared up and they would return home to their father. She petted and kissed them, but she was crying because she was haunted by a dreadful foreboding.

The Germans ordered her to step forward. Thinking that this meant freedom for herself and her children, she relaxed. But alas, it had been decided that she was to perish together with the Jews, because she had seen too much and would be liable to tell all about what she had seen, which was supposed to be shrouded in secrecy. Whoever crossed the threshold of Treblinka was doomed to die. Therefore this German woman, together with her children, went to her death along with all the others. Her children cried just as the Jewish children did, and their eyes mirrored the same despair, for in death there is no racial distinction; all are equal. Her husband probably will be killed at the front, and she was killed in the camp.

While I was in Camp No. 1, I managed to find out the identity of certain Jews I had seen wearing yellow patches. They turned out to be professional people and craftsmen who had been left over from earlier transports. They were the ones who had built Treblinka. They had hoped to be liberated after the war, but fate decreed otherwise. It had been decided that whoever had crossed the threshold of this inferno had to die. It would not do to leave witnesses who would be able to identify the spot where these fiendish tortures had been perpetrated.

Among these men there were jewelers who appraised the articles of precious metal which the deportees had brought with them. There was quite a lot of this. The sorting and classifying was done in a separate barrack to which no special guard had been assigned, for there was no reason to expect that these men would be able to steal any of the loot. Where would they dispose of their pilferings? Eventually, whatever they might manage to steal would only get back to the Germans again.

The Ukrainians, by contrast, went wild at the sight of gold. They had no idea of its value, but it was enough to give them something that glittered and to tell them that it was gold. When deportations took place, the Ukrainians broke into the homes of the Jews and demanded gold. They did this without the knowledge of the Germans and, of course, they applied methods of terror. They took whatever was given them. Their faces were greedy and savage and inspired fear and loathing in those who had to deal with them. They hid the loot most carefully in order to have something to show their families as spoils of war. Some of the Ukrainians hailed from nearby villages; others had girl friends in the vicinity to whom they wanted to give gifts. A part of their plunder was always traded in for liquor. They were terrible drunkards.

When the Ukrainians noticed that the Jews were handling the gold under practically no control, they began coercing them to steal. The Jews were compelled to deliver diamonds and gold to the Ukrainian guards or else be killed. Day after day, a gang of Ukrainians took valuables from the room where the valuables of the deportees were kept. One of the Germans noticed this and of course it was the Jews who had to pay the penalty. They were searched, and the search disclosed gold and precious stones on their persons. They could not claim that they had stolen these articles under duress; the Germans would not have believed their story. They were tortured and now they were worse off than the camp laborers. Only half of them—there had been 150 of them— were left alive. Those who survived suffered starvation, misery and incredible tortures.

The entire yard was littered with a variety of articles, for all these people left behind millions of items of wearing apparel and so forth. Since they had all assumed that they were merely going to be resettled at an unknown place and not sent to their death, they had taken their best and most essential possessions with them. The camp yard in Treblinka was filled with everything one's heart

167

might desire. There was everything in plenty. As I passed, I saw a profusion of fountain pens and real tea and coffee. The ground was literally strewn with candy. Transports of people from abroad had come well supplied with fats. All the deportees had been fully confident that they were going to survive.

Jews were put to work at sorting out the plunder, arranging things systematically because every item had to serve a definite purpose. Everything the Jews left behind had its value and its place. Only the Jews themselves were regarded as worthless. Jews had to steal what they could and turn the stolen articles over to the Ukrainians. If they failed to do so, the Ukrainians killed them. On the other hand, if the Jews were caught redhanded, they were killed on the spot. Despite the danger, the traffic continued, a new accomplice taking over where the previous one had left off. In that way a chosen few from among millions survived—between the devil and the deep blue sea.

One day a transport of 80 Gypsies from near Warsaw arrived at the camp. These men, women and children were destitute. All they owned was some soiled underwear and tattered clothes. When they came into the yard, they were very happy. They thought they had entered an enchanted castle. But the hangmen were just as happy, because they wiped out all the Gypsies just as they did the Jews. Within a few hours all was quiet and nothing was left but corpses.

I was still working at Camp No. 1 and was free to move about as I pleased. Though I saw many terrible things there, the sight of those gassed at Camp No. 2 was far more horrible. It was practically decided that I should remain permanently in Camp No. 1. Hermann, the architect, and a master cabinet maker from Bohemia, did what they could to this end, because they had no other craftsmen like myself and they therefore needed me. However, in mid-December, 1942 an order came for all inmates of Camp No. 2 to be returned. Since this order could not be appealed, we proceeded to Camp No. 2 without even waiting long enough to eat our noontime meal.

The first sight that met my eyes upon my return was that of the corpses of newly gassed victims on whom "dentists" had worked, extracting their false teeth with pliers. Just one look at this ghastly procedure was enough to make me even more disgusted with life than I had been before. The "dentists" sorted the teeth they extracted according to their value. Of course, whatever teeth the

Ukrainians managed to lay their hands on remained in their possession.

I worked for a while in Camp No. 2, doing repair work in the kitchen. The commandant of the kitchen had introduced a new system. During that period fewer transports arrived and no new workers became available. At that time, workers in Camp No. 1 were given numbers and triangular leather identification badges. There was a different color patch for each group. The badges were worn on the left side of the chest. Rumors circulated that we workers in Camp No. 2 would also receive numbers but at the time nothing came of it. At any rate, some system had been introduced so that no stranger from an incoming transport could smuggle himself in, as I had done, to prolong his life.

We began to suffer greatly from the cold and they started issuing blankets to us. While I had been away from Camp No. 2, a carpentry shop had been installed there. A baker from Warsaw served as its foreman. His job was to make up stretchers for carrying the corpses from the gas chambers to the mass graves. The stretchers were constructed very primitively; just two poles with pieces of board nailed at intervals.

The Hauptsturmführer and the two commandants ordered me to build a laundry, a laboratory and accommodations for 15 women. All of these structures were to be built from old materials. Jewish-owned buildings in the vicinity were being dismantled at the time. I could tell them by their house numbers. I selected my crew and began to work. I brought in some of the new lumber from the woods myself. Time flew fast on the job.

But there were new events to upset our emotional balance. This was the period when the Germans talked a lot about Katyn,[1] which they used for anti-Soviet propaganda purposes. One day, by accident, we got hold of a newspaper from which we learned about that mass killing. It was probably these reports that made Himmler decide to visit Treblinka personally and to give orders that henceforth all the corpses of inmates should be cremated. There were plenty of corpses to cremate—there was no one who could have been blamed for the Treblinka killings except the Germans who, for the time being, were the masters of the land which they had wrested from us [Poles] by brute force. They did not want any evidence of the mass murders left.

At any rate, the cremations were promptly begun. The corpses of men, women, children and old people were exhumed from the mass graves. Whenever such a grave was opened, a terrible stench rose from them, because the bodies were already in an advanced stage of decomposition. This work brought continued physical and moral suffering to those who were forced to do it. We, the living, felt renewed grief, even more intensively than before. We were ill-fed, because transports had ceased to arrive, so that the hapless purveyors of food had become a thing of the past. We did not like to draw on our reserves. All we ate was moldy bread, which we washed down with water. The malnutrition caused an epidemic of typhus. Those who became ill needed neither medication nor a bed. A bullet in the neck and all was over.

Work was begun to cremate the dead. It turned out that bodies of women burned more easily than those of men. Accordingly, the bodies of women were used for kindling the fires. Since cremation was hard work, rivalry set in between the labor details as to which of them would be able to cremate the largest number of bodies. Bulletin boards were rigged up and daily scores were recorded. Nevertheless, the results were very poor. The corpses were soaked in gasoline. This entailed considerable expense and the results were inadequate; the male corpses simply would not burn. Whenever an airplane was sighted overhead, all work was stopped, the corpses were covered with foliage as camouflage against aerial observation.

It was a terrifying sight, the most gruesome ever beheld by human eyes. When corpses of pregnant women were cremated, their bellies would burst open. The fetus would be exposed and could be seen burning inside the mother's womb.

All this made no impression whatsoever on the German murderers, who stood around watching as if they were checking a machine which was not working properly and whose production was inadequate.

Then, one day, an Oberscharführer wearing an SS badge arrived at the camp and introduced a veritable inferno. He was about 45 years old, of medium height, with a perpetual smile on his face. His favorite word was "*tadellos* [perfect]" and that is how he got the by-name *Tadellos*. His face looked kind and did not show the depraved soul behind it. He got pure pleasure watching the corpses burn; the sight of the flames licking at the bodies was precious to him, and he would literally caress the scene with his eyes.

This is the way in which he got the inferno started: He put into operation an excavator which could dig up 3,000 corpses at one time. A fire grate made of railroad tracks was placed on concrete foundations 100 to 150 meters in length. The workers piled the corpses on the grate and set them on fire.

I am no longer a young man and have seen a great deal in my lifetime, but not even Lucifer could possibly have created a hell worse than this. Can you picture a grate of this length piled high with 3,000 corpses of people who had been alive only a short time before? As you look at their faces it seems as if at any moment these bodies might awaken from their deep sleep. But at a given signal a giant torch is lit and it burns with a huge flame. If you stood close enough, you could well imagine hearing moans from the lips of the sleeping bodies, children sitting up and crying for their mothers. You are overwhelmed by horror and pain, but you stand there just the same without saying anything. The gangsters are standing near the ashes, shaking with satanic laughter. Their faces radiate a truly satanic satisfaction. They toasted the scene with brandy and with the choicest liqueurs, ate, caroused and had a great time warming themselves by the fire.

Thus the Jews were of some use to them even after they had died. Though the winter weather was bitter cold, the pyres gave off heat like an oven. This heat came from the burning bodies of Jews. The hangmen stood warming themselves by the fire, drinking, eating and singing. Gradually, the fire began to die down, leaving only ashes which went to fertilize the silent soil. Human blood and human ashes — what food for the soil! There will be a rich harvest. If only the soil could talk! It knows a lot but it keeps quiet.

Day in and day out the workers handled the corpses and collapsed from physical exhaustion and mental anguish. And while they suffered, the hearts of the fiends were filled with pride and pleasure in the hell they had created. It gave light and warmth, and at the same time it obliterated every trace of the victims, while our own hearts bled. The Oberscharführer who had created this inferno sat by the fire, laughing, caressing it with his eyes and saying, "*tadellos* [perfect]!" To him, these flames represented the fulfillment of his perverted dreams and wishes.

The cremation of the corpses proved an unqualified success. Because they were in a hurry, the Germans built additional fire grates and augmented the crews serving them, so that from 10,000 to 12,000 corpses were cremated at one time. The result was one huge inferno, which from the distance looked like a volcano breaking through the earth's crust to belch forth fire and lava. The pyres sizzled and crackled. The smoke and heat made it impossible to remain close by. It lasted a long time because there were more than half a million dead to dispose of.

The new transports were handled in a simplified manner; the cremation followed directly after the gassing. Transports were now arriving from Bulgaria, comprising well-to-do people who brought with them large supplies of food: white bread, smoked mutton, cheese, etc. They were killed off just like all the others, but we benefitted from the supplies they had brought. As a result, our diet improved considerably. The Bulgarian Jews were strong and husky specimens. Looking at them, it was hard to believe that in 20 minutes they would all be dead in the gas chambers.

These handsome Jews were not permitted an easy death. Only small quantities of gas were let into the chambers, so that their agony lasted through the night. They also had to endure severe tortures before entering the gas chambers. Envy of their well-fed appearance prompted the hangmen to torment them all the more.

After the Bulgarian transports, more transports began to come from Bialystok and Grodno. In the meantime I had finished the construction of the laboratory, the laundry and the rooms for the women.

One day a transport arrived in Treblinka when we were already locked in our barracks for the night. Accordingly, the Germans and the Ukrainians processed the victims without help. Suddenly we heard yells and heavy rifle fire. We stayed put and waited impatiently for morning to come so that we could learn what had happened. The next morning we saw that the yard was littered with corpses. While we were working, the Ukrainian guards told us that the people who had come on that transport had refused to be led into the gas chambers and had put up a fierce fight. They smashed everything they could lay their hands on and broke open the chests with gold that stood in the corridor leading to the chambers. They grabbed sticks and every weapon they could get hold of to defend themselves. The bullets fell thick and fast, and by morning the yard was strewn with dead bodies and with the improvised weapons the Jews had used in their last fight for life. Those killed while fighting, as well as those who died from gas, were all horribly mutilated. Some of them had had limbs torn from their bodies. By dawn it was all over. The rebels were cremated. To us it was just one more warning that we could not hope to escape our fate.

CHAPTER X

About that time, the camp discipline became stricter. A guard station was built, the number of guards increased and a telephone was installed in Camp No. 2. We were short of hands for work, and so men were sent from Camp No. 1. But their work was not considered satisfactory, and so they were finished off a few days later. Since they were such poor labor material, they were not worth the food required to keep them alive.

The Scharführer, a German master carpenter from Bohemia, whom I have already mentioned, came to me for advice about the construction of a four-story observation tower of the type he had seen in Maidanek. He was very happy when I gave him all the required information and he rewarded me with some bread and sausage. I figured out the specifications for the lumber and screws and proceeded with the construction work. Whenever I started on a new job, I knew that my life would be spared for a few weeks longer because as long as they needed me, they would not kill me.

When I had completed the first tower, the Hauptsturmführer came, praised me extravagantly and ordered me to build three additional towers of the same type around Camp No. 2.

The guard at the camp was increased and it became impossible to get from one camp to the other. Seven men joined in a plot to dig a tunnel through which to escape. Four of them were caught and were tortured for an entire day, which in itself was worse than death. In the evening, when all hands had returned from work, all the inmates were ordered to assemble and witness the hanging of the four men. One of them, Mechel, a Jew from Warsaw, shouted before the noose was tightened around his neck: "Down with Hitler! Long live the Jews!"

Among us workers there were some who were very religious, who recited the daily prayers each day. A German by the name of Karol, who was deputy commandant and a cynic, observed the habit of this little group and made jokes about it. He even gave them a prayer shawl and phylacteries for their devotions, and when one of the men died, he gave permission to give him a traditional Jewish funeral, complete with a tombstone. I advised the men not to do this, because our tormentors would exhume the body and cremate it after they had had their fun watching the ceremony. They refused to heed my advice but they soon found out that I had been right.

In April, 1943, transports began to come in from Warsaw. We were told that 600 men in Warsaw were working in Camp No. 1; this report turned out to be based on fact. At the time a typhus epidemic was raging in Camp No. 1. Those who got sick were killed. Three women and one man from the Warsaw transport came to us. The man was the husband of one of the three women. The Warsaw people were treated with exceptional brutality, the women even more harshly than the men. Women with children were separated from the others, led up to the fires and, after the murderers had had their fill of watching the terror-stricken women and children, they killed them right by the pyre and threw them into the flames. This happened quite frequently. The women fainted from fear and the brutes dragged them to the fire half dead. Panic-stricken, the children clung to their mothers. The women begged for mercy, with eyes closed so as to shut out the grisly scene, but their tormentors only leered at them and kept their victims in agonizing suspense for minutes on end. While one batch of women and children were being killed, others were left standing around, waiting their turn. Time and time again children were snatched from their mothers' arms and tossed into the flames alive, while their tormentors laughed, urging the mothers to be brave and jump into the fire after their children and mocking the women for being cowards.

A number of men from Camp No. 1 were sent into our camp as workers. They were terrified and afraid to talk to us, for Camp No. 1 was known to have a very stern discipline. After a while, however, these men calmed down and gave us to understand that a revolt was being planned in Camp No. 1. We wanted to establish contact with the inmates of Camp No. 1, but no opportunity presented itself, for there were watchtowers and guards all around. The food in our camp had improved. We got a shower and even clean linens once a week, and a laundry had been set up in which female inmates were working. We decided that by spring we would either make a try for freedom or perish.

About that time I caught a cold, which developed into pneumonia. All the sick were being killed either by shooting or by injections, but it seems that they needed me. Accordingly, they gave me whatever medical attention was available. A Jewish physician attended me, examined me every day, and gave me medicine and comfort. My German superior, Loeffler, brought me food: white bread, butter and cream. Whenever he confiscated any food from smugglers, he shared it with me. The warm spring weather, the urge to live and the medical help I was getting did their bit and despite the incredible hardships under which I lived, I recovered. I went back to work to finish the construction of the observation towers.

One day the Hauptsturmführer, accompanied by the camp commandant and my superior, Loeffler, came to see me. They asked me whether I would undertake to build a blockhouse. It was to be constructed of logs and serve as a guard station in Camp No. 1. When I began to explain to him how the job should be done, he turned to his companions and remarked that I had understood him in a flash.

There was no lumber or building material on hand. We had to cut the wood with saws. I suggested making a shingle roof, and we had to prepare the shingles ourselves. As a result, I was able to make things easier for a good many camp inmates, who were relieved from the work with the corpses in order to assist me. I built the blockhouse in Camp No. 2 in such a way that it could be taken apart and moved to Camp No. 1. Everybody liked it so much that the Hauptsturmführer and Loeffler bragged to their colleagues that they had done the work themselves.

After a while, the time had come to take the structure apart and move it to Camp No. 1, but the architect Hermann and the master carpenter were unable to reassemble the structure themselves. It was evidently easier for them to kill innocent people than to do this kind of work. Once again, they turned to me for assistance.

This suited me to perfection because in that way I was able to gain access to Camp No. 1 and to make contact with our companions in adversity there. I needed assistance in my work and, although four men would have been enough, I asked for eight.

When I entered Camp No. 1, I did not recognize it at all. It was spotlessly clean and the discipline was extremely strict. Everyone was terror-stricken at the mere sight of a German or a Ukrainian. Not only did the inmates of Camp 1 refuse to speak to us, they were even afraid to look at us.

Starved and ill-treated though they were, they had a secret organization which was functioning efficiently. Everything was carefully planned. A Warsaw baker by the name of Leiteisen, who acted as liaison man between the conspirators, was working near the fence in Camp No. 1. It was difficult to make contact with him because there were German and Ukrainian guards all around and the fence was screened by saplings and you never knew who might be lurking behind them.

The workers in Camp No. 1 were continually under the threat of the whip. Compared with them, we enjoyed complete freedom. For instance, we were permitted to smoke while we worked and even received cigarette rations. We took advantage of our relative freedom for our own purposes. Some of us drew our guard into conversation to divert his attention, while others used that opportunity to make contact with inmates of Camp No. 1.

In due time, we became members of a committee of the secret organization, a circumstance which gave some prospects of deliverance or at least of a heroic death. All this involved considerable risk because of the watchfulness of the guards and the strong fortifications at the camp. However, our motto was "freedom or death." In the meantime, I completed the blockhouse. To celebrate the occasion, the Hauptsturmführer treated us to liquor and sausages. While we worked on the blockhouse, we received additional daily rations of ½ kilogram of bread apiece.

CHAPTER XI

In contrast to our camp, the reign of terror in Camp No. 1 was getting worse, with Franz and his man-eating hound lording it over the workers. During my first stay in Camp No. 1 I had noticed a few boys, aged 13 and 14, who had been tending a flock of geese and had been doing odd chores. They were the favorites of the camp. The Hauptsturmführer cared for them almost as a father would for his own children, looking after their needs and often spending hours on end with them. He gave them the best food and the best clothes. Because of the good care, the food and the fresh air they were getting, these boys looked the picture of health and I thought that no harm would come to them, but now, when I returned to Camp No. 1 I immediately noticed that they were no longer around. I was told that after the chief had tired of them, he had had them killed.

Having completed our assignment, we returned to Camp No. 2 in high hopes of being free soon. However, we had nothing definite to go on and the contact was broken off again.

The cremation of corpses had been going on in Camp No. 2 while we had been away, but as there were so many of them, the end was not yet in sight. Two more excavators were brought in, additional fire grates were constructed and the work was speeded up. The fire grates took up almost the entire yard. It was midsummer by then, and the fire grates gave off a terrific heat, turning the place into an inferno. We felt as if we ourselves were on fire. We anxiously waited for the moment when we would be able to force open the gates of the camp.

Several new transports arrived, I did not know from where. Two transports of Poles arrived also, but since I never saw them alive I do not know how they were treated when they had to disrobe and enter the death chambers. They were gassed just as the others had been. When we handled these corpses, we noticed that the men had not been circumcised. Also, we heard the Germans remarking that those "damned Poles" would not rebel again.

The younger inmates of our camp were growing impatient and were anxious to start the revolt, but the time was not ripe. We had not yet completed the plans for the attack, and escape. Contact with Camp No. 1 was difficult, but soon we were able to communicate with them again.

One Sunday afternoon Loeffler, my superior, told me that the Hauptsturmführer wanted to build an additional gate for the blockhouse and that the job would be given to me. He told me to draw up a plan, and I added the necessary information for the Hauptsturmführer, who accepted my suggestions. I submitted my specifications for the materials I would need and I started the job. I eagerly seized this opportunity, for I realized that this was the last chance of establishing contact with the conspirators. I visited Camp No. 1 under all sorts of pretexts and discussed our plans with my fellow conspirators, who, however, did not give any definite information. All they told us was not to give up but to wait. Meanwhile, bigger and better fire grates were set up at the camp, as if they would be needed for centuries to come. Seeing this, the young inmates were eager to take action. Our patience was wearing thin.

In Camp No. 2 we began to organize into groups of five, each group being assigned a specific task such as wiping out the German and Ukrainian garrison, setting the buildings on fire, covering the escape of the inmates, etc. All the necessary paraphernalia was being prepared: blunt tools to kill our keepers, lumber for the construction of bridges, gasoline for setting fires, etc.

The date for starting the revolt was set for June 15, but the zero hour was postponed several times and new dates were set, because the time was not yet ripe. The committee on organization used to meet after we had been locked in the barrack for the night. After the rest of our fellow inmates, worn out by the day's toil and abuse, had fallen asleep, we gathered in a corner of our barrack, in one of the upper bunks, and proceeded to make our plans. We had to keep the younger men in check, because they were eager for action and wanted to get things going even though we were not yet properly prepared.

We decided not to do anything without the inmates of Camp No. 1, since to do so would have been tantamount to suicide. We in Camp No. 2 were only a handful, because not all of us were physically fit for combat. As I have mentioned before, we had better food and treatment than the inmates in Camp No. 1, but we were only about 300 as against their 700.

The inmates of Camp No. 1 were practically starved and had to endure beatings and brutal punishment, which assumed fiendish forms if they were caught doing business with the Ukrainians. I saw with my own eyes how one of them on whom a piece of sausage had been found was tied to a post and forced to stand motionless through a blisteringly hot day. As he was physically quite strong, he survived the ordeal and did not betray the Ukrainian with whom he had done business. In this connection I must add that whenever the Germans found out about a Ukrainian dealing with the inmates and smuggling food to them, they would beat up the Ukrainian, too. The Ukrainians, in turn, took it out on the Jews. Living under such conditions, the inmates did not last long. It was then Franz's chance to drag those poor devils to the fire grates, torture them brutally and, after beating them to a pulp, kill them and throw their corpses into the fire. In view of these conditions, we knew that the inmates of Camp No. 1 would revolt but, since we were unable to accomplish anything without them, we completed our own preparations, and waited for a signal from them.

CHAPTER XII

In the meantime, "life" ran its "normal" course. There was no end to macabre ideas. The German staff suddenly felt the need for diversion and amusement, since they had no other worries. Accordingly, they organized compulsory theatrical performances, concerts, dance recitals, etc. The "performers" were recruited from among the inmates, who were excused from work for several hours to participate in rehearsals. The "performances" took place on Sundays. They were compulsory, with the audiences consisting of Germans and Ukrainians. Women were forced to sing in choirs, while the orchestra consisted of three musicians who were compelled to play each day at roll call after the whippings. The inmates were forced to sing Jewish songs as they marched off to work. Plans had been made for a new performance and new costumes obtained for it, but the show never took place because of our successful revolt and escape.

While the Germans ate their midday meal, between noon and 1 p.m., the Jews had to stand in the yard, in front of the mess hall, and provide music and song. The members of the choir had to work just as hard as the rest of the inmates, but had special hours for singing and performing their music. By and large, our tormentors had quite a bit of fun with the rest of us, dressing up as clowns and assigning functions which, heart-sore though we were, actually made us laugh.

One Jewish watchman, especially selected by the Germans, was stationed in front of the door of our barrack. He wore red pants like those of a Circassian, a tight-fitting jacket and wooden cartridges on both sides of his chest. He wore a tall fur calpac on his head and carried a wooden rifle. He was forced to clown and dance to the point of exhaustion. On Sundays he wore a suit of white linen with red stripes on the pants, red facings and a red sash. The Germans often got him drunk and used him for horseplay. No one was permitted to enter the barrack during working hours, and so he stood on guard at the door. His name was Moritz and he came from Czestochowa.

Another such poor wretch was the so-called "Scheissmeister" [shitmaster]. He was dressed like a cantor and even had to grow a goatee. He wore a large alarm clock on a string around his neck. No one was permitted to remain in the latrine longer than three minutes, and it was his duty to time everyone who used it. The name of this poor wretch was Julian. He also came from Czestochowa, where he had been the owner of a metal products factory. Just to look at him was enough to make one burst out laughing.

Moritz meekly accepted whatever the Germans did with him; he did not even realize what a pitiful figure he cut. Julian was a poised and quiet man, but when they began their horseplay with him, he wept bitterly. He wept also while he worked on the fire grates. His garb, his appearance and the task he had to perform provoked the German fiends to abuse him all the more and to amuse themselves at his expense.

For quite some time I had been working in Camp No. 1, returning every evening to Camp No. 2. This gave me a chance to make contact with the insurgents in Camp No. 1. I was watched less than the others and also treated better. Time and again, the Ukrainian guards entrusted some of their possessions to me for safekeeping because they knew I would not be searched. My superior bought me food himself and saw to it that I did not share it with anyone else. I never acted obsequious toward the Germans. I never took off my cap when I talked to Franz. Had it been another inmate, he would have killed him on the spot. But all he did was whisper to me in German, "When you talk to me, remember to take off your cap." Under these circumstances, I had almost complete freedom of movement and an opportunity to make all the necessary arrangements.

No transports had been coming to Treblinka for quite some time. Then, one day, as I was busy working near the gate, I noticed quite a different spirit among the German garrison and the Ukrainian guards. The Stabscharführer, a man of about 50, short, stocky and with a vicious face, left the camp several times by car. Then the gate flew open and about 1,000 Gypsies were marched in. This was the third transport of Gypsies to arrive at Treblinka. They were followed by several wagons carrying all their possessions: filthy tatters, torn bedclothes and other junk. They arrived almost unescorted except for two Ukrainians wearing German uniforms, who were not fully aware of what it all meant. They were sticklers for formality and even demanded a receipt, but they were not even admitted into the camp and their insistence on a receipt was met with sarcastic smiles. They learned on the sly from our Ukrainians that they had just delivered a batch of new victims to a death camp. They paled visibly and again knocked on the gate demanding admittance, whereupon the Stabscharführer came out and handed them a sealed envelope which they took and departed. The Gypsies, who had come from Bessarabia, were gassed just like all the others and then cremated.

July was drawing to a close and the weather was blistering hot. The hardest work was at the mass graves, and the men who exhumed the corpses for cremation were barely able to stand on their feet because of the sickening odors. By now about 75 per cent

180

of the corpses had been cremated; all that remained to be done was to grade down the soil so that not a trace would be found of the crimes which had been committed on that spot. Ashes don't talk.

It was our job to fill in the empty ditches with the ashes of the cremated victims, mixed with soil in order to obliterate all traces of the mass graves. The parcel of ground thus gained had to be utilized one way or another. It was fenced in with barbed wire, taking in an additional plot from the other camp to form an area for planting. An experiment was conducted with planting some vegetation in this area; the soil proved to be fertile. The gardeners among us planted lupine, which grew very well. And so the area of the mass graves, after 75 per cent of the corpses buried there had been exhumed and cremated, was leveled, seeded and fenced in with barbed wire. Pine trees were also planted there.

The Germans were full of pride over what they had accomplished and thought that they deserved some modest entertainment as a reward for their troubles. They began by celebrating the "retirement" of the excavator which had been exhuming our dead brethren. It was pointed skyward, its shovel high in the air. The Germans fired salvos: then came a regular banquet with much drinking and merrymaking.

We, too, benefitted from this celebration: we gained a few days' respite from work, but we realized only too well that these would be our last days on earth, since only 25 per cent of the graves still remained to be emptied. Once this would be finished, the few of us who were the sole witnesses to the appalling crimes which had been committed would also be killed. However, we controlled ourselves and waited patiently for deliverance.

At that time I was working steadily at Camp No. 1. A portion of the area of Camp No. 2 had been joined with Camp No. 1 and one of the towers had to be moved to Camp No. 2. I worked on this job with my men. I was, therefore, able to remain in contact with our comrades in Camp No. 1.

Within a few days work was begun to empty the remaining 25 per cent of the graves and the bodies were cremated. As I pointed out before, the weather was extremely hot, and as each grave was opened, it gave off a nauseating stench. Once the Germans threw some burning object into one of the opened graves just to see what would happen. Clouds of black smoke began to pour out at once and the fire thus started glimmered all day long. Some of the graves contained corpses which had been thrown into them directly after being gassed. The bodies had had no chance to cool off. They were so tightly packed that, when the graves were opened on a scorchingly hot day, steam belched forth from them as if from a boiler.

In one instance, when a batch of corpses was placed on the fire grate, an uplifted arm stuck out. Four fingers were clenched into a tight fist, except for the index finger, which had stiffened and pointed rigidly skyward as if calling God's judgment down upon the hangmen. It was only coincidence, but it was enough to unnerve all those who saw it. Even our tormentors paled and could not turn their eyes from that ghastly sight. It was as if some higher power had been at work. That arm remained pointed upward for a long, long time. Long after part of the pyre had turned to ashes, the uplifted arm was still there, calling to the heavens above for retributive justice. This small incident, seemingly meaningless, spoiled the high good humor of the hangmen, at least for a while.

I continued working at Camp No. 1, returning to Camp No. 2 each night. I was constructing a birchwood enclosure, a low fence around the flower garden where domesticated animals and birds were also kept. It was a quiet, pretty spot. Wooden benches had been placed there for the convenience of the Germans and Ukrainians. But alas, that serene spot was the seat of infamous plotting, the only theme of which undoubtedly was how to torture us, the hopeless wretches.

CHAPTER XIII

The *Lagerälteste* of Camp No. 1 frequently watched me at work from a distance. It was forbidden to talk to any of us, but he frequently spoke a few words to me on the sly. He was a Jew of about 45, tall and pleasant, by the name of Galewski. An engineer by profession, he hailed from Lodz. He had been appointed to his office in August, 1942, when Jewish camp "authorities" had first been set up. He was the mainstay of the organization work. Because he did not prostitute himself as some of the others had done, but always considered himself one of us unfortunates, he was frequently beaten and hounded like the rest of us.

When he came to me for a brief exchange of words, he had just been set free from a three-day confinement in a prison cell. While there, he had been let out only once each day — in the morning —

to empty the ordure bucket. Now, when no one was near me, he took the opportunity and categorically stated that the younger element should be patient because the hour of deliverance was approaching. He repeated this several times. I had the feeling that zero hour was approaching and that the end was really in sight.

On my return home from work that evening, I called a meeting to check the state of our preparedness. Everybody was excited and we did not sleep at all that night, seeing ourselves already outside the gates of the inferno.

The heat was becoming increasingly unbearable. It was almost impossible to keep standing on our feet. The terrible stench and the heat radiating from the furnaces was maddening. The Germans therefore decided that we were to work from 4 a.m. till noon, at which time they herded us into the barracks area. Once again, we came close to despair. We were afraid that now we would never be able to get out. However, we managed to find a way. We convinced the Germans that it would be better if the corpses would be cremated as soon as possible and said that there were volunteers among us who, for extra bread rations, would gladly work overtime. The Germans agreed.

We arranged two shifts, from noon till 3 p.m. and from 3 p.m. to 6 p.m. We selected the right men and waited from day to day for the signal. Beyond the area of our barrack there was a well that supplied the kitchen and laundry with water. We made use also of this "gateway," although it was guarded all the time. We made frequent trips to that well, even when we did not need water, in order to get the guards used to seeing us come and go.

At that time no transports at all came in, and so the only executions performed were those of individual Jews. After all, our executioners simply could not remain idle. But in due time the Germans were all in a good mood once more because new victims had arrived: a transport from Warsaw which was supposed to have been sent abroad. All the people in that transport were well-to-do and looked prosperous. They numbered about 1,000 men, women and children. We understood that it was a transport of people who had paid plenty of money to be taken to a place of safety. As I subsequently learned, they had been housed in the Hotel Polski, a first-class establishment on Dluga Street in Warsaw, but then they were taken to Treblinka. We learned who they were when we sorted out their possessions and found their personal papers. These people were killed like all the others.

The same fate befell transports coming in from other countries. These people had been told that they were going to be "resettled" in a place called Treblinka. Whenever they passed a station, the poor wretches would poke their heads out of the train windows and casually ask how much longer it was to Treblinka. Spent as they were, they looked forward to reaching a haven where they would be able to rest from their arduous journey. When they finally got to Treblinka, they were put to rest — forever — before they even had time to feel surprise or terror. At this writing, lupine grows over the spot where their ashes were buried.

Next came a transport from the Treblinka Penal Camp. It consisted of about 500 Jews, all barely alive, worked to the bone and brutally tortured. They looked as if they were begging to die and they were killed like all the others.

However, we were drawing closer to the end of our suffering. The day of our deliverance was approaching. Just then, my superior, Loeffler, who had been treating me so well, was transferred to Maidanek. He was bent on taking me with him to work there, and I was in a terrible predicament. I knew that a cruel death awaited each one of us. In Maidanek, I would be unable to find a quick way to freedom in the new surroundings and it would take me a long time to become acquainted with new people and new conditions. However, the decision did not rest with me: what was more, I had to pretend that I was elated over Loeffler's honoring me with such an offer. Luckily for me, the Hauptsturmführer refused to let me go. He still needed me. I, for my part, was very happy about that.

At about that time, for some reason unknown to us, we were ordered to write letters. Some among us were naive enough to do it. Later on I saw with my own eyes how the letters were burned. I do not know whether it had just been a game, a practical joke, or whatever.

CHAPTER XIV

The final, irrevocable date for the outbreak of the revolt was set for August 2, and we instinctively felt that this would really be the day. We got busy with our preparations, checking whether everything was in readiness and whether each of our men knew the part he had to play.

It so happened that I did not go to Camp No. 1 for several days because I was busy constructing an octagonal building with a suspended roof, resembling a guard station, that was to house a well. I was also constructing a portable building in Camp No. 2 which could be taken apart and which I subsequently had to move to Camp No. 1, where it was supposed to remain permanently. I was becoming impatient because I was unable to get in touch with Camp No. 1 and zero hour was approaching.

August 2, 1943 was a sizzling hot day. The sun shone brightly through the small, grated windows of our barrack. We had practically no sleep that night; dawn found us wide awake and tense. Each of us realized the importance of the moment and thought only of gaining freedom. We were sick of our miserable existence, and all that mattered was to take revenge on our tormentors and to escape. As for myself, all I hoped for was to be able to crawl into some quiet patch of woodland and get some quiet, restful sleep.

At the same time, we were fully aware of the difficulties we would have to overcome. Observation towers, manned by armed guards, stood all around the camp, and the camp itself was teeming with Germans and Ukrainians armed with rifles, machine guns and revolvers. They would lock us up in our barracks as early as 12 noon. The camp was surrounded by several rows of fences and trenches.

However, we decided to risk it, come what may. We had had enough of the tortures, of the horrible sights. I, for one, was determined to live to present to the world a description of the inferno and a sketch of the layout of that accursed hellhole. This resolve had given me the strength to struggle against the hangmen and the endurance to bear the misery. Somehow I felt that I would survive our break for freedom.

A presentiment of the coming storm was in the air and our nerves were at high tension. The Germans and the Ukrainians noticed nothing unusual. Having wiped out millions of people, they did not feel they had to fear a paltry handful of men such as we. They barked orders which were obeyed as usual. But those of us who belonged to the committee were worried because we had no instructions about the timing of the outbreak. I was fidgety. I kept on working but all the time I worried that we might fail to establish contact which, in turn, would mean that we would perish miserably and in vain.

However, I found a way of communicating with Camp No. 1. My superior, Loeffler, was no longer there; he had been replaced by a new man whose name I did not know. We nicknamed him "Brown Shirt." He was very kind to me. I walked up to him and asked him for some boards. Boards were stored in Camp No. 1 and he, not wanting to interrupt our work, went off with some workers to get them. The boards were brought. I inspected and measured them, and then said they weren't right for the job. I volunteered to go over myself to select the material I needed, but I made a wry face as if I did not like the idea. And so I went to the storage shed with my superior, all the while shaking with excitement. I felt that unless I made the most of this opportunity, all would be lost.

Presently I found myself in Camp No.1 and nervously looked around, appraising our chances. Three other men were with me. The storage shed was guarded by a Jew about 50 years of age, wearing spectacles. Because he was an inmate of Camp No. 1, I knew nothing about him, but he was a participant in the conspiracy. My three helpers engaged the German superior in a conversation to divert his attention, while I pretended to be selecting boards. I deliberately went away from the others, continuing to select boards. Suddenly, someone whispered in my ear: "Today, at 5:30 p.m." I turned around casually and saw the Jewish guard of the storage shed before me. He repeated these words and added: "There will be a signal."

In feverish haste I collected whatever boards were nearest to me, told my comrades to pick them up and started to work, trembling with fear lest I betray my emotions. Thus time went by until noon, when all hands returned from work. Again our committee met furtively and the word was passed around. I asked everyone to keep cool and remember their individual assignments. The younger ones among us were greatly agitated. As I looked at our group, I began to believe that we would really win.

Volunteers for the afternoon work shift were then selected. We assigned the weaker and less capable men to the first shift because it had no task to perform. The first afternoon shift returned from work at 3 p.m. The men we had picked then went to work, thirty in number. They were the bravest, the pluckiest and the strongest in the lot. Their task was to pave the way for the others to escape. A crew was also picked for fetching water from the well. At around 5 p.m. there suddenly was a great need for water. The gate leading to the well was opened wide and the number of water carriers was considerably augmented.

All those assigned to work with the corpses wore only striped overalls. A penalty of 25 lashes was meted out for wearing any other clothing while doing this particular job. On that day, however, the men wore their clothes under their overalls. Before escaping, they would have to get rid of the overalls, which would have given them away at once.

We remained in our barracks, sitting close together and exchanging glances; every few minutes someone would remark that the time was drawing near. Our emotions at that point defied description. We silently bade farewell to the spot where the ashes of our brethren were buried. Sorrow and suffering had bound us to Treblinka, but we were still alive and wanted to escape from this place where so many innocent victims had perished. The long processions, those ghastly caravans of death, were still before our eyes, crying out for vengeance. We knew what lay hidden beneath the surface of this soil. We were the only ones left alive to tell the story. Silently, we took our leave of the ashes of our fellow Jews and vowed that, out of their blood, an avenger would arise.

Suddenly we heard the signal — a shot fired into the air.

We leaped to our feet. Everyone fell to his prearranged task and performed it with meticulous care. Among the most difficult tasks was to lure the Ukrainians from the watchtowers. Once they began shooting at us from above, we would have no chance of escaping alive. We knew that gold held an immense attraction for them, and they had been doing business with the Jews all the time. So, when the shot rang out, one of the Jews sneaked up to the tower and showed the Ukrainian guard a gold coin. The Ukrainian completely forgot that he was on guard duty. He dropped his machine gun and hastily clambered down to pry the piece of gold from the Jew. They grabbed him, finished him off and took his revolver. The guards in the other towers were also dispatched quickly.

Every German and Ukrainian whom we met on our way out was killed. The attack was so sudden that before the Germans were able to gather their wits, the road to freedom lay wide open before us. Weapons were snatched from the guard station and each one of us grabbed all the arms he could. As soon as the signal shot rang out, the guard at the well had been killed and his weapons taken from him. We all ran out of our barracks and took the stations that had been assigned to us. Within a matter of minutes, fires were raging all around. We had done our duty well.

I grabbed some guns and let fly right and left, but when I saw that the road to escape stood open, I picked up an ax and a saw, and ran. At first we were in control of the situation. However, within a short time pursuit got under way from every direction, from Malkinia, Kosow and from the Treblinka Penal Camp. It seemed that when they saw the fires and heard the shooting, they sent help at once.

Our objective was to reach the woods, but the closest patch was five miles away. We ran across swamps, meadows and ditches, with bullets pursuing us fast and furious. Every second counted. All that mattered was to reach the woods because the Germans would not want to follow us there.

Just as I thought I was safe, running straight ahead as fast as I could, I suddenly heard the command "Halt!" right behind me. By then I was exhausted but I ran faster just the same. The woods were just ahead of me, only a few leaps away. I strained all my will power to keep going. The pursuer was gaining and I could hear him running close behind me.

Then I heard a shot; in the same instant I felt a sharp pain in my left shoulder. I turned around and saw a guard from the Treblinka Penal Camp. He again aimed his pistol at me. I knew something about firearms and I noticed that the weapon had jammed. I took advantage of this and deliberately slowed down. I pulled the ax from my belt. My pursuer — a Ukrainian guard — ran up to me yelling in Ukrainian: "Stop or I'll shoot!" I came up close to him and struck him with my ax across the left side of his chest. Yelling: "Yob tvayu mat" [you motherfucker!] he collapsed at my feet.

I was free and ran into the woods. After penetrating a little deeper into the thicket, I sat down among the bushes. From the distance I heard a lot of shooting. Believe it or not, the bullet had not really hurt me. It had gone through all of my clothing and stopped at my shoulder, leaving only a scratch. I was alone. At last, I was able to rest.

1. In 1943 German forces occupying the village of Katyn announced that they had found in the woods nearby a mass grave of some 10,000 Polish officers. They claimed that these Poles had been captured and murdered by Russians. The Russians later accused the Germans of this wholesale murder.

I SURVIVED TREBLINKA

SAMUEL WILLENBERG

SAMUEL WILLENBERG was born in Częstochowa in 1923. In 1942 he was deported to Treblinka, where he soon became active in the underground that initiated the rebellion. Although wounded during the uprising, he managed to escape into the woods and eventually reached Warsaw. He participated in the general Polish uprising in August, 1944, and fought in the ranks of the partisans in the Kampinos woods.

After the liberation of Poland he joined the Polish army and served as a captain until 1947. In 1958 he settled in Israel.

The excerpts published here are part of his memoirs I Survived Treblinka, *which were written in 1945 in Lodz, and are now in the archives of the Israeli semi-annual* Moreshet. *The full memoirs will be published shortly.*

O NE DAY in the late afternoon we were lined up in the roll call square. We noticed that the Germans were very nervous that day, but somehow less ruthless than usual. They bustled around the camp like puppets, paying special attention to little details. Their nervousness soon communicated to us. We didn't know what was the matter.

We were standing in the square waiting for things to happen. We were prepared for every surprise but nothing special happened.

At a certain moment a group of officers and several civilians entered the square. A stout officer, his chest covered with medals, stepped forward. Of medium height and wearing eyeglasses, he held a speech where shameless lies and bold verbiage were mixed with expressions of contempt and hypocrisy. He turned out to be

Heinrich Himmler. We learned many interesting things but nobody was stupid enough to believe the baloney he was giving us. Himmler tried to convince us that after all the Jewish camps had been completed, the Germans would organize an autonomous Jewish region. Then we could have our freedom and we would all be happy. We would lose nothing by being in the camps because all the possessions taken from us would be sent to other camps, where they would be used for the good of the Jews. He encouraged us to work and claimed that as soon as we would have learned to perform our duties conscientiously we would be taken into the German army, where we would form a special *Ordnungsdienst* (police force).

At the end of this strange ceremony we were ordered to sing. The whole camp sang the pretty but later universally hated Polish song: *Góralu, czy ci nie żal* [Aren't you sorry, mountaineer?] . . .

* * *

One night the *Lagerälteste*, the engineer Galewski, and several kapos were called out of the barrack. Galewski had held the post of *Lagerälteste* ever since he had come to the camp. He would assign the work and make sure that everyone performed it properly. He was the immediate superior of our kapos and of the foremen. Galewski was a decent man and exceptionally intelligent. At the same time, however, he was cautious and did not take part in any underground activity. And here we should note that there had been an organized underground in Treblinka ever since the early days of the camp. Galewski could not have been ignorant of its existence. We made many guesses as to why several of our men had been called out in the nighttime. We were afraid they might have been condemned to liquidation. But for what transgression?

That night brought us further surprises. We suddenly heard the hoot of a locomotive. It could only be the arrival of a new transport. But the strange thing was that it should have arrived during the night. Such a thing had never happened before. After a short while, I heard a human shriek, a desperate cry for help. Rude curses . . . and then a shot rang out: one, a second and a third . . . Outside, the shrieks mingled with the sound of feet running. Someone pounded violently on the door of our barrack. The knocking was insistent; one could recognize in it the fear and despair which precede death. The door could not withstand the pres-

190

sure of several strong men, and finally gave way. Since it was dark inside the barrack, we could not make out who the intruders were. I felt someone climbing up on my bunk and lying down beside me. I asked no questions. I was trembling with excitement and fear.

Outside, the firing went on without a stop. Single shots, the rat-tat-tat of a machine gun, the groans of the wounded, the shouts of the pursued, the calls of sentries—all these frightened us and threw us into terrible tension. And suddenly one of our most cruel kapos—allegedly, he had been in the white slave trade before the war—burst into the barrack and, with a swing of his whip, ordered us to hand over immediately the people who were hiding out with us. In order to get the men moving, he lashed out at several of those who were lying down, and so he hit me, too. The whip struck me in the face, leaving a purple weal. I howled with pain, but even worse than the pain was my fear that the next day I would fall into the hands of the SS, for anyone who attracted their attention [by having a visible wound or bruise] could expect to die. In the end about 20 Jews whom no one had ever seen before were captured in the barrack. They were dragged outside and shot. During the struggle with the unfortunates one of our people was stabbed in the hand with a dagger. When "The Doll" heard about this, he appeared in our barracks and cared for the wounded man with a devotion which astonished us.

In the morning we learned that a transport of Jews from Grodno had arrived during the night. When they were taken out of the boxcars, the people realized what was about to happen to them. The red glow of the flames, the barbed wire fences, the watchtowers—all that could be seen in the darkness which was illuminated by the flames—goaded them into resistance. They were ordered to undress, but they rushed at the SS men with knives, and the battle blazed in all its intensity. The Jews defended themselves with the strength of despair. Since they had no weapons, they attacked the Germans with bottles. The transport comprised about 2,000 people, including many women and children. Not all of them took part in the battle. Some of them just prayed. There was never any doubt that the revolt would end with the defeat of the unfortunates. The machine guns reaped a harvest of blood; [the new arrivals] fell in the roll call square. Of the Germans, three SS men were mortally wounded. They were removed to the nearby hospital. When we came out of our barracks in the morning a terrible sight met our eyes. The roll call square was strewn with blood-soaked

Jewish bodies. During the night the soft snow had swaddled them in a coat whiter than white.

* * *

... I remember the night we were awakened by whistles and blows of the whip. They hurried us along as if a fire had broken out at the camp. We were chased out to the roll call square and ordered to line up in columns. We were terror-stricken. We thought our last hour had come. But the hangmen had other plans for us. . . . In the course of a few hours we loaded 60 empty freight cars. Loading the freight train could offer a possibility of escaping. I was overcome by a desire to slip unseen into one of the cars, bury myself beneath the clothes and, after the train had moved some distance away from the camp, come out of my hiding-place and jump for my life—to freedom. I started to maneuver my way, trying to get onto a freight car with one of the bundles and not get off again. But fate did not smile upon me. The sentries kept a very careful eye on me. Every time I got into a freight car, there was someone trailing me. Finally dawn broke, it became light all around, and the light of the new day destroyed any chance of escape. When we returned to the barracks, we saw that ten men were missing. The block supervisor noticed this immediately, but since he was a Jew he did not report it to anyone. During the roll call and head count we maneuvered with such agility that the SS men did not notice anyone was missing. That day a new transport arrived and we succeeded in bringing 15 people from it to the barracks. Thus we not only made up for the shortage but even had a surplus. Did the escapees succeed in fleeing from the freight cars? I do not know. At any rate, they never returned to the camp.

* * *

In spite of the fences, the barbed wire, the guards, the severe regulations and unremitting control, a trade in foods flourished at the camp. Speculation also thrived. Almost everyone in the camp had some money. We had obtained it in various ways. Most of it had come from the clothing of the Jews who had been killed. Thanks to this money, goods from the outside reached us. They were smuggled in by inmates who worked outside of the camp, including the *Tarnungskommando* [camouflage detail], to which I belonged. During our stay in the woods we would meet local inhabitants. They came with the aim of doing business. The go-betweens were usually our guards, who were eager for extra profit. We often

192

succeeded in bribing an SS man or a Ukrainian guard. When there was a short pause in our work the SS man would go off to one side, supposedly to talk with some girls, and the Ukrainian would take the money, contact the trader and come back with the bundle. We would divide up the food in equal portions. But within the boundaries of the camp the trading was done only at night. Once the prisoners were asleep, several would slip out to the latrine and wait for the Ukrainian. Finally a black shadow would emerge in the darkness and a quiet voice would ask whether the money was ready. A hundred-dollar bill or a gold twenty-dollar coin would be held out to him, and a bundle would be received in return. In it there would be a loaf of bread, a kilo of sausage and half a liter of vodka. More than once we ordered oranges or other fruits for the sick. Occasionally other goods such as milk, fat, sugar, etc. were brought to us. There were cases where prisoners were caught in the act of receiving bundles, and then their hope for freedom and life would evaporate at once, since any attempt to obtain food or make contacts was punished by death. More than once SS men tried to catch suspects, and so extreme caution was required not to get caught. Yet, despite the mortal dangers which hovered over us in Treblinka, the trading never ceased. The greater the hunger, the more trading there was. In return for ten cigarettes you could get a slice of bread; the price of a ration of bread was five gold rubles. Half a liter of vodka cost up to a hundred dollars. We drank the vodka only in the evenings, after we had climbed onto our bunks, and we did not care that this was ruining our health even more. Thanks to the vodka we were thrown into a state of excitement in which our drab lives took on brighter colors. It aroused positive thoughts in us and drove the terror of danger further away. Under the influence of the alcohol our optimism increased, our bodies were swept by a wave of warmth, our sleep was deeper and more peaceful. Every morning, as we went to work and passed the barracks of the Germans and Ukrainians, we would throw ourselves upon the garbage cans. Sometimes we found scraps of food in them, crusts of bread, half-gnawed bones, potatoes. . . . On one occasion Alfred Boehm found a bottle of cream, which apparently had been tossed into the garbage because it was hard to pour the thick cream from the bottle. That day was a royal feast for Boehm.

* * *

The hunger, the lack of water and the dirt brought on a typhoid epidemic in the camp. The disease struck almost the entire camp. The prisoners strove to remain in the barracks until their last breath, knowing that transfer to the *Revier* [sick bay] was tantamount to death. The Germans shot any man who showed signs of the disease. Sick, their knees shaking, the prisoners went out to work, burning with fever, pleaded for help and protection from their comrades, but eventually their strength gave out and all hope of saving them would be lost. The lives of the sick depended to a great degree upon the doctors who worked in the *Revier*. It should be noted that the moral level of these doctors was very low. I do not remember their names. Two male doctors and one female dentist were usually employed in the *Revier*. Their function was that of quacks and poisoners rather than that of preservers of health. In addition there was Dr. Chorążycki, a brave and honest man, but he treated Germans only. Aside from this group, there were a few doctors in the barracks who had concealed their professions, and it was they who helped us considerably—they treated the sick people we had hidden, prepared medicines for them and gave them helpful advice. But their role was limited by the shortage of drugs, syringes and other equipment. Each day the typhoid fever exacted a terrible toll from us and the bunks grew emptier.

That winter four prisoners escaped from Treblinka. The escape had been organized without special preparations. It was customary at the camp that the doors of the barracks would be opened before the reveille hour so that the inmates could relieve themselves in the latrine behind the barracks. Our group was located in the very heart of the camp and was surrounded by many barracks. It was difficult to escape, if only because there were fences between the various sections of the camp. Anyone trying to escape had to overcome all these obstacles. In the evenings, when we returned to the barracks for the night, the camp sentries would leave their posts, and only the barracks of the Jews were watched over by guards. That morning, before dawn, in utter darkness, two prisoners entered the latrine. When they saw that there were no sentries around, they cut the strands of barbed wire of the nearby fence which separated us from the roll call square. Luck was with them, and without the slightest difficulty they crossed the vacant area in a run. On the other side of the square they again cut wires and another fence, and broke through to freedom. Within a few minutes they had reached the woods. At that time there were two other Jews in the latrine who took advantage of the opportunity and escaped. At dawn the Germans noticed the breaks in the fences. Clear tracks indicated the direction of flight, and it was impossible to conceal what had happened. The camp administration immediately made a head count and it was discovered that four prisoners were missing from our barracks. The Germans organized a hunt while we were left in the roll call square for a time. Finally, we were sent to breakfast, as though nothing had happened. Afterward, we were lined up alongside the fence. We thought that we would go out, as we did every day, to the roll call square. We were absolutely still. Suddenly we became alarmed. We saw that the Germans were removing machine guns from the arsenal. Unterscharführer Miete and another SS man were setting up machine guns and rifles on stands nearby. Fear choked our throats. We bore the escapees no grudge. We knew that we would have done the same if we had had the chance to do so. And despite the fact that we had resigned ourselves long ago to the thought that death lay in wait for us on every hand, now, in the face of our certain extinction, we felt a pang of grief in our hearts. The world, which had kept itself aloof from us and had shown us only its anger, now seemed colorful and tempting with the prospect of a good life. Were we indeed doomed to part from all this? Indeed, how strange it was: in the face of death a man forgets his suffering and agony and sees only the pleasures of life awaiting him. A whisper passed through the ranks. Perhaps the escapees had been captured and we would be silent witnesses to their execution. After a half-hour's wait Miete walked up to us and commanded: "First barrack, forward march!"

We extended our hands to one another in parting. There was no doubt in our minds that as soon as we had turned our backs we would be cut down by a round of gunfire. We moved. I marched in the first row of five. At the railroad platform we were ordered to halt. Our hearts pounded like footsteps. The blood roared in our temples and it was a wonder that it did not burst the blood vessels. Once again a command—about face! After a moment an SS man—short and stout, with the face of a bulldog—ordered us forward. We marched on a few paces and were again forced to turn on our heels. And suddenly the SS man started to deliver a speech. It was unreasonable, extraordinary—the SS man Fesele was speaking! And speeches were equivalent to salvation. A German won't shoot while he is delivering a speech.

The executioner with the bulldog face gave us a long speech. It seemed that he had resolved to get into our thick skulls all the instructions and orders which we were supposed to obey. If one of us should try to escape the all-powerful German authorities would not only catch him and make him shorter by a head, but they would punish all the rest of us as well. For each escapee caught, every tenth prisoner would be executed, in order to kill our desire to oppose the power of the Reich. Everything had to be *in Ordnung* [in order]. And now—forward to the roll call square.

A regular roll call was held and we returned to our daily work. In our absence SS men had burst into the *Revier*, taken 20 patients out of the barracks and shot them. Did they wish by this act to get their revenge for the escapees?

* * *

Underground activity began in the camp almost as soon as the camp had been set up. At first the underground group consisted of only a few people. These were monomaniacs whose plans were the fruit of imaginings and visions completely divorced from reality. It is truly unbelievable, but that group decided to purchase arms from the Ukrainian camp guards and even made contact with them for this purpose. These contacts bore no fruit whatever. The shrewd Ukrainians would take the money but did not supply the weapons. We had to employ other means of organizing the underground. For the time being, therefore, the men contented themselves with reading underground publications and listening to clandestine radio broadcasts. Later, the group decided to execute the traitors, spies and informers among the inmates. The men of the underground achieved significant results in carrying out this task. The executions would be carried out cautiously, secretly and without arousing any suspicion. The frequent cases of suicide among the prisoners helped camouflage the executions. Almost every one of us had a dose of cyanide or some other poison on hand [for ourselves] in case of trouble. Many people in the camp committed suicide by hanging themselves, but then cases of suicide in a state of nervous collapse were common even among people who were free and lived in relatively good conditions. Therefore the underground employed a unique stratagem: they would give the execution of an informer the appearance of a case of suicide, and as a rule the SS men did not realize what had happened. The executions were carried out only after a rigorous investigation of the activities of the traitor or informer. We had to be convinced

196

beyond the shadow of a doubt that the accused was indeed guilty as charged. In many cases the traitor was first warned and given a chance to turn over a new leaf. If the warning did not help, a court was convened and meted out the death sentence. Thanks to the liquidation of such informers, the lives of many prisoners were saved, and a certain solidarity was preserved among the inmate population. I recall the case of a certain Hermann, a stooge of the Germans who for a long time had been informing the camp authorities of everything that was going on among the inmates. He gathered around him a group of petty informers and talebearers. Either directly or through these individuals he was informed about who owned gold or silver, who was planning to escape, who was engaging in barter or organizing the smuggling of food into the camp. Due to Hermann's informing, many prisoners lost their lives. Among his victims was a Jew from Częstochowa, Dzialos-zynski, a very worthwhile person and an excellent comrade.

We had no pity on suspected informers during the famine period, when we would distribute equal shares of the foodstuffs obtained from various sources. We did not help them in their hard labor and paid no attention to them during punishment drills. The traitors were abandoned and isolated. One of our kapos, a man named Rakowski, knew very well that we were liquidating the in-formers, and he secretly gave his consent to this. It also happened that the doctors in the *Revier* played a certain part in the liquidation of dangerous characters. If one of the traitors fell ill, camp head-quarters were notified of that fact, and he would be ordered killed by a bullet or by an injection of poison.

In the course of time the underground developed considerably. In every block and barrack, groups were organized which consti-tuted cells of the underground. Each group numbered from five to ten members; the total number of cells was ten. Nearly everyone in the *Kommandos* [labor details] belonged to the underground, and each group comprised from 15 to 25 men. The kapo Rakowski aided the conspirators. He got us accustomed to long marches, for he was planning a revolt and hoped to lead us all out into the woods, to the partisans. During the famine period the conspirators organized a commune. Everyone contributed money to a common treasury with which to purchase foods. Afterwards we would divide up the food which had been smuggled in. Those of our comrades who could not afford to pay were not forgotten; they received their share. This form of self-help helped many to survive this difficult period. More than once dramatic conflicts broke out which posed a grave threat to the conspirators. I remember the case of a journalist whose name was Kronenberg or Korenberg. Wanting to save his life, we had spirited him out of a transport. But the journalist's body has wasted away and his mind had become unhinged. He deteriorated until he finally caught dysentery. In the course of his illness he relieved himself in his bunk. We could not hide this fact, and the SS men dragged him off to the *lazaret*. At the sight of the rifle aimed at him he broke down completely and, getting down on his knees, he begged for mercy. He promised his executioners that if they would let him live he would turn over to them, as a gesture of gratitude, the names of 100 prisoners who belonged to the underground. The Germans heard this and hesitated momentarily, but the day was saved by [the kapo Zev] Kurland, who made a circle with his finger on his forehead, implying to the Germans that the poor fellow had gone out of his mind. A shot rang out, and thanks to it 100 other men were saved from sure death.

* * *

After the escape of the four prisoners we were transferred to another barrack. We were housed in the very center of the camp, which was known as the "ghetto." Our new group of buildings were laid out in a square. In our new section the bunks were stacked three high. It is not known for what reason they began digging up the ground under our old barracks. Perhaps it was because of an informer, but it makes more sense to assume that the Germans suspected us of concealing valuables in camouflaged hiding places. And they really came across buried treasures which astonished even the camp authorities: no less than 40 kilos of gold, a large number of gold, silver and chromium watches, precious necklaces, diamond rings and other treasures were removed from beneath the barracks. It can easily be imagined what a great panic seized our group. And indeed, we did not have long to wait for the consequences. During roll call we were told that there would be body searches and that everyone who wanted to keep out of trouble should immediately hand over all the money he possessed, gold articles, watches, rings and documents. Only the foremen were allowed to keep their watches for themselves.

I was one of the few "clean" prisoners, but I had in my possession forged documents in another name which identified me as an Aryan. I had hidden them in case I should managed to escape from

Treblinka. These documents were enough to bring down disaster upon me. Standing there in line it was hard for me to dispose of them. Therefore I did not hesitate long; I tore up the papers and swallowed them. While I was doing this, an amusing thing happened to me. The man next to me noticed that I was chewing something and thought I had taken a bite out of a sausage. "Give me a piece," he said. I grinned and passed him a piece of paper. He looked at the paper angrily. He thought that I was not only refusing to give him some of my delicacies, but was even mocking him, and he stopped speaking to me.

* * *

In the meantime we continued to expand the camp. At that time (in 1943) a small addition was erected between two German barracks which connected the structure by a sort of corridor. It looked as if it would serve either as a detention room or as an arsenal. And in due time we saw that it really would be an arsenal. It was planned to put a water tank above the arsenal. Since no one from the outside was allowed to enter the camp, we inmates did all the jobs with our own hands. Those parts which we were unable to manufacture were brought in from the outside. This happened in the case of the arsenal also. Its iron door was brought in from the outside, but unfortunately for the Germans it did not have a lock. The task [of making a lock] was assigned to our locksmiths. And here the underground, which lately had branched out into every portion of the camp, came into the picture. The locksmiths received their instructions and carried them out precisely: they made two keys for the lock [instead of just one]. Needless to say, only one of the keys was supplied to the Germans; the other was placed in our cache and was to lift our spirits in the difficult moments ahead. That key was destined to open for us the gate which led to freedom. One characteristic of this period was the improvement in the morale of the inmates. This was clearly evident, and even the Germans were amazed that despite our hunger and suffering we still showed so much optimism.

On the orders of the Germans, Artur Gold gathered the most musical from among the prisoners. These musicians were given instruments and quickly formed an orchestra. Every day after roll call we listened to concerts conducted by Gold. First our rows were counted and our attendance checked. Afterwards the SS man on duty read out the list of prisoners who had been fined that day for various offenses, with the number of lashes coming to each one of them. After the whipping, the artistic portion of the program began. First, serious works were played, and then marches, to whose beat we were forced to march around the roll call square. This marching had a special function; its purpose was not torture but drill. It was initiated by our *Lagerälteste*, Rakowski. He was a young man, from Jędrzejów, I think. He impressed me as an intelligent man. It was said that he had been a farmer. Rakowski was appointed to the post during the typhoid epidemic, after his predecessor, Galewski, also had come down with the disease. His selection was due at least in part to his impressive height. Rakowski was tall, broad-boned and strong. He would beat us in such a manner that the Germans believed no prisoner could emerge from his hands alive. But in fact Rakowski took pity on us; he was very humane and understood our suffering. Under certain circumstances, of course, he was powerless to rescue us, for if the Germans were around he would be forced to torture the men of whom he was in charge. Rakowski dreamed of a great revolt, the destruction of the camp and the removal of the prisoners in organized groups to the partisan units in the woods. Therefore he got us accustomed to long marches and conducted various exercises with us for the purpose of steeling us and accustoming us to the hardships of partisan life. Much to our sorrow, Rakowski's dreams were not fulfilled. Like many others, Rakowski, too, had lots of enemies in the camp, and he was forced to watch out for informers and traitors. One of these scoundrels informed the camp authorities that Rakowski was keeping a canteen full of gold in his bunk. Of course an investigation was made immediately, and as a result Rakowski was shot. It was a shattering blow for all his friends. We parted from him in sorrow as from a hero who did not think of himself; his every thought and action was for the good of others. All the time he believed that he would manage to lead us out of that hell to the woods and that he would yet become famous for many heroic deeds. It is not known who informed on him. We suspected Kuba, a butcher who hailed from Warsaw.

Galewski, who had recovered from his typhoid fever, was once again appointed *Lagerälteste*. But he, too, was in constant danger from stool pigeons, traitors and informers. One of his sworn enemies was a prisoner named Blau, who was a kapo. He was a real caricature: corpulent and bandy-legged, with the face of a degenerate. The Germans had driven him out of Vienna, and Blau had reached Kielce and started collaborating with the Gestapo. There is no doubt that this man, who had neither honor nor conscience, was responsible for the death of many people. After the liquidation of the Kielce ghetto he was deported with his wife to Treblinka, and here the couple was separated from the rest of the transport. This was the only instance in the history of the camp where a husband and wife were both put to work over a long period. Blau enjoyed certain privileges. He was appointed chief kapo and finally made head of the kitchen. He immediately surrounded himself with a gang of informers who kept him up to date about everything that went on in the barracks, the conversations and plans of the prisoners. Blau would serve his friends double portions and good cuts of meat—at the expense of the other prisoners, of course. His hatred for Galewski was based on personal ambition. Blau himself aspired to become *Lagerälteste* and was angry that he was, to a certain extent, subordinate to Galewski.

How was a *Lagerälteste* appointed in Treblinka? It was a rather solemn ritual. All the prisoners were assembled in the roll call square, where they were lined up to form a perfect square. After the singing of the camp anthem, the man who had just been appointed would go out to the center of the square, express his thanks in German for the confidence which had been placed in him and promise to obey diligently all the orders and instructions, to take care to preserve order and to settle quarrels. Promptly, when the Germans had left the roll call square, he would wink his eye at us meaningfully and order us to fall out.

In addition to the arsenal, we built two latrines during the period when Treblinka was constructed. One of the latrines was built within the camp area; the other, next to the *lazaret*. The latrines were the only place in the camp where you could sit quietly, hold long conversations and find out all sorts of news. Our executioners quickly realized that we had it too good in the latrines. One day special monitors appeared there—the idiots among the prisoners. Their job was to admit no more than five men at a time and to see to it that these did not stay too long. The SS men hung alarm clocks on the monitors' chests, and afterward dressed them up in priests' cassocks, taken from the cargo of one of the transports which had arrived from Greece. The monitors were also given whips to hold. The Germans burst out laughing at the sight of the idiots in this getup, and rejoiced over the excellent idea.

* * *

One bright April day a strange transport arrived in Treblinka. The freight cars were in poor condition and their boards ripped away. On the roofs lay armed sentries who fired whenever a frightened human face peeped out of one of the cars. We got the impression that a fierce battle had been fought on the way with the Jewish deportees in the train.

Not long before, we had received new instructions regarding the reception of transports, and that day we were about to carry them out for the first time. We were divided into small groups, three men to a group, and placed at intervals of 20 meters from one another. When the new arrivals were let out of the boxcars and directed toward the roll call square, they were ordered to take off their various articles of clothing one after the other and hand them over to the groups. The first trio got coats, the second jackets, the third trousers, underwear, shoes. The stripping of the women was organized according to the same system. This assembly line made for greater efficiency in the job. That day the cowardice of the "master race" was exposed. As the new arrivals took off their clothes, there was a sudden explosion. One of the Jews had probably hidden a hand grenade in his pocket, and now it exploded. Three of our people and several more from among the newcomers were wounded. Immediately there was a great tumult which cannot be described in words, but the most startled of all were the Germans. In an instant the roll call square was emptied of SS men. Most ridiculous of all was the sight of Sepp, who usually pretended to be a "fearless hero." Now the sound of the explosion had sent him running across the roll call square, knees knocking, terror-stricken. Hard on his heels ran the Ukrainian sentries. Several minutes passed before the Germans recovered from their astonishment. "Kiewe" burst into the transport ground and ordered the wounded workers moved to the *lazaret*. But we took them into the barracks and waited for what would come next. We were afraid that our wounded comrades were lost, that they could expect a bullet in the head. But the Germans were magnanimous this time; not only did they not punish us for having disobeyed them, but they even ordered us to take the patients to the *Revier*. "Kiewe" himself, and "The Doll," too, visited them in the barracks, pretended sympathy and ordered the doctors to treat them well. It was astonishing and beyond our understanding. The simple truth was that the Germans feared that bitterness might drive us to some desperate deed upon the arrival of one of the new transports;

perhaps they had other suspicions, too. In any event, they tried to show us their friendliness, in which, however, no one had any faith.

That day we learned from the newcomers about the Warsaw ghetto revolt. We were shaken by the news. We had long known that a considerable number of Jews had been concentrated in Warsaw, and that many of them were ready to do battle for life and death, because the underground had prepared the ground for the organization of a resistance movement. The news of life and conditions in the ghetto filtered in to us only in bits and pieces. Nevertheless we would dwell upon them, argue about them and weave thoughts around them. In Warsaw were many of the relatives, friends and acquaintances, of our comrades. Warsaw was our hope, our secret dream. And lo and behold, we suddenly learned that in the crowded streets of the Warsaw ghetto the fire of revolt had flared, the rat-tat-tat of machine guns accompanied by the sound of exploding grenades. We pictured that bitter struggle to ourselves. Our hearts went out to the rebels; we worried about the fate of the heroes, the relatives who had remained there, and the children . . .

The revolt of the Warsaw ghetto fired us, infused new strength into us. We, too, wanted to act and no longer allow ourselves to be led to our death stunned, submissive and helpless. In the evening the barrack hummed like a beehive. On every bunk a group sat conversing in low voices. We were all very excited; it seemed as if daylight had broken into the everyday drabness of the camp. Now our suffering was of only secondary importance. We launched into wild conjectures and we were beset by a fever of activity. The plan for the destruction of Treblinka and an armed revolt against our oppressors took shape. We heard the call of the woods, where the partisans were multiplying daily and which the SS and *Wehrmacht* companies entered with ever-increasing fear.

Slowly the underground raised its head in the camp. Several days after the news of the Warsaw ghetto revolt had reached us, a meeting was held in the carpentry shop in which the leaders of the revolt took part. I was one of those initiated. That is why I was admitted to the deliberations. Altogether about 15 persons were present. Underground members from all the units had assembled; the *Hofjuden*[1] were especially numerous among them. For various reasons some of the conspirators could not be present. I remember some of those who attended: Zygmunt Strawczynski, 40, a tinsmith from Lodz; his brother Oscar, also a tinsmith, and many others. At that meeting we decided to get ready for battle. First of all, we needed weapons, and we therefore decided to devote all our efforts to obtaining rifles, hand grenades and ammunition. It was agreed that we would purchase arms. The dangerous task of securing arms was assigned to Dr. Chorążycki, who was not present at the meeting.

As I have mentioned above, Chorążycki served as physician at the German Clinic. He was destined to play an important part in the underground. He was a man of unblemished character, a respected personality. He knew the Germans through and through. He knew how to talk with them, and there was no doubt that they, too, respected him and had confidence in him. The fact that they entrusted the care of their health to his hands was proof of this. During the famine period there always was something cooking in his section, and everyone who happened to come in received a little food. The doctor never withheld advice or aid from anyone.

We collected about 750,000 zlotys for the purchase of arms. I brought the roll of bills to Dr. Chorążycki with my own hands. But here something unexpected occurred, which almost led to the exposure of our conspiracy. Before Dr. Chorążycki could hide the money in a safe place, "The Doll" burst into the clinic. The doctor was upset because he had so much money on him, and the SS man immediately noticed his embarrassment. In order to verify his suspicions, "The Doll" searched him and, of course, found the roll of bills in the doctor's pocket. Chorążycki knew he was done for. He realized that not only did he have no chance of saving his own life, but he was liable to cause the death of many of the conspirators. This thought moved him to immediate action. With a sudden blow he knocked Kurt Franz down, pushed him across the threshold and then swallowed a vial of poison which he had with him for any eventuality. It is not known whether it was luminal or potassium cyanide. Several of us worked directly alongside the barracks of the Germans and were witness to this unusual occurrence.

"The Doll" let out a great shout. SS men came running from every corner of the camp and broke into the clinic. By that time Chorążycki was unconscious. Never had the Germans worked so hard to save the life of a prisoner. They tried to revive the doctor by pouring buckets of water into his mouth. One of the SS men bore down on his belly in order to wash out his stomach. But their efforts were in vain. Dr. Chorążycki did not return to life. The Germans went wild with rage. They thought that the doctor had collected the money in order to escape from the camp. They feared that he had had accomplices and they wanted to torture him in order to extort from him the means by which he had obtained so much money and the identity of his accomplices. Finally a roll call was held, and as we all watched, they resumed their efforts to revive him. The executioners' efforts bore no fruit. They then laid the body on a bench and gave it 50 lashes. We looked on, with grief choking our throats, but there was a feeling of victory in our hearts.

The camp authorities suspected that the money had been supplied by the *Goldjuden*,[2] and therefore put them through a thorough search. But the Jews were careful and did not let themselves get caught in the trap. Nothing was found on them. All that time I feared for my life, for it was I who had gotten the money from the *Goldjuden*. Many of the prisoners knew that I had given [Chorążycki] the money and also from where I had obtained it, but our solidarity stood the test and no one betrayed me. This was a considerable achievement, for at the time there had been an upsurge of informing. We knew who was collaborating with our oppressors, but we didn't know all of their accomplices. One of the official informers was a Warsaw butcher whom we called Chaskel. He was a young man, not yet 30 years old. His assignment was to stand outside camp headquarters and carry out petty errands. The Germans called him "Hermann." This man would transmit announcements, bring in the prisoners who were required to report, and hand over documents; he simply served as a messenger boy. And wherever he appeared he aroused alarm. At the sight of him, conversations were broken off and the prisoners withdrew into themselves, giving him an artificial smile. Everyone secretly kept track of where, and to whom, he was going. Anyone who had gained Chaskel's favor was suspect in our eyes, even if we were sometimes unable to accuse him of any offense. This particular informer specialized in ferreting out prisoners who were engaged in speculation or food smuggling.

At regular intervals Chaskel would burst into the barrack and, humming the Jewish hit song "Sorele, Sorele" between his teeth, would turn to various prisoners, asking them for vodka, oranges and other foods. The one of whom the demand was made was then caught between the devil and the deep blue sea, for whatever the prisoner replied, he stood a good chance of being harmed by Chaskel, this monster in human form. If the prisoner offered to accede to Chaskel's request, he would be charged with possessing stolen goods. If he refused, he would be punished for unwillingness to accommodate Chaskel. Chaskel and a fellow named Blau had set up a partnership and were aided in their evil business by a gang of assistants to whom all feelings of comradeship were alien.

The tragic death of Dr. Chorążycki had not put an end to our desire to destroy Treblinka. Our spirits were not broken, but henceforth we worked with redoubled caution. We continued to gather for meetings, at which we talked about the plans, worked out the details of the conspiracy, evaluated our strength and foresaw the difficulties, researched the activities of the various units, decided who was fit to bear arms, who could be useful and where, and who would be unhesitatingly ready to join the revolt. But we were very careful of Chaskel and his friends, and we concealed our activities with the slyness of foxes. In the *Tarnungskommando* [camouflage detail], in which I worked, there were 12 who knew about the plan to destroy the camp; among these were Klein, Klin,[3] [Gustav] Boraks, Brojer, Klajnman, Kohn and others. . . . Twelve men from the *Baukommando* [construction detail], several of the potato-peelers, two drivers, four locksmiths and several of the *Hofjuden* also took part in the conspiracy.

The transports were now arriving very infrequently, and the work at the camp grew less. On more than one occasion we found ourselves with nothing to do. We were ordered to level a plot of ground where there had been hundreds of ditches, which had never given anyone concern before. We dug the tightly-packed soil, moved it from place to place and gradually evened out the folds of earth. Everyone in the conspiracy tried to get hold of some gold or silver to use after they would be free, to pay for clothing, forged documents, and shelter from the gendarmes who would be searching for them.

During this final period we had been receiving better and more filling food rations. We got the impression that the Germans wanted to annihilate us all and were trying by their behavior to lull us into complacency. We were therefore particularly careful; our preparedness increased and with it our desire for freedom. Now we would go to work outside the camp only on rare occasions, and when we finally did go out to work in the woods, we tried desperately to hold in our nervousness and our agitation lest we would try to overpower our guards, kill the Ukrainians and SS men who escorted us, and flee to the partisans. But whenever we did resolve upon some mad scheme, some unforeseen obstacle was bound to come up, until we began to have doubts whether our operation would really succeed. And since our comradeship with our fellow inmates had become firmer in the course of time, we worried about the reprisals which the SS men might perpetrate against those who would remain in the camp. There was no doubt in our minds that the Germans would murder them in cold blood.

* * *

The conspiracy cells finally worked out the plan down to its smallest details. Every conspirator knew exactly what his assigned task would be, what place he had to attack, on whom he could rely for help, whom he should help and what weapons would be available to him. The date for the destruction of the camp had been set several times, only to be postponed for a few days and canceled at the last minute. This aroused great resentment in us. It was hard to restrain us. As we chopped down the bushes around the fence we felt ready for any mad act, and as we worked we would position ourselves in such a fashion that each guard would be surrounded by several prisoners armed with axes. Our foreman, Kleinbaum, tried to hold us back and cool our zeal. The earnest looks he gave us struck the weapons from our hands; his arguments convinced us. For the idea of our revolt was to liberate all the prisoners, not just the workers at the Treblinka camp proper but also those employed in the Death Camp. We were forbidden entry there, and only rarely did we set foot in the *Totenlager*. Although the two portions of the camp constituted one integral unit, their workers constituted separate *Kommandos*. In our section life lasted a little longer, while the hell in the *Totenlager* was of relatively short duration. Very rarely was one of the workers from the *Totenlager* put to work with us. One such exception in the final period of the camp's existence was a carpenter named [Jankiel] Wiernik. This man would be brought under guard each day to our section of the camp. He would do certain work there and would be taken back to his camp in the evening. We were unable to draw him into the conspiracy because we were forbidden any contact with him. But Wiernik was saved nevertheless, since at the time of the revolt he happened to be in our part of the camp.

Our confidence in ultimate success grew from day to day. We would pat each other's shoulders and encourage each other with the words: "All right then! We shall see!"

* * *

207

And then came the unforgettable day; August 2, 1943. We arose from our bunks, excited and tense. Thousands of thoughts raced about in our brains which burned with the fever of anticipation. None of us reflected on the fact that he was eating his last breakfast, that he was reporting to the roll call square for his last roll call, that he was going out for the last time to do a day's work. Quiet reigned all around us, the everyday, regular and tedious routine. In the watchtowers, the sentries whom we knew stood at their posts and stared with indifferent eyes at the doings of the prisoners below. On the grounds the SS men strolled around as they had the day before, and the day before that, the week, and the month before. There was nothing to indicate any change. Routine dominated the surroundings and misled our enemies. Our hearts were overflowing with hatred and with the desire for revenge. With great difficulty we managed to put on a vague smile whenever we encountered one of our executioners. The smoke billowed forth as usual from the chimneys, the din of conversation was no different than at any other time. But the blows of axes on the stumps of trees, our shouts, every sound held a sort of shocking announcement, and it was strange that the all-knowing Germans did not notice a thing, that they did not sense what was about to happen in another brief moment.

For the few weeks that had gone before, relative calm had prevailed in the camp. The executioners had left us alone. No one had been shot. But we feared that very silence, that absence of cruelty, that rest taken by the Angel of Death.

The time of the revolt had been set for the afternoon. The signal agreed upon was a rifle shot. We were divided into groups, each of which was assigned a specific task. Some had instructions to kill the sentries in the watchtowers, others to storm the barracks with hand grenades, and still others to fall upon the SS men who walked about in the camp. We had not forgotten a single detail or person. We had planned to cut the telephone lines, to set afire the gasoline dump and other inflammable materials, to loot the arsenal. . . .

Until noon we worked as usual in the camp area. No mishaps occurred, no one committed any offenses or fell into the hands of the murderers. And then the conversations, the confessions, the whispers died down. And the sun blazed all the more fiercely.

It began shortly after three o'clock in the afternoon. Two prisoners, young boys who performed courier duties for the Germans, were given the key to the arsenal, which was held by the conspirators. They immediately took several buckets, and a stretcher which had been used for hauling garbage and rags, and slipped into the arsenal unnoticed. It was an ideal hour for this operation. The guards and SS men were tired from the heat of the day and paid no attention to what was going on around them. The boys were allowed to walk around near the Germans' barracks, for their duties required this. The entrance to the arsenal was not guarded, for several reasons. First of all, it was well-sealed by iron doors and a barred window which faced the rear of the building. Secondly, there were construction workers busy alongside the arsenal putting up a water-boiler. Thirdly, the guards in the watchtowers were supposed to keep an eye only on what was going on in the area, not on what was happening inside the buildings.

The boys locked themselves in the arsenal and began to pass out rifles, ammunition and hand grenades through the bars of the window to the construction workers, who were in on the conspiracy. Afterwards, they slipped outside, walked around the building and carried the arms to the center of the camp on the stretcher, which was covered with rags. The grenades were taken in buckets covered with rags. Everything was placed beneath piles of potatoes, which served as the location at which the weapons were distributed. Slowly the rifles and bullets were removed. Everyone who knew how to use a hand grenade received grenades. We also had several revolvers. Additional weapons were supplied us by the storekeeper, a young, very ugly man from Warsaw whom we nicknamed "The Ape." It was he who that morning had distributed to the conspirators a larger number of axes and wire-cutters than usual and several pairs of pliers. Many of us had hammers, knives, clubs, gasoline cans. . . .

But meanwhile, something happened on the grounds which had a telling effect upon the success of our carefully detailed plan. Each of us had prepared a little silver and gold before escaping. Actually, "little" was a relative concept, for there was a lot of gold in the camp, so much so that two "mere" canteenfuls were considered a trifle.

It was close to four o'clock when one of the prisoners crossed the camp in a run and dropped a gold twenty-dollar coin on the way. Unfortunately for him this was noticed by Chaskel, who stopped the man and turned him over to "Kiewe." The investigation did not last long. "Kiewe" simply dragged the captured man off to the *lazaret* and, as usual in such cases, shot him.

This was the shot we had heard, and which we had taken for the prearranged signal to start the revolt.

That moment is well preserved in my memory. I remember the picture of the camp in all its details: there was much movement all around. I was at work chopping trees with my comrades. The heat was extraordinary. We worked clad only in shirts or half-naked. The SS man [Franz] Suchomel passed by on his bicycle and gaily shouted something to the prisoners who were busy working. Weary guards had dozed off in the watchtowers. Near the gate to the vegetable garden, which was our handiwork, one of the SS men was strolling around. When I heard the shot I started to make a run for the barracks and take my jacket, in which I had hidden the gold intended for my escape, but at that moment a shout of "Hurrah!" rang out, which turned my feet in an entirely different direction.

The assault had begun.

Shots rained down on the guards in their watchtowers. The roar of an explosion shook the air. One, a second, a third. . . . Our comrades lobbed hand grenades into the barracks and buildings of the camp. Prisoners came running from everywhere, formed into groups which kept growing larger, and with a shout fell upon the sentries, the Ukrainians, the SS men. We heard a loud and long shout, which grew stronger by the moment and faded out into a distant echo in the woods. Somewhere hand grenades cut the telephone lines and the barbed wire fences. A commotion was created which cannot be described in words. One of the wooden barracks, dried out by the sun and the heat, caught fire. Among the dense crowd of people I noticed several Germans running panic-stricken in the grounds, taking cover behind trees and forming into a group at the other end of the camp.

Two Jewish drivers, one a Pole and the other a Czech, set the gasoline and oil pools afire. The flames flared up; clouds of black smoke covered the sky. Rifle and machine gun fire burst from the six watchtowers. . . . They were answered by single shots from our side. The Ukrainian who stood at the entrance to the vegetable garden turned at the sound of the shots and the shouts, made a movement as if he was about to run for his life, but he was mowed down by a bullet. The Ukrainian arched backward and collapsed on the ground. His face had contorted with the fear which precedes death; it was a sort of mad, satanic grin. As he lay there on the ground, he still twitched as if he was having a bothersome coughing fit. One prisoner ran by him, then a second, and a third.

A whole group followed in their wake. And suddenly the group was hit by machine gun fire. Many were mowed down by the bullets. The crowd retreated in panic. A cry of fear was heard, but above the sounds of fear and terror there rose a mighty shout:"Hurrah! Hurrah! ..."

Someone sets fire to the pine branches which serve as palings for the fence wires. The dried wood burns with a bright, explosive flame, spreading farther and farther. Now the barracks are on fire, the garages, the shops, the warehouses, the building that contained the gas chambers. ... The flames grow more intense everywhere, the heat strikes our faces, and prisoners come and assemble from every part of the camp.

The machine gun from the nearby watchtower spews forth burst after burst of fire. The bullets strike our men, thinning out our ranks. The situation in this sector is becoming dangerous. Nearby, one man is holding a rifle but does not fire. ... I grab his weapon, aim calmly and at length, and finally squeeze the trigger once, twice, a third time. ...The dim silhouette collapses on the railing, the machine gun falls silent. ... From here on in the way is wide open.

"Hit! Hit! Kill!" someone shouts into my ear.

"Move back! The fences have been cut! Slow! Don't push!"

The sound of Polish commands mixed with Jewish curses, someone praying in a language unknown to me, one man calling out to God in Hebrew and another in Yiddish. ... The smoke sears the eyes and fills the lungs; the bullets whistle and ring past our ears like cut strings from musical instruments ...

At the other end of the camp the Germans get organized, but their firing is still sporadic. For the time being, panic and surprise keep them from sizing up the situation and making an efficient response. They hide like rats in the corners of burning buildings and advance with caution. The arms and ammunition we have are not enough. That cursed Chaskel! Had we been able to complete our preparations, our situation would be entirely different now.

And again the rat-tat-tat of a machine gun. It forces us to make a slow retreat. We jump from tree to tree in the direction of the fence. The cut wires dangle loosely.

Now we must run across the 50 meters of open space to the barbed wire entanglements and anti-tank barriers. The machine gun steps up its fire. Behind my back tragedies are taking place. The brave climb the steel-and-wire entanglements, and there the bullets catch up with them. They collapse with cries of despair. Their bodies hang on the wires, spilling streams of blood onto the ground. No one pays any attention to them. Other prisoners who have just arrived leap over the quivering bodies. And they, too, are mowed down and collapse, their madness-stricken eyes looking at the camp, which now looks like one gigantic torch.

"Onward! Onward! Onward!" a voice booms out nearby.

"The inferno is behind us!" I shout like a madman. "The inferno is behind us!" These words infuse me with strength, bring me back to my senses, force me to behave with caution.

And now I crawl along in the exposed area and reach the barriers. I look around. Behind me the dead have created a sort of bridge over which another fleeing prisoner passes every moment. Behind the barriers are the redeeming woods—freedom.

And again the thought troubles me: if we had been able to complete our preparations, we would have been able to get weapons to every part of the camp. At the prearranged signal, our gunfire would have hit all the SS men and sentries. We would have neutralized all the watchtower guards simultaneously and wiped out all the nests of German resistance. When "Kiewe's" shot rang out [which we had taken for our own signal] there still were lots of weapons hidden beneath the piles of potatoes; many of the hand grenades had not yet reached the hands of the conspirators. Now many prisoners were forced to run from the fences to the center of the camp in order to pull out the rifles, and afterwards they had to retreat under withering gunfire. Under the circumstances, it is no surprise that so many of our men were killed. If the plans had succeeded in full, we would have been in possession of two armored cars and we would have been able to cross the Bug River in close ranks to join the partisans.

Again I lift my head cautiously and inspect the goings-on around me. The machine gun is still firing away, but we can no longer remain here. With one leap I ascend the bridge of corpses. I hear a shot, feel a blow, but one more jump and I am at the edge of the woods. In front of me, beside me and behind me, men are running. It is difficult today to figure out how many were saved. I presume that about 200 men broke out by the route along which I escaped. On another side, about 150 escaped.

Now I am running with all my might among the trees. I feel a pain in my leg. I am wearing boots, and I feel blood filling up my

212

right boot. The woods come to an end. I cross a highway and am once again swallowed up in a thick and damp forest.

Warmth and pleasant odors are all around me. Night falls.

Translated from the Polish original

1. Lit. "Court Jews," Jewish inmates employed to perform personal services for the SS men and Ukrainian guards.

2. Lit. "Gold Jews." Jewelers put to work at sorting and evaluating the valuables of the deportees.

3. Klin survived Treblinka and finally succeeded in making his way to freedom. Afterward he hid in a bunker near Wengrów and apparently died of starvation and exhaustion, because he was afraid to emerge from hiding. Others of the 12 were saved.

THE REVOLT IN TREBLINKA

TANHUM GRINBERG

TANHUM (TADEUSZ) GRINBERG was born in Błonie, Poland, in 1913. In 1941, he was "relocated" to the Warsaw ghetto with his mother, three younger brothers and a sister. A shoemaker by trade, he was put to work at Schultz's shop.

One day, when he came home from work, he found his apartment empty. His mother, brothers and sister had all been taken away. Soon thereafter, Grinberg himself was deported.

In Treblinka he was active in the underground and took part in the uprising. After his escape, he hid out in the little town of Sterdyń, and later joined a partisan unit.

After the war he settled in Israel. He was killed in an automobile accident in 1976.

He was a witness at the trial of Kurt Franz, "The Doll." When asked on the witness stand, "Do you recognize Kurt Franz?" he replied, "I would shudder even on my deathbed if anyone were to mention the name of Kurt Franz."

The following are selected passages from the comprehensive testimony which Grinberg gave in Warsaw in December, 1945 and which has been preserved in the Yad Vashem Archives in Jerusalem. These passages describe the preparations made for the Treblinka revolt, and then the revolt itself. They supplement the information given in Willenberg's testimony.

IT WAS THE DAY BEFORE Yom Kippur [1942].[1] A general roll call was ordered at sunset. We all stood in rows and the Germans selected 220 of us, including myself. We were chased to the platform where we stood and waited. A Ukrainian stood guard over us. The rest—540 men—were ordered to undress for death. Suddenly, a terrifying scream was heard from there like the bellow of an ox when the butcher's knife is raised to its throat, and rifle shots split the air. What had happened? When the Jews had been ordered to undress, a 40-year-old Jew from Warsaw[2] had taken a kitchen knife and stabbed a German, [Max] Bielas, in the side. Thereupon, pandemonium broke out. The Germans started to run for their lives and the Ukrainians opened fire. In the general confusion, "The Doll" [Kurt Franz] took the wounded man and brought him to the commander's barrack. As "The Doll" passed the platform carrying Bielas, we heard Bielas' last words: "We must shoot and kill the Jews, all of them!"

And indeed, just an hour later, the machine guns were brought in and the Ukrainians started shooting at once.

. . . We wanted to organize, but how could we be able to do this under the conditions at Treblinka, with no weapons on hand except for knives and small hammers? But then we learned that the *Tarnungskommando* [camouflage detail], which would go out of the camp to bring in rocks and bricks, had been able to accomplish something. They met with local peasants and they had collected a total of 100 "hard ones" [gold dollar coins] and 200 "soft ones" [dollar bills], and obtained one or two pistols. The peasants would bring packages, set them down some distance away and hold two fingers up to their eyes. That meant that they wanted 20 dollars. In this manner, a few pistols were brought into the camp. The pistols were kept in the workshop during the day, hidden among the hides; at night we hid them under the floor of our barrack. Our first organizer was Dr. Chorążycki of Warsaw. It was he, too, who set up the committee, but we didn't know who its members were. We only knew the name of the doctor.

Actually, the *Lagerälteste*, the engineer Galewski, was also on the committee. When he became ill, Rakowski was appointed [*Lagerälteste*] in his place, at the same time remaining in his post of kapo. The latter two and Dr. Chorążycki set up the organizing cadre.

The doctor was able to bring the group of *Goldjuden* [who handled the valuables of the deportees] under his command and even to get needed funds from them. But while the doctor was in his room, transferring some money from one pocket to another, the door opened and "The Doll" materialized on the threshold with his dog. "The Doll" immediately saw something stick out from the pocket of the doctor's lab apron. He went over to the wall where the garment was hanging and reached into it and, to his own amazement, found a large amount of money there. When the doctor saw

215

what "The Doll" had done, he grabbed a lancet off the table and tried to plunge it into "The Doll's" chest. There was a struggle, but the German, who was a good fighter, threw the doctor off. He attacked again, and they both fell down and struggled on the ground. When the doctor realized that "The Doll" was stronger than he, and that he was sure to overpower him and then interrogate him and force him to tell all that he knew, he leaped to his feet, opened the window and ran outside. "The Doll" started to shoot after him. As he ran, the doctor took a vial from his pocket and swallowed its contents. Just at the moment he was surrounded, he fell to the ground, unconscious.

This happened on the square where the roll calls were held. We were immediately ordered to gather in this open place and were forced to watch how cruel [the Germans] were to our doctor. The Germans tried to revive him at all costs. They wanted to know where he had obtained so much money, and for what purpose. It was easy to deduce that the money came from the gold detail, but its purpose interested them even more. The Ukrainians opened the doctor's mouth, and, while one of them stepped on his forehead, another stood on his jaw and they tried to force two bucketfuls of water down his throat. The man was tortured for two hours but he did not wake up. Finally, "The Doll" came over, kicked him a few times and shouted, "Such an old dog!" He then ordered his body to be thrown into the fire ditch, since the doctor was obviously dead.

From that time on, we intensified our preparations for revolt; this became our overriding concern. At the same time, however, "The Doll" was still trying to find out the source from where the doctor had obtained his money. The men of the gold detail had not been present at the time the money had been discovered; they were now gathered and received a full measure of beatings, but they denied that they had ever had any contact with the doctor. The Germans took the eight most likely suspects, one of whom had indeed been involved in the affair. They were ordered to undress, were beaten savagely, and then were forced, one by one, to do 400 meters of frog-leaps. "The Doll" accompanied the first one, then led him to the fire ditch and fired a shot in the air; he threatened to shoot him if he would not tell all he knew. Then he left him there. After he had gotten through with the first one, "The Doll" went back to the seven others and ordered a second man to do frog-leaps. After they had gone a certain distance, he told him that the first man had been killed, after confessing that not he, but the second, had turned over the money [to the doctor]. The Jew replied that he was innocent of any crime and if he were killed, he, too, would be killed for no cause. All eight of them were tortured in this way and they finally met at the incinerator. They were all subjected to additional tortures in a similar manner, but not one of them gave away the secret, and the men were finally released.

The new *Lagerälteste*, Rakowski, who has already been mentioned before, was a six-foot-six giant. He was a great gourmand and never sat down to a meal without a bottle of champagne. He had arranged for the Ukrainians to provide him with all the food he wanted. His wife and child had perished, and he now had a mistress who lived with him. Rakowski decided to escape from the camp without waiting for the general uprising. The kapo Moniek kept a close eye on him. "Either we all escape," he said "or we all will stay here." Rakowski had bribed a Ukrainian to assist him in his separate escape, who then revealed this to the *Zugwachmann* (train guard) Streibel, and they both proceeded to extort a great deal of money from Rakowski. The actual escape was postponed from one day to the next. Streibel, for his part, revealed Rakowski's plot to "The Doll." With "The Doll's" complicity, the escape date was finally set. One night, at midnight, Rakowski gave Streibel a 50-dollar bill, and he took it straight to "The Doll" and [August] Miete,[3] who were lying in ambush. They appeared immediately and carried out a search in Rakowski's room, and found a sack full of gold and gems next to his bed. "The Doll" unceremoniously conducted Rakowski to the cremation ditch. Rakowski, who had always been so arrogant, was now bowed and broken. After a little while, he was shot and killed. The next morning, "The Doll" gave us an eloquent speech, informing us that Rakowski had been executed for extortion, speculation, and for defrauding Greater Germany. From now on, he informed us, the engineer Galewski would be *Lagerältester* again.

The Germans had a large arsenal inside the camp. We ceaselessly racked our brains to figure out a way of getting to it, but we did not get the slightest opportunity to do so. The arsenal was well guarded. Ukrainian guards surrounded it on all sides. But one day its lock got jammed. Our locksmith, a man whose wife and two daughters had perished in Treblinka, was ordered to repair the damaged lock. The door was taken down and brought to the workshop, and a special German guard was assigned to watch the locksmith while he did the job. Nevertheless, the locksmith was able to make a wax impression of the key. We were thus able to obtain our own key to the arsenal. A few days passed before we were able to make use of it, take out 80 hand grenades and hide them in the cobbler's workshop. Once this had been accomplished we were able at last to set a date for the uprising. Everything was properly prepared. We were organized in groups of ten, each with its own commander. Our plan of action was also prepared well in advance. We were ready to attack the Ukrainian barracks and the German command post. Other groups were supposed to pour gasoline on the barracks before the moment of attack and then to set fire to them. The signal for the uprising was supposed to be a pistol shot. Even the camouflage detail had one pistol. We knew that they were supposed to be outside the camp when the rebellion broke out. One of them was supposed to shoot the German guard while the others surrounded the two Ukrainians who had escorted them, take away their rifles and kill them.

The signal was to be given at 4:45 p.m. We were not able to wait for the end of the working day, which came at 6 o'clock, because it would have been too dark by then. A few minutes before 4 o'clock, Rakowski called me over (this was before his own unsuccessful attempt to escape), showed me a hand grenade and asked me whether it would work. I was familiar with these grenades from my [Polish] army service, and I saw at first glance that its detonator was missing. Rakowski repeated his question: "Will it work?" "Yes," I answered, "it will work, but not without its detonator." Rakowski put the hand grenade back in its hiding place. I let our comrades know right away about the new adverse turn of events, but what could we do? Should we begin our operation at a time when we were completely unprepared? The worst thing was that we couldn't make contact with the camouflage detail, who were supposed to kill their officer and the Ukrainians. If something went wrong, our whole plan would come to naught.

Moniek the kapo was able to leave the camp, accompanied by a Ukrainian. He got to the group and said, "No! We'll have to go ahead with it!" And indeed, the uprising didn't take place then. We were confused and excited all day long. To our great shame, we were forced to go back the next day, sneak into the arsenal and return the hand grenades to their storage place before the Germans could notice their absence . . .

. . . Things went badly. Detonators had not yet been found for the hand grenades. Finally, we figured that it would be better to prepare a revolt based on cold steel alone rather than to die in vain. We began to sharpen our knives. The work was done in the cobbler's shop. Shoemaker's knives are round and blunt on one side. We sharpened them on both sides, until they looked like real daggers. We took apart scissors and turned them into knives, for which we also made wooden sheaths. This equipment was prepared for the designated day.

But there were differences of opinion. Some felt that if this was all the weapons we would have, we would lose the battle and not one of us would survive. We were thus prevented from beginning our revolt, but meetings and deliberations multiplied. However, the impetus to action came from an unexpected source. They began to bring large hewn rocks to Treblinka—literally monument stones. We figured that these were intended as pillars for a large crematorium. Rumors spread in the camp that the oven was intended for Poles, because their time had now come. Very few Jews had remained alive. For some time they had been bringing people's bodies here and burning them on pyres, under the open sky. The Germans had assured us that there was still much work for us to do and that we would remain alive. The shoemakers unloaded the stones, because "Kiewe" had said that we were talking all day long instead of working. We all agreed on one thing—on no account would we permit the furnace to be constructed. With this in mind, the date of the uprising was finally set, for August 2 at 4:30 p.m. This date, a Monday, was decided on a Friday, four [sic] days in advance. Saturday went by amidst great tension. We were all afraid of how the affair would turn out and wondered who among us would remain alive.

We usually completed our work on Sundays by 12 noon. This time, we used our one-hour break for a final assignment of duties in the uprising. We were all organized in groups of ten, each with its own commander. First, we would surround the barracks and cut the telephone wires. At the same time, we were to get the Ukrainian guards to leave their posts in the six watchtowers overlooking the camp. This had to be accomplished by some sort of ruse. We knew that all you had to do was to call out to a Ukrainian and point your finger at your eye, signifying that you had a 20-dollar gold coin to give away. This would be enough to make the Ukrainian run over as fast as his legs could carry him. Then you had to grab his rifle from his hands and kill him. Other men were supposed to surround the Ukrainian barracks, throw grenades into the German command post and kill all the officers and SS men. We were ready to carry out every command. We were similarly agreed that if the conspirators succeeded in seizing control of the camp, we would put on the Ukrainians' uniforms, escape to the Bialowieza woods, and join the partisan units there. Others, at the same time, would be charged with seizing the camp trucks, loading them with food and weapons, and driving them to the partisans in the woods. There was even an armored car in the camp, which was used for taking shipments of plundered gold to Germany.

Monday morning brought us great anxiety and agonizing suspense. We worked like the devil, not talking to each other and silently gathering in groups. The word got around that we had finally found detonators for the hand grenades. There were Jews in the camp who worked at hauling bricks and mortar. Each of them had a horse and a little wagon and they were free to come and go inside the camp. One boy from Czenstochowa, about 11 years old, would ride on his little wagon, gather up ashes in the camp, and carry them to the big ash heap. These Jews were members of our group. At 2 p.m., one of us whom the Germans trusted went into the arsenal, took out two boxes of hand grenades and loaded them onto this boy's little wagon. The boxes were brought to the workshop. Thirty-seven rifles were similarly removed but, because they were long, they were covered up in the wagon of the mortar carrier and taken to the garage. Then, a young man, also from Czenstochowa, cleaned them thoroughly and loaded each one of them with five bullets. Now we opened up the hiding place on the workshop floor and took out the pistols. Of course, very few of us were lucky enough to get firearms. Each group commander, as well as each of the kapos, had a pistol.

The Jews in the death camp also knew what was about to happen and when the uprising would break out. But they had no weapons at all. Their job was to take away the weapons of the Ukrainians and our people were to reach them as soon as they got through with their jobs in our camp. Between our camp and the death camp there was a garbage dump where a fire was burning continually. Since we were some distance away from the fire, we had our own ashpit, where they also would burn wood for coals which were used in the tailors' irons. The ashes from the death camp were also brought here. But when people from the death camp approached, the Germans chased us away because the place could be used for meetings and communication between the two camps. This time, too, the Germans chased us away but when we got to the place where the ash-carriers came from the death camp, we were able to call out to them from afar: "Today is the Day of Judgment!" In this way, we let them know what was about to happen.

We were 1,200 rebels in all and now we had to cope with a situation we had not anticipated. All the Jews had started to prepare gold and silver for themselves. All the valuables which had been buried in the ground were now dug up. Of course they weren't supposed to be doing this now, but rather to come back afterwards and empty out the hiding-places. But the power of money was great, and everybody kept thinking about his own future. These considerations had a powerful impact on the inmates and also interfered with their plans.

At a little before 4 p.m., "Kiewe" came across a boy whose pockets were bulging. He grabbed him and took the money out of his pocket. A hail of blows immediately descended on the youth. While this was going on, another Jew happened along. *"Komm, komm!* [Come over here!]" the German called to the man, and when the German found that this Jew also had money on his person, he led both [the man and the boy] behind our barrack and started beating them alternately. The designated hour had not yet arrived, but we were afraid that the two would break down, confess and then we would all be locked up. So there was no alternative but to jump the gun and go into action immediately. One of us went over to the window and fired his pistol at "Kiewe." "Kiewe" died on the spot.[4] But just at that moment, [Franz] Suchomel came up on his bicycle. They shot at him, too, but they missed him and he returned their fire. We rushed outside, cut the telephone wires, and set fire to one storehouse and barrack, which we had doused with gasoline an hour earlier. The guards were cleared out from inside the watchtowers. At first, the Ukrainians didn't grasp what was going on; and some of them ran away and hid. But others opened fire. We turned to them and called out *"Nye strelat', Prishol konyetz voyny!* [Don't shoot, the war is over!]" But the barracks were already going up in smoke.

The Germans in the penal labor camp, which was about two kilometers from ours, saw the fire and started to send over support units. Their telephones were operating normally and they called Malkinia, Wengrow, Sokolow, and even Siedlce, which was far away, to send help. In the surrounding area there were many of our people who had not been able to carry out their assignments, and they started to run for their lives, under fire as they fled. In the death camp the sound of gunfire raised the inmates spirits. A Czech Jew named Zelo [Bloch], a former officer in the Czech army, grabbed a rifle from a Ukrainian, lay down on the ground, and started to shoot. Meanwhile, the wires of the barbed wire fences were cut and we were given the signal to run away. At the last moment, I grabbed a coat and, wearing my shoemaker's apron and holding a knife in hand, I ran out of the camp.

Beyond the cut electric and telephone wires there was another barrier—an anti-tank barrier. These wires were hard to cut and so we were forced to cross them the best way we could, every man for himself. Many left one of their boots on the wires and ran away with one foot bare. The bullets were ringing both in front and in back of me. Many men fell as they ran. My group was small, but it, too, shrank as we were running. When we finally reached the woods, we reckoned that only four men from our group had gone the distance of 15 kilometers. When we arrived in the woods, I told my comrades that we ought to find a big thicket and hide out in it, since we could hear gunfire in every direction and a posse had probably been organized to sweep the area.

Night fell and we could not get our fill of the intoxicating joy of freedom. All the time we had dreamed about the moment we would find it, the first meter of ground outside the damned camp, and now we were 15 kilometers away. We could still see the flames from the woods. The distant skies were red and the echoes of gunfire and explosions reached our ears. We were happy that, thanks to our iron willpower, we had succeeded in overcoming even the Germans, despite the stringent security. Only now did we realize that if we really would be saved, we would be able to tell the whole world how the Germans had made us suffer. But for the moment we were still in danger.

The search went on for a long time. The peasants helped the Germans in their own way. Even as we fled, we could see the corpses of slain Jews, with the boots removed from their legs. The peasants knew that the Jews had money, and that was reason enough for them to set ambushes and murder Jews.

We lay low in that place for two whole days, without any food or water. We ate only wild berries from the plants growing above us, and they made us sick. The Germans and the navy blue police[5] roamed all around us. They surrounded the escapees with a ring that got tighter and tighter. Once, they literally passed right by us but they didn't notice us. Only about two kilometers away, we heard sudden gunfire and we realized that they had found some of the escapees and finished them off. Our strength was ebbing away . . .

We decided to go out at night and blaze a trail to the virgin forests.

. . . We reached a stream which divided the woods to two parts. We flung ourselves to the ground, drank our fill of the icy water and ate some bread. Then we crossed the stream silently and entered the virgin forests. A torrential rain was pouring down. We quickly broke off some branches and built ourselves a little hut. From that moment on, we saw ourselves as free men, denizens of the wild Sterdyń woods.

. . . Of the four of us, I alone remained alive.

Translated from the Hebrew

1. Krzepicki gave the date as the day before Rosh Hashanah (i.e., ten days earlier). He was correct.

2. The man's name was Meyer Berliner.

3. August Miete, who was killing prisoners at the *lazaret*. See chapter "Dramatis Personae," p. 271 ff.

4. "Kiewe" was only wounded. He died after the war.

5. Polish police units who wore navy blue uniforms.

THE TREBLINKA REVOLT

SHALOM KOHN
(Stanisław Kon)

SHALOM KOHN (STANISŁAW KON) was born in 1910 in the little town of Praczka, Poland. He settled in Lodz, where he worked as a building contractor. He served in the Polish army for 18 months. After his discharge in 1933, he regularly participated in military exercises until the outbreak of World War II, when he was called to active duty. His outfit held out for 20 days before being overrun by German tank troops. After Poland's surrender, he made his way home. On October 1, 1942, Kohn, his young wife and her mother were deported to Treblinka. The boxcar in which they traveled held about 100 passengers. Kohn's wife and mother-in-law went to the gas chambers, but since Kohn himself was young and strong, the Germans put him to work as a slave laborer, carrying corpses and sorting the clothes of new arrivals. He frequently received beatings from the SS men and the Ukrainian guards. He actively participated in the Treblinka uprising, during which he was able to escape from the camp. He is now living in Israel.

"The Holocaust will follow me to my grave," he said on the witness stand at the Fort Lauderdale trial. "Every year, on August 2, the anniversary of the Treblinka uprising, we meet in Tel Aviv to pray together. . . . The memory is with me all the time."

Even before I arrived at Treblinka, i.e., before October 1, 1942, cases of individual revenge on the part of Jews had been reported. Thus, for example, a Jewish man from Warsaw who worked in one of the death details and had seen his wife and child taken away to the gas chambers, attacked the SS man Max Biel[as] with a knife and killed him on the spot. From that day on, the SS barracks bore the name of this Hitlerite "martyr." But neither the plaque on the wall of the barracks nor the massacre of Jews that followed this attack deterred us. On the contrary: this episode en-

224

couraged us to fight and take our revenge. The young man from Warsaw became our ideal.

As we witnessed Hitler's horrible methods of extermination, a desire for revenge burned within us and grew each day, starting to concretize into something precise, particularly from the moment when the 50-year-old doctor, Chorążycki of Warsaw, began to be active. This doctor worked in the camp as a "medical counselor," a position invented by the Germans to mock the hapless victims even more cruelly before dispatching them to the gas chamber. He was a calm, prudent man who on the surface, appeared rather cold. He went around in his white apron with the Red Cross emblem on his arm as he had in the old days at his Warsaw office, and he seemed completely detached from what was going on around him. But beneath his apron beat a warm Jewish heart, aflame with a desire for revenge.

After the gruesome experiences of the day, the four plotters of the revolt met by night around his plank bed and discussed the plans. Their first problem was how to get hold of the weapons and explosives which were needed. These four men were the above-mentioned Dr. Chorążycki, the Czech army officer Zelo [Bloch]—a Jew, of course—[Zev] Kurland from Warsaw and Lubling from Silesia. After a short time, when it was considered necessary to enlarge the organization committee, we were joined by Leon Haberman, an artisan from Warsaw; Salzberg, a furrier from Kielce; a 22-year-old youth from Warsaw named Marcus, and the Warsaw agronomist Sudowicz. We could procure arms either from the outside or else we could steal them from the Germans and Ukrainians inside the camp itself. We tried both ways. We began to make a study of the camp arsenal and the headquarters barrack. But they were guarded by Germans and there was no way for us to get in. At first, we thought of digging a subterranean passage, but we felt this would be difficult, because of the constant danger of discovery. Then we decided at all costs to manufacture a duplicate key to the arsenal. This could only be done, however, if one of us could somehow gain access to the iron door of the arsenal. We had no alternative but to wait for a propitious moment.

An opportunity soon presented itself. Somehow the lock of the arsenal got jammed and the Germans had to call in one of the Jewish mechanics to fix it.

The Germans were extremely cautious. They had the door taken off its hinges and taken to the workshop. However, the mechanic managed to distract the attention of the German guard for just one moment, and managed to make an impression of the key in cobbler's wax. A few days later, our group received a key to the arsenal. We guarded it like a precious relic, waiting for the proper opportunity to use it. Dr. Chorążycki himself assumed the task of acquiring weapons from outside the camp. He managed to get in touch with a Ukrainian guard who agreed, for a large sum of money, of course, to buy some light weapons for us. A few of our purchases were safely smuggled in, but then something happened which put an end to our [hope for additional] equipment and cost the life of Dr. Chorążycki. One day, while the doctor had with him a large amount of money intended for the guard, the camp's vice-commandant, SS Untersturmführer Franz, a bloody murderer notorious for his sadist methods, entered the room, accompanied by his dog, Barry. By pure chance, Franz spotted the packet of banknotes peeping out of the doctor's apron pocket.

"Give me that money!" the SS man roared. He suspected that the doctor was planning to escape from the camp. Chorążycki attacked him with a surgical lancet, stabbing him in the neck. Franz was able to jump out of the window and call for help. Well aware of the tortures which would await him, and realizing the threat to the entire conspiracy, Chorążycki swiftly swallowed a large dose of poison which the conspirators always carried on their persons. The SS men rushed up and tried to revive him in order to take their revenge, but to no avail.

In this way the initiator of the revolt died, but his death did not put an end to the matter. On the contrary, it encouraged the others to continue.

If Dr. Chorążycki was the initiator and the leader of the Treblinka revolt, then the title of chief of staff must be given to Captain Zelo. The participation of this military expert greatly facilitated the fulfillment of a mission which was both difficult and complicated. At difficult moments, when many of us fell prey to resignation and abandoned all hope of a revolt, Captain Zelo continued to encourage us to carry on. When he was transferred to another part of the camp, all the plans and decisions were submitted to him for his approval despite the danger involved in such contacts.

The engineer Galewski of Lodz was chosen to replace Dr. Chorążycki. He, too, dedicated himself to the cause with all his heart. He was a very cautious, reserved man, and this proved useful to our cause.

The date of the revolt was postponed several times for various reasons. The first date was fixed in April, 1943, while Dr. Chorążycki was still alive. And then the last transports of Jews from the Warsaw ghetto were brought to Treblinka. From them we first learned about the Warsaw ghetto revolt. The Germans treated them with particular savagery; most of the railroad cars were full of the corpses of ghetto fighters who had refused to leave the ghetto alive. Those who now arrived were no longer resigned and indifferent creatures like those who had come before them.

The leaders decided that the hour for the revolt had arrived. In the camp there were a number of so-called "Court Jews," boys who rendered personal services to the Germans, like cleaning their quarters, etc. These individuals enjoyed a certain freedom of movement within the camp. At times they even were able to get close to the arsenal. The leadership decided to entrust to these boys the task of expropriating 100 hand grenades from the arsenal on the day of the revolt.

They proved to be equal to the task. Haberman, who worked in the German laundry, the shoeblack Marcus, and Jacek, a Hungarian boy of 17, managed to get his hands on a certain number of hand grenades. Exceptionally lithe and skillful, the boy Salzberg, age 14, son of the leader we have already mentioned, took a huge pile of SS uniforms as though he were taking them to the tailor's for pressing, but in fact the pockets of these uniforms were filled with hand grenades. Unfortunately these hand grenades lacked detonators, and for this reason the revolt had to be postponed at the very last moment.

Meanwhile, we were joined by other activists. Dr. Leichert, of Wengrow, whom the Nazis had selected from a new transport to replace Dr. Chorążycki, soon became a member of the committee. We were also joined by a Czech, Rudolf Masaryk, a relative of the late President of Czechoslovakia.[1] He had refused to leave his Jewish wife and had accompanied her to Treblinka. Here, he became one of the privileged characters and was attached to a labor detail. With his own eyes he had seen his pregnant wife being taken to the gas chamber. Masaryk became one of the most active members of the committee. We must also mention Rudek, the driver-mechanic from Plotzk, who worked in the garage. His job was very important for our operation because it was there [in the garage] that we stored our weapons.

Months of waiting and tension passed in this way. Every day we

227

looked death in the face and witnessed the German atrocities. Every day hundreds of thousands of men and women, stark naked, arrived in long lines at the "Jewish State"—this was the name the Germans had cynically given to the building that housed 12 gas chambers. Untersturmführer Franz kept giving us speeches: "The gas chambers will continue to operate as long as so much as one Jew is left in the world."

The desire for revenge increased all the time. The terror-stricken eyes of the Jews who were led to their death and were thrust into the gas chambers cried out for revenge.

At last the leader, Galewski, gave the signal for the revolt. The date had been set for Monday, August 2, 1943, at 5 p.m. This was the plan of action: to lay an ambush for the chief murderers and to liquidate them; to disarm the guards; to cut the telephone wires; to burn and destroy all the extermination plants so that they would never function again; to free the Poles from the Treblinka detention camp a mile away, and, together with them, flee into the woods to organize a partisan unit.

An atmosphere of great tension lay upon the camp that Monday morning. The leaders needed all their energies to calm the people down. Finally, special inspectors came to see that the normal quota of work was carried out as usual in order not to arouse suspicion. All the details of the plan were known only to the 60 people who constituted the nucleus of the fighting organization. The activists were divided into three groups and, as soon as the signal would be given, each group was to occupy the position assigned to it.

At one o'clock in the afternoon we lined up as we had been doing every day, for the roll call, the last roll call in this camp because there was never to be another. But when Galewski, the head of a group of workers, told us that work that day would end an hour earlier than usual because Scharführer Rotner was going to Malkinia to bathe in the river Bug, he gave us a little wink as though alluding to the "bath" we had prepared for the Nazis.

At two o'clock in the afternoon the distribution of weapons began. Young Salzberg and the other looked for weapons in their masters' barracks. They managed to steal about a score of rifles and one machine gun and took them to the garage. It was very difficult to steal the hand grenades from the arsenal. That day a pile of garbage was being removed from near the arsenal. This was very convenient but it disturbed the camp administrator, SS man Miller, who had just arrived and wanted to sleep. The agronomist,

Sudowicz, who was in charge of the garden, called on him with the excuse of wanting to talk over some problem relating to the plants. At the same time Marcus and Salzberg picked up the rugs and beat them in front of the arsenal, so that the guards had to move out of the way for a while. At that moment the door of the arsenal was opened with our key and Jacek, the Hungarian boy, slipped inside, climbed onto the window sill at the end of the room, used a diamond to cut out a small square in the glass and handed the bombs and other weapons to Jacob Miller from Wlodzimierz-Wolynski, who was waiting outside and put them on his garbage cart. The arms were taken to the garage. This time the hand grenades had their detonators all right and acted as a spur to flagging spirits.

Spirits grew agitated and it seemed that no one would be able to keep the secret. The leaders therefore decided to start the revolt an hour before the time originally agreed upon.

At four o'clock sharp that afternoon, messages were sent to all the groups with orders to assemble immediately at the garage to pick up their weapons. Rudek from Plotzk was responsible for the distribution. Anyone who came to fetch weapons had to give the password "Death!" to which the proper reply was "Life!" "Death! Life! Death! Life!" Cries of enthusiasm arose as the long-awaited rifles, revolvers and hand grenades were handed out. At the same time the chief murderers of the camp were attacked. Telephone wires were cut and the watchtowers were set on fire with gasoline. Captain Zelo attacked two SS guards with an ax and joined us to take over the command.

Near the garage stood a German armored car, but Rudek swiftly put the motor out of commission. Now the car served as an ambush from which to fire at the Germans. Our gunfire felled Sturmführer Kurt Seidler and other Nazi dogs. The arsenal was taken by assault and the captured weapons handed out to the insurgents. We already had 200 armed men. The others attacked the Germans with axes and spades.

We set fire to the gas chambers, to the "bathhouse," burned the simulated railroad station with all the fake signs: "Bialystok-Wolkowysk," "Office," "Tickets," "Waiting Room," etc. The barracks which bore the name of the Nazi hangman Max Biel[as] were ablaze, too.

Captain Zelo gave commands and encouraged the men to fight. Nobody cared about his own life. A fiery spirit of revenge had taken hold of us. We had acquired more weapons; we even had a machine gun now. Rudolf Masaryk took care of it. He stationed himself on the roof of the pigeon coop and poured fire on the confused Germans. Through the exchange of fire we can hear his voice shouting, "Take that for my wife, and take that for my child who did not even have a chance to come into the world! And take that, you murderers, for the humanity which you have insulted and degraded!"

Roused to action by the flames and the firing, the Germans began to arrive from all sides. SS and police arrived from Kosów, soldiers from the nearby airfield and finally a special squad of the Warsaw SS. A full-scale battle developed. Captain Zelo was darting in and out among the flames, giving us courage and urging us to fight on. He gave orders, concise, warlike—until a Nazi bullet put an end to his life.

Night fell. The battle had already been going on for six hours. The Germans were getting reinforcements, and our ranks had become thinner. Our ammunition was running out.

We had been ordered to make for the nearby woods. Most of our fighters fell but there were many German casualties. Very few of us survived.

Translated from Dos Naye Lebn, *Warsaw,*
May 10, 1945

---

1. This is not correct. The man's name was actually Masarek, and he was half-Jewish. It was the misspelling of his name that gave rise to the legend that he was related to Masaryk. See section on "Dramatis Personae," p. 271 ff.

THE END
OF TREBLINKA

SAMUEL RAJZMAN

SAMUEL RAJZMAN was born in the little Polish town of Wengrow in 1902. Before the war he lived with his wife and young daughter in Warsaw, where he was employed in an export-import business. On September 21, 1942 he was deported to Treblinka. His wife and daughter perished; so did two brothers and one sister. Altogether, 70 members of Rajzman's family were killed in the Holocaust.

Rajzman was an active participant in the plans for the Treblinka revolt, and during the uprising he led one of the groups of fighters.

In 1944 he wrote one of the first reports about Treblinka, which was published in the Lublin literary weekly Odrodzenie. *He was the only witness to testify about Treblinka at the Nuremberg war crimes trials, where his testimony made a shattering impression. After the liberation he worked as director of personnel with the Central Committee of Liberated Jews in Germany.*

Later, he moved to Paris. In 1950 he emigrated to Canada, settling in Montreal.

He was one of the prime witnesss at the Düsseldorf trials, and witness for the prosecution at the Fort Lauderdale trial.

I WAS TAKEN TO Treblinka in 1942. I had been living in Warsaw. They took me out on Yom Kippur: in the middle of praying they took us away to Treblinka. We had a minyan[1] in the courtyard. We were reciting our prayers in the courtyard: there were no more synagogues open by that time. We were working in Toebbens' shop, a factory that produced buttons for the Germans. Toebbens had 30 or 40 enterprises working for him in occupied Warsaw. In the shop where I worked there were 125 to 130 people. They took everybody away. A couple of us they killed right on the spot; the rest were taken to Treblinka.

At the *Umschlagplatz*, we were pushed into boxcars, 70 to 80

231

people to a car. It was summer then; by the time the train arrived in Treblinka, many cars had only half their passengers still alive. In the morning, when I arrived in Treblinka (we had traveled all night), there were about 20 dead bodies in my boxcar. There just wasn't any room to stand. There was no air, and the windows were covered with wire grates and boards. My cousin had come to Treblinka with me. She couldn't get out of the boxcar; they had to carry her off and take her to the *lazaret* (the word means "field hospital" but in reality it was a place where people were shot immediately by Scharführer [Willy] Mentz and the Ukrainian guard) and there they shot her. She had no longer been able to walk. Many of the dead in the boxcars were small children who had suffocated.

Upon our arrival, we all had to hand in our valuables and get undressed. Everybody was told to tie up his clothes in such a way that he would be able to recognize his package. That was how the Germans fooled us into thinking that we would get our clothes back. The women had to line up, and all their hair was clipped off. It was destined for use in German mattresses. Naked, they went the road of no return, into the gas chamber. While they undressed and walked to the gas chambers, the Germans hit them very hard; many people died from the beatings alone. Everybody was pushing to get to the gas chamber fast, because the Ukrainians and the Germans were beating them so hard. Everybody was stampeding forward. The whole place was covered with blood. People didn't know that it would be the end there; the idea was simply to get out of the place where they were beating you. And in doing that, they went straight into the gas chambers.

As soon as we came to Treblinka, we could smell the stench of tens of thousands of corpses. When I arrived, the Germans weren't cremating the corpses; they were burying them, tens of thousands of people in ditches. They later figured that burying the victims was not such a good idea, because someday those ditches would be dug up and what had gone on there would become known. So they made these fires with grates and they brought steam shovels. They dug the dead out of the ditches and loaded them on the fire, where they burned 24 hours a day. The Germans poured oil on the corpses and oil underneath, and the fire burned continuously.

We all got out of the boxcar. Those who were sick, or old, or had children with them were taken to the *lazaret*, where Kurland worked as a prisoner-overseer. There they were undressed. A German, Mentz (he was later sentenced to life imprisonment), stood there with a gun and killed them, 30, 40 or 50 at a time. Then they threw them into the burning ditch.

I was already in the line, naked, ready to go into the gas chamber. At the last minute, I was saved by a Jew who had been appointed the *Lagerälteste*—Galewski the engineer.

I had met Galewski by accident. In the Warsaw Ghetto his 13-year-old daughter had gone to school with my daughter. I hadn't known him personally, but his daughter used to come to my house to do her homework together with my daughter. So from time to time, he would come to my apartment to take his child home. When he saw me standing there naked, he remembered where I had lived—near him. And he wanted to know what had happened to his family; when they had taken him away they had left his family behind. So he told me not to push to the front of the line going into the gas chamber; he told me to hang back and he brought me a shirt and a pair of pants. You couldn't just step out of line. Galewski went over to the Scharführer, an SS man, and said, "Look, you need a translator from Russian to Polish, from Russian to German. I have a man here who can do that. If you'll allow it, have him taken out of the line."

So the SS man said, "Call him out!"

From that enormous transport that brought me and seven or eight thousand other people to Treblinka, they took out just two—me and another young fellow who worked in the same shop I did. He lasted just 48 hours; then they shot him. I was the only one from the whole transport to remain alive.

I knew a fellow who had married a girl from Wengrow. I knew her well, and he worked in a shop near my place of work in Warsaw. One day he suddenly disappeared; no one saw him any more. Then, some weeks later, he suddenly reappeared on Leszno Street. He came into our shop, where there were about 150 people sitting and working. The factory had been owned by Raskin, a Jew, but it had been confiscated by Toebbens.

Now this fellow said he had been in Treblinka and he had seen with his own eyes that this was not a labor camp. They were taking the people from the boxcars straight to the gas chambers, and then they burned them. Few people actually were put to work there, but he had been one of the very few selected to work, and he had [escaped and] returned to tell us to do something, because we were all going to be burned there.

Everybody said that he probably was crazy. It was impossible that they would burn women and small children! Only a mental case would say that. All who heard him were very understanding. "Too bad, so young and a mental case."

Two weeks before I was taken to Treblinka, my wife had been taken away during a "selection" on Mila Street. We were so foolish! My wife said, "Oh, if I'm resettled in the East, what will I do? I have a sewing machine; I'll earn a piece of bread with it." So she painfully lugged her heavy sewing machine on her shoulders and dragged it all the way to Treblinka.

That shows how positive we were that it wasn't going to be extermination, even though this fellow had visited all the workshops and told everybody about Treblinka.

When they took me to Treblinka, a couple of weeks later, they took that fellow back to Treblinka; they had picked him up during one of their selections. We were in the clothes-sorting area; that was some work! When you emptied 20 or 30 cars, you had to go at such a tempo that you couldn't keep it up. Many Jews had heart attacks on the spot and died.

This fellow said to me, "Rajzman, I'm going to try my luck and try to get away again. Perhaps I can get away in one of the cars loaded with clothing."

In order to get away, you had to have somebody else who would cover you with rags. You had to keep untrustworthy people away from the wagon while you made your escape. So I told him that I had a pen, which I had brought with me and had hidden. I asked him to go to the address where my daughter was and give her my regards and the pen, which would prove to her that he had really been with me.

He took the pen and went away. I didn't know what happened to him. That day, when he escaped, there were two missing at the roll call and the Germans shot 20 people. I didn't know whether this fellow made it.

Six weeks later, another transport arrived in Treblinka and he was back—his third time in Treblinka.

I went over to him, and he said, "Yes, I saw your daughter. She's in Warsaw with your friend. I gave her your pen, and you can imagine how happy they were when they heard you were alive. But I explained to them the real situation—that the chances of coming out alive from Treblinka are practically nil."

After the war, I found out that he had really been there and seen her. His story checked out completely. However, the Germans later took my daughter to Poniatow, and they killed her. I can never forget the greetings he brought me from her.

It was very hard to separate him from the crowd of new arrivals, because the whole transport was sent to the gas chamber. Everybody knew him; everybody knew he had escaped twice—his story had gained notoriety in Treblinka—so we had to make a special effort to get him out. We tried very hard because we wanted to know what was happening on the outside, what was the news from Warsaw, and what was happening with the uprising in Warsaw. We had heard rumors about an uprising. So we managed to get him out.

He was with us for two weeks; the Germans forgot about him and took him to work. He had been a prizefighter and the Germans knew about that. He died during the uprising, like most of the other prisoners. He had been in Treblinka three times.

When we came, there was no labor camp [in Treblinka]. There were people whom they took too for work, but everybody was killed. There were only very rare exceptions. Everybody was taken to the gas chambers immediately. There was no labor camp. A number of workers were kept alive to keep the camp going— tinsmiths, carpenters and so forth. But Treblinka was not a labor camp; it was an extermination camp.

There were tens of thousands of eyeglasses which people had brought with them to Treblinka. There were also microscopes that had been brought along by medical men, telescopes, and equipment for optical tests. I had to wash all of this, clean it and pack it up for shipment to Germany. While I was in Treblinka, I was called upon only once for translation work. They had found 10 or 15 pages of Polish writing in a doctor's possession. So these murderers went and split up the pages seven or eight ways; they picked out prisoners, and they gave each one a couple of pages to translate into German. The next day they looked to see whether the pages fitted together and whether they had been translated correctly. It was simple material—the doctor had written about family matters—but they wanted to know what it was. So this was the one and only time I did any translation work there.

There's one scene I'll never forget as long as I live. We had to throw all kinds of garbage into the fire to keep it going. We threw rags and waste on the fire in the *lazaret*. All of a sudden two women rose up from out of the fire. There were flames all around. These women had been shot but had remained alive; they had only been wounded. They had been thrown into the fire alive, but they got up. So a German walked over to them at once with a gun—this I'll never forget. I can never forget this; it follows me everywhere. The German shot them in the head and he shot off the tops of the skulls of these two women, and the brains and the blood came pouring out . . .

[Zvi] Kurland had to stay there day in and day out, looking at such things, and then they say that he killed people. Ah, ridiculous! When Kurland came to Treblinka he was a middle-aged, handsome man with black hair. By the time of the uprising his hair had turned completely white. Every day it became whiter and whiter. Every evening, as he returned to the barracks, he would recite the [mourners'] Kaddish for those whom he had seen die that day.

At work every day they took 20 people from the arriving boxcars and put them into the labor force, then took out 20 from the labor force and cremated them. I was working one day under the direction of Scharführers [August] Miete and [Willy] Mentz, those murderers. Miete didn't go out of his way to make special trouble for me. The reason was that before the war, I had had dealings with a Jewish-owned lumber firm where he had been employed as a foreman. So he looked at me in a somewhat different way. One day, I was sitting with Kudlik in the camp and doing my work, cleaning the microscopes, telescopes and eyeglasses and putting them in packages to be shipped to Germany. This Scharführer came in and took 25 or 30 people, including me. He took us to the path which led to the gas chambers. I was sure that this was it—this was the end. I was somehow confused—I had nothing to lose anyhow, and so I said, "Scharführer, it's a pity that our torn clothes and torn shoes should be burned along with us. Why don't you ask us to get undressed so you'd have more shoes?" I said this was evident sarcasm. At this point, I didn't care much.

He said, "Don't worry, your time hasn't come yet." They had brought some very heavy railroad rails, and these rails had to be brought into the death camp because the Germans were making another enormous ditch in which to cremate the dead. We almost died carrying those rails. It was extremely hard work. Each rail had to be carrried by a team of six or eight people. Weakened as we were, this was almost a death sentence. We carrried them as best we could, put them down, and the Germans led us back to our regular work.

Another incident I can't forget is the time when we hadn't been given any water to drink for a whole day. In the morning, they had brought me a pitcher of water to wash the eyeglasses, and this water had to last all day. It was dirty; you couldn't drink it. I was very nauseous because the heat was so stifling, and I said to several other fellows sitting with me, "Look, I'll take a chance. I'll try. I'll take that pitcher, go to the well in between the barracks and fill it up with water."

I filled it up, and on the way back this Scharführer stopped me and asked, "Who gave you permission?"

I knew that if I were to say, nobody, it would be very bad for me. So I took a chance. I said, "The kapo told me to get a pitcher of water because I didn't have enough water to wash the eyeglasses."

He called the kapo over. If I got in trouble with the kapo I would be whipped and kicked around, but I'd get by. He called the kapo over, and this kapo said, "I never talked to Rajzman at all."

I had to lie down on the ground, and the German gave me 25 lashes with a wire. This was a standard treatment, and seldom did anybody live through it. Usually, you were so badly cut that after several days you were sent to the *lazaret* and shot. Very few fellows survived that. As soon as he gave me the first whack, blood ran into my eyes.

Later [Franz] Stangl [the commandant of Treblinka] came by. He looked at me and said, "What happened to you that you are so banged up?"

So I told him. I had to tell the truth. I said there had been several of us dying for a drink, so I had gone to the well to bring a pitcher of water and the Scharführer "Kiewe" [Küttner] had caught me and given me 25 lashes. I was sure that after I'd told him the story he would send me to the *lazaret* and I'd be killed like all the others. He himself never shot anybody. However, he went past me and kept right on walking.

My friends said, "Look, Rajzman, you'd better hide. If they come to look for you, you won't be around. And if they find you, what have you got to lose? They're going to kill you anyhow."

So I listened to them. We went to the barracks, and I crawled beneath the rags and arranged them so that I could breathe. Nobody came to take me away.

At night I went back to the barracks. Dr. Chorążycki, from Warsaw, obtained medicines to rub on me so that I should look human because my face was one burning mass, like ground meat. But I survived.

The Germans devised various cruel forms of torture for the prisoners. They didn't need much of a reason. Let's say a Scharführer went by and you forgot to stand at attention. Then they took the whole group in the evening and made us run. They drove us with sticks at such a speed that dozens of people died of heart attacks. You couldn't go slow. They had billy clubs, and they used them. They had whips, too. The Ukrainians were standing and beating steadily. I usually knew when we would have to run so I took medicines (which we found in the clothing of new arrivals) to strengthen my heart. Among us there was a watchmaker who was a very strong man, although he was around 50 years old. One night he was running, but he couldn't stand it and fainted. They took him to the *lazaret* immediately and shot him. Shootings like that were everyday occurrences. The Germans would take 20 people from the train and send them as replacements for 20 workers whom they had killed.

Once they strung up some of my friends by their feet. The latter had given a Ukrainian guard money in exchange for food. Money was no problem—there was a lot of it around, and there also were diamonds and gold. Tens of thousands of people arrived in every transport. What did they carry on them? Gold and silver, diamonds and medicines—this type of thing. So there was no shortage of valuables.

(Once they brought a woman to Treblinka who was said to be a member of the Vienna branch of the Rothschild family. They had told her they were moving her to a rest home, a type of sanatorium. When she got off the train, the Scharführer told her that she would have to go to the baths or take a shower; then they would take her to the sanatorium. Meanwhile, she would be well advised to check all her valuables. She took out a sack of diamonds and valuables. Galewski was holding it in his hands—it weighed at least one kilogram.)

So, either the Germans found the money on my friend or one of the Ukrainians squealed. They took my friends to the roll call square, and the Germans put up two gallows. The Germans undressed them, assembled everybody (800 workers), and strung up my friends by their feet. The Germans hit them on their naked bodies with rifle butts until they both suffered strokes. When you string up people by their feet, the blood explodes inside their heads within 15 minutes. So, after a short time, they died.

That was one moment which I can never forget—one of them shouted right up to his last breath, "Children, remember God and make an uprising!" He kept repeating this. He had belonged to a group in Treblinka that had to take new arrivals off the train and get them to undress. He was a very gentle man from Lukow. Eight days before he was killed, a transport had arrived from Lukow, and the first ones off the train had been his own mother and father. He had to take them to get undressed. He turned away, but his father noticed him and started to yell. "Yechiel! Yechiel! Yechiel!" I can still hear him. His son didn't want to go over to him. What could he have done? And his father kept yelling, "Yechiel! Yechiel!"

One day they brought in a Czech transport. The Polish Jews came in cattle cars; the Czechs came in Pullman cars. You could see from their clothing and behavior that there were some highly educated people among them. There was an elderly man of about 60, who kept yelling that he couldn't leave because his equipment was in the Pullman car. It was very specialized equipment, and if he couldn't supervise its unloading it would all be broken. Well, 20 minutes later he was on the fire grate.

From that transport, they took six or eight people out to work. They took one handsome man, 30 or 35 years old, a dentist from Prague. The Germans took him aside and told him that he would be a kapo. He didn't know what a kapo was. He had come with his wife and child; they had taken away his wife and child right there, on the arrival square.

Two hours later we went into the barrack. This Czech was lying near me on the boards. He started to talk to me and said, "What happened to my wife and child?"

I said, "Don't you know what's going on here? You see the 24-hour-a-day fire over there. ... "

He then asked, "What is this kapo that I'm supposed to become tomorrow morning?"

So I told him what a kapo was supposed to do.

He said, "What happens if I tell the Scharführer that I don't want to be a kapo?"

"Well, then they'll send you where your wife is."

He didn't say anything. I fell into a troubled sleep. I got up in the middle of the night. I looked up and saw him hanging there. Rather than become a kapo, he had hanged himself with his belt. I never knew his name. There were many who didn't want to be kapos and were sent away to the fire.

There was a doctor who met a terrible death. When the Germans came in, they had singled him out to lead the *Judenrat* [Jewish Council]. He had taken the job. Several weeks later the Gestapo ordered him to furnish 30 people for "resettlement" immediately. He said, "I don't have 30 people, but I can give you four people immediately—myself, my wife and my two children." And he was the first to go. There were such people.

I think about what I went through every day and every night. Especially at night.

In Treblinka the Germans kept saying, "You Jews started the war. You wanted the war, so now you have it." The Germans kept repeating that.

We had a Ukrainian guard, a terrible man: he used to beat people to death with a rod of iron. Whoever fell into his hands— *bang!* he was dead. That was it. He used to hit them over the head. When he beat them in the face, it meant they would be taken out later on and killed.

The first thing was to torture people. They put you on a table, locked your legs and arms to the table, and gave you 25 lashes. When you had had these lashes, if you survived, you wouldn't be able to sit for four weeks. You couldn't move and you couldn't sit. One morning, they found on a prisoner some bread that hadn't originated in the camp. He had probably bought it from some Ukrainian for a lot of dollars. So another Ukrainian held his head in a pitcher of water until he drowned. I saw this with my own eyes! The tortures they invented—it's incredible!

The Germans had a big dog, the dog which belonged to "The Doll" [Kurt Franz]. This dog was trained to attack a man's genitals. Once you were attacked by that dog, even if you lived, you were in such bad shape that you would be taken to the *lazaret* and shot. Kurt Franz was the worst of the murderers there.

In the beginning, there were two unusual men with us. One, Masarek, had been a captain in the Czech army. The other one was Dr. Chorążycki. It was these two people who first came up with the idea of a revolt. They were military people. Chorążycki had been a captain in the Polish army.

So one day, they saw how hopeless the situation was. You saw that this [place] was for the complete extermination of Jews: it wasn't a temporary thing. They saw that they had nothing to lose in starting an uprising, absolutely nothing to lose.

It was very hard to run away alone. You had to have somebody with an iron will to want to run away, because this was practically tantamount to death. Another factor was that in the last months they had given everybody a number, and twice a day there was a strict head count, first before going out in the morning, and then after coming back in the evening. There were 700 people. There couldn't be 701 or 699. You had to have *exactly* 700. And they gave an order that if one was missing, they would line up everybody and shoot every tenth man. So those who remained were afraid to let anybody run away because... I myself stood by several times while they were picking out every tenth man to be shot. This happened a couple of times.

Masarek and Dr. Chorążycki started the whole thing. Then there was a question of whom to take into their confidence, whom they could recruit. The first one they could take in was the engineer, Galewski. He was a very sympathetic man, a Jew who had converted [to Christianity], a fine man. Nobody said he had been converted, but I heard that he had converted. He was a very sensitive man.

So these three were really the beginning of the whole thing. But there was a question of whom you could ask to join this revolt. A number of them could never be trusted.

My joining the planners of the uprising happened quite by accident. After a couple of weeks there, I had seen the whole operation of Treblinka. I knew everything about the extermination process. One day, I was sitting with Galewski, and I said to him, "You know, I'm not very thankful to you that you took me out of the extermination line. You should have let me remain there, and I would have been through with the whole thing. . . . I wouldn't have suffered the way I'm suffering here."

He told me, "You've remained alive because we need you, and you're going to see that you're going to be very useful." Those were his words. And from then on they took me into their organization.

There was Zvi Kurland, an older man, a merchant (from Warsaw, I think), a very fine man. He was the overseer, unfortunately, of the death house, the *lazaret*. He had to keep order in that place.

When they killed 20 or 30 people, Kurland had to place these people with their faces to the burning ditch. That was his work. He sat there all day with somebody else. Kurland was one of the most important people in organizing the uprising. Everybody knows that: I'm not alone in saying this, it's no secret. Every survivor of Treblinka knows that.

We couldn't sit down and hold regular meetings, so our meetings took place in the shop where the Strawczynskis worked, or in the carpenter's shop. To all appearances, we were playing cards. If somebody came in at night, they could catch us playing cards. You weren't allowed to do that, but you wouldn't get the death penalty for doing it.

Afterwards, there were more people who joined, but the strict organizing committee consisted of 12 people. We had organized it from the first minute to the last.

We had four companies, 12 people in each company, so we had about 50 fellows who would be in on the job. But not one of these 50 knew who the others were. Each one of these 50 knew only one other person on the committee. [The idea was that if] the Germans should catch one of these 50, even if they should torture him to death, he wouldn't be able to put the finger on more than one person. So that's how we organized it. It's evident that everybody tried in every way not to talk about the uprising. Even among ourselves, we didn't want to talk about it.

They took me into the committee a few weeks after I had arrived in Treblinka, after I had reproached Galewski for saving my life. So the organizing effort took about one year.

We had to postpone the uprising several times, because we found that we didn't have enough weapons. Do you know how we obtained weapons? During the time that Treblinka existed, the Germans were forever "improving" it, making it larger. They were expecting the British Jews. So one fine day they set up a special military building; all the ammunition was there, everything. This arsenal had been built, of course, by Jewish workers. Among us there was a tailor and his young son, 13 or 14 years old. The Germans let the boy live because he took their uniforms to the tailors for washing and pressing. This boy walked all over the camp, free. He was just about the only prisoner who could do that.

We decided that this boy should try to see what kind of lock there was on this arsenal. We had a shoemaker's shop in the camp. We took black bootwax and had this boy make on this wax an impression of that lock.

The boy brought a sketch of this key, and we had a blacksmith shop in the work area. Two or three people were in that shop who were able to do such precision metalwork. It was a very intricate lock. It took a couple of weeks until they could get the material to make the key. It was very hard—you couldn't go shopping for the materials. When our people made this key, the boy and one other fellow went to the arsenal one day. They said that there were boxes of hand grenades there, and they brought out one hand grenade to show Galewski, Dr. Chorążycki and Masarek. They saw that this really was a hand grenade, but it had no detonator.

Evidently, it took a couple of weeks till our people had another chance to get [into the arsenal]. It didn't happen as fast as I'm telling it. One fine day the boy brought out a grenade with a detonator, and Masarek said it was a very good thing that this had been obtained because we could use it for practice. There were revolvers, too, but the idea was to take out hand grenades, because we could hide the grenades and bring them out at the last minute. All this took weeks. We didn't have storage space for that material.

One fine day they started to build another building near the arsenal, and there was a lot of lime and mortar lying around; we saw we could hide things in the concrete and get them out of there later on. But we had to know the exact time when we could get that stuff out. So one day we decided on the time when we would make the uprising: five o'clock in the afternoon. We figured this way: at five o'clock there was a train outside our camp taking workers to the other Treblinka [a labor camp two kilometers away from the extermination camp]. So we figured that at five o'clock we would stop that train—there were always 200 to 300 people on it coming from work. We would take the people off the train, and they would help us revolt. So it was agreed that when you would hear the first shot from the blacksmith shop, you'd know that the uprising had started. We had four groups, twelve people in each group; everybody had to have weapons.

But at the last minute, with the uprising planned for five o'clock, things began to look bad. No matter how much we tried to keep it a secret—and nobody knew about anybody else—there was a kind of nervous tension in the camp. And the Germans sensed that something was going on. Suddenly, they saw two boys standing there shaking hands and saying good-bye to each other, another fellow standing there and crying, so they smelled something. This was reported right away to Galewski, the engineer, and we decided that if we were to wait until five o'clock, the Germans would know exactly what was up and it would turn out badly. We were afraid that somebody might squeal, too. . . .

There was a great deal of nervous tension in the camp, so at twelve o'clock, the lunch hour, they gave an order that the arms and ammunition should be brought out and distributed. There was no place to hide. So instead of five o'clock, we had to start at three o'clock, before the train arrived. We were afraid that by five it would be too late.

That was the only time since my arrival in Treblinka that I was transferred from my regular, daily place of work. I had always worked at one specific place, but that day I was supposed to be with my group at one of the watchtowers that surrounded the camp. I didn't know where I would be stationed. Only two or three people knew the exact arrangements. So Galewski went to "Kiewe" [Küttner] and told him that he didn't need me for polishing eyeglasses, so I should go with a group of branch cutters. Branches were used to camouflage the camp, especially the more gruesome areas. These branch cutters were working near the watchtower. At one o'clock I was there, and that was the place where I was supposed to be stationed for the uprising. They brought me two hand grenades and two or three revolvers, that was all. And that's how the revolt took place.

At the same time, twelve o'clock, there was a prisoner walking around with a canister on his shoulder. There was a great deal of gasoline in this canister that he carried. His regular job was to disinfect the clothes [of the new arrivals] by spraying them. We had poured gasoline into his canister instead of the usual disinfectant, and after twelve o'clock, he went all over the place and he sprayed everywhere.

When it started at three o'clock, we set everything on fire, and the whole place was in flames. It had been soaked in gasoline. The signal to start it had been a shot. Of course, the Germans were shooting at the *lazaret* every five minutes, but this signal shot was to come from the workshops, where the Strawczynskis and the carpenters and tailors were working. This was the first signal to start. The moment the shot was fired, everything burst into flames.

The fellow who did the spraying had a very important role in the uprising, and he was killed. He was from Bendin. He was about 25 or 26 years old, and when I arrived in Treblinka, he was already there and doing his disinfecting job. There were mountains of clothes, tens of thousands of people's clothes, and he was spraying all the time. As soon as the shot was heard, he set the place on fire with the group that was assigned to this job. When I was at the tower, I didn't hear the shot: I saw the fire right away. It was an extraordinary fire.

We threw our few grenades. There was one German whom we thought we had killed, but he had been only wounded and he is still alive today. He received a 25-year term. We went to the woods immediately. . .

Only one man from my group other than myself was left alive, and even he died some time later in Warsaw. My group had been joined by other prisoners who had been working nearby; altogether twelve of us got out. We made straight for the woods. We ran from about four p.m. until ten at night. We ran for about four or five hours until it was really dark. We all ran together, twelve people. At one time we saw the fire from Treblinka. We went only about seven or eight kilometers in all that time, because we were zigzagging here and there.

By about ten o'clock we were very tired; we lacked food and drink. So we decided that we'd send two people to a peasant's cottage at the edge of the woods to find food and water for us. I had some knowledge of these woods, because we had lived 30 miles from Treblinka. To make it fair, we decided that the oldest and the youngest in our group should go. This would be very dangerous, because the Germans were searching all over the place. I was the oldest, and the youngest was my friend Kudlik, who is now living in Israel. We worked side by side. So he said he would go with me.

We both left, and in about an hour's time we came to a peasant's cottage. A dog was howling there like mad; it was eleven p.m. A peasant woman came out. She saw us at the entrance of the yard and knew we had come from Treblinka, because she had seen a terrific fire burning there. She told us to get away from the house, because the Germans were looking everywhere and if they found us they would shoot her, too. So we told her, "Give us some bread and a pitcher of water, and we'll go away."

So she gave us what we had asked for and said, "Please bring the pitcher back because it's the only one I have." It was a very poor hovel at the edge of the woods.

We took the bread and the water and we went back to our friends. Everybody ate the bread and drank the water. We had to return the pitcher to the woman. As we were taking the pitcher back, we heard terrific shooting from the place we had just left. So we lay down in a potato field—the grass was very tall. We lay there for 45 minutes until the shooting stopped. At twelve o'clock we returned to our friends. We didn't find a single one left alive from the whole group. Nobody was left alive; the only other survivor besides myself was Kudlik, who had accompanied me.

We immediately headed out of the woods and left the pitcher just inside the fence of the peasant woman's cottage. Just under her window there were potatoes growing, and the greens from these potatoes were very tall. So we lay down head to head, and we remained there until six in the morning.

When the woman came out in the morning to do her chores, we went over to her and asked her for directions. I wanted to go to Wengrow, where I was born, but I didn't know how to get out of the woods. She said, "Don't go, because I know that the Germans are running around all over the woods looking for people from Treblinka. One-half kilometer from here the hay has been cut." The peasants had made enormous stacks of hay, and these stacks remained in the field all winter. She said, "Go to this hayfield, hide in one of the stacks, and remain there for another day or two."

She gave us another loaf of bread, and I went away with Kudlik. We remained in one of the haystacks for one day and a half.

She had explained to me how to get to Wengrow from there. I knew the area, but I didn't want to use main highways. I wanted to go by side roads. Twelve kilometers from my town there was a hamlet called Brzozów. In this hamlet (which still exists), there was a Gentile who had been a good friend of my father's. My father had been in the construction business, and this Gentile man used to build houses for him. This man was quite wealthy; his name was Pavel Pienak. My plan was to come to him and see whether he would hide us for a while. Frankly, I didn't know what to do. My main idea, however, was to get to Warsaw. I was still hoping that my daughter was alive.

We started out from the hayfield at night, and it took us two or three days to get to this hamlet. We used side roads and fields. We came in the middle of the day to this Pienak: we had to go in to him because we didn't have food or drink. When we came into his courtyard, we found him in very bad shape—he was paralyzed, lying in a bed in the courtyard. A man was sitting near him.

Pienak recognized me immediately, although he hadn't seen me in years. "You're Rajzman!"

I said, "Yes, yes—I am."

He said, "What do you want?"

I saw this fellow sitting near him and I didn't know who he was. Several minutes later this fellow got up and went away.

As soon as he had left, Pienak told me, "If you want to live, run away immediately. That fellow is the village chief here. He went to call the police and tell them that you're here."

In back of that house there was some corn growing. He told us, "Go to that cornfield and lie down. They'll never find you there." It was an enormous field. He continued, "At night, you'll come into my house and we'll see what we can do. If you don't want to go directly into the house, go into the shed in the back. My son will be there; he'll talk to you."

So we lay there until about eleven at night; then we went into the shed. Pienak's son gave us bread and other food. I told him I wanted to go from Wengrow to Warsaw (Wengrow was about 12 miles from this hamlet) to find my daughter. We lay down again for the night, and we started off the next morning, using side roads.

We came to a house near a forest about three kilometers from Wengrow. We came into the yard of the house in the middle of the day. I knew that whoever was there must know me, because the poor peasants who lived there had horses and wagons; they had transported wood for my father in earlier times.

A young man, 27 or 28 years old, approached me. He looked at us and saw who we were. He said, "You must be from Treblinka."

We said, "Yes."

He said, "I'll tell you—you better get going. There's such a search going on all over this neighborhood; it's unbelievable. They're looking for those who escaped from Treblinka."

What could we do? He had recognized me already.

His father came out, a man of about 70. He said, "You're Rajzman's son!"

I said, "Yes, I'm Rajzman's son."

He was deeply moved, and he gave us something to eat. He told us to go one-half kilometer from his house, where there was a little pond. There was tall, green grass growing around this pond. Very tall grass. He said, "Stay there and come to my house at night. I want to help you. Then we'll see what we can do for you."

And that's the way it was. I went there with my friend. I said, "What have we got to lose? If they shoot us here we'll lie in the cemetery with all my dead relatives from Wengrow." I didn't feel we would remain alive. It was inconceivable.

We lay in the grass at night, and then we came to this Gentile, Edward Gołoś, who was waiting for us.

He said, "What can I do for you?"

I said, "I must get to Warsaw. I *must*; perhaps my daughter is alive." We were practically naked and barefoot. I said, "If you could help me and give me some advice, I'd be very grateful to you."

He said, "I can help you. Go into the woods and give me the address."

I told him about the young Gentile woman in Warsaw who had been forelady at Toebben's factory where we had worked. She was a young woman in her twenties; we had gotten along very well with her because we had lived in the same building before the war. So I said, "I would like to ask this woman whether she knows anything about my daughter."

When they took me away, I had been working in the shop and this woman had been there, too, so I felt she would know what had happened.

Gołoś said, "Do you know what? I'll go to Warsaw. I'll see her. You go into the woods and I'll go with you. You'll show me where I can leave food for you. Every two or three days I'll bring you food, and you will remain in the woods." The woods were very dense, perhaps a mile or half a mile from Gołoś's house.

Kudlik and I went into the woods, and Gołoś went to Warsaw for a day. He returned to Wengrow with Marisha. It was midnight. Kudlik and I went to the house and I spoke to Marisha. She said she believed that my daughter was alive at Poniatow. My friend had taken her in when they took me away to Treblinka. She heard that they had taken him to Poniatow with my daughter, and it was possible that they were still alive. I had some money on me, so I gave her money for her expenses. In Treblinka there had been hundreds of thousands of dollars all over the place, so that was no problem. It had been all over the ground, but if they found a penny on a prisoner they shot him immediately.

Marisha said she would inquire about my daughter in Poniatow and return in a few days to report to me. She left, and when she returned she said that all the Jews in Poniatow had been killed. (While she was there, she had talked with Mr. Gołoś about the situation of the Jews. She fell in love with him and eventually married him.)

So we spent a whole year in the woods. Gołoś brought us food. During the winter, when it was freezing, he allowed us to go into his barn and stay there overnight, because of the bitter cold. So that's how we got by. The last few weeks we waited impatiently because the battlefront was getting close. We couldn't go to Gołoś then, so we just remained in the woods. In the winter he allowed us to come into his house when it was very cold, but only if there was no snow; if there was snow, people might see our footprints.

As the front came closer, the shooting went on directly over our heads. There was German artillery fire from the one side, and the Russian artillery fire on the other, and we were caught in the middle, lying there in the woods. The shells ripped dozens of trees, but they never harmed us. When the Russians came in, Gołoś came into the woods. He had to look for us, because he never knew where we were. We never stayed in the same spot twice. He would put food down at a certain spot, and we would go later to get it.

So that's how Kudlik and I were saved. From the whole group of twelve people, nobody remained alive except the two of us.

This Pole, Gołoś, was a very fine man. He's a judge now. He went to high school with my sister. He had a certain feeling for us. He was a member of a rightist-nationalist organization.

One evening—it was a Sunday night—the weather was very cold and we were resting in the shed. At eleven o'clock at night, Gołoś's father, the old man, who was very religious, came in. He called us into the house for a cup of coffee or a glass of milk. He told us he had been in church that day, and the priest in his sermon had told all the people that anybody who knew a Jew was hidden and didn't hand him over to the Germans would not go to Paradise. Everybody who knew where a Jew was hidden had to report it.

When I heard this, I really became nervous. My heart began to tremble. After all, the priest had said it was a sacred duty for a Christian to hand over a Jew. I said to the old man, "How do you feel about the priest's suggestion?" Even as I spoke, I wondered why he had called us in. Perhaps he had alerted the Germans; perhaps they had already surrounded the house; perhaps they were even waiting for us.

"How do I feel?" he answered. "I think you can find the devil even in the church." That was a fine man! Oh, yes!

The old man died a long time ago, but I still keep writing to the young man all the time. . . .

The Russians came in, and the Nuremberg trials began. After my liberation I wrote a long article about Treblinka for a Polish literary journal. This article made a big impression, because people didn't know very much about Treblinka. I was living in Lodz, but I traveled to Warsaw: the late Dr. Friedman, the historian, was then in Warsaw. He led the Jewish Cultural Committee in Lodz. I was his close friend in Poland, and he had called me to Warsaw. He had received a letter from the Nuremberg prosecutors asking him to locate me. I had mentioned a few other Treblinka survivors in my article, but they wanted me to go to the trial in Nuremberg. I was ready to go—I was glad to find an opportunity to get out of Poland. I didn't have a passport, but I was granted one in two or three days.

It was through the Nuremberg trial that my Treblinka experience became known. So, in 1950, when they caught the first Treblinka guard, Jozef Hittreiter [Josef Hirtreiter] — he had been "my" watchtower German, and he had survived—I received a letter that I should come to the trial in Germany. I was in a bad financial situation; it was my first year in Canada. . . . I went to the German consulate here [in Canada] and gave them a sworn declaration that I knew this Scharführer very well, and I described his activities. I really had known him very well; he had been stationed at our position every day. He was sentenced to 25 years in prison. . . .

Even when I worked in Munich for the Central Committee of Liberated Jews, I went nowhere except from my room to my work, and directly back again. I couldn't go out into the street; I just couldn't take it. I was the first to leave Munich. There were no passports, no visas, but I went to the French commandant and received a travel document to go to Paris. I was the first of the Central Committee to leave.

They asked me at the Treblinka trial whether I could recognize the accused. Of course, I recognized them all by name. I had difficulty recognizing only one of them. In Treblinka he had been fat, but afterwards he had been sick and had become thin. I described the specific duties of every one of them, because every one of them had a particular job to do. [Willy] Mentz's job was the *lazaret*—when the transports came and they took the sick and the aged from the train, he shot them in the *lazaret*. He was sentenced to life imprisonment.

What happened to "Kiewe" [Küttner]?

We thought that he had been killed in the revolt. Nobody saw him, According to our plan, he was supposed to be the first to be finished off. But I wasn't inside the barracks or the shops at the time. I was near the watchtower, so I didn't see what was going on inside. I only saw how the place was burning. They say that "Kiewe" died a natural death.

When I saw them in court, I had such a shock that they had to stop the court proceedings for half an hour until I could regain my composure.

Eichmann had also visited Treblinka. It was a bright day. In the middle of that day they took everybody from their work and locked them in the barracks: They didn't let us out. We didn't know what was going on. We were sure that we'd never go back to work again—they'd take us from the barracks straight to the gas chambers. After a couple of hours they sent us back to work, and later they told us that one of the very high-ranking SS men had come, and that it was Eichmann. Nobody saw him. When he came, no Jew was allowed around or even at a distance.

It was worthwhile to hold the Eichmann trial. Many of the young people in Israel could not imagine and did not believe what had happened. The world is a prostitute—today it believes, tomorrow it forgets. Yesterday they loved you, and today they sell you down the river. But for young Jews in Israel it was a very important part of their education.

In writing about the Holocaust, we don't need authors with great imaginations. We need people who can depict the reality as it was. It was so overpowering that the facts speak for themselves.

Based on Howard Roiter's translation of Rajzman's testimony from a Yiddish tape recording.

1. Quorum of ten adult Jewish males needed for public worship.

PHOTOGRAPHIC CHRONOLOGY OF TREBLINKA

Betrifft: Arbeitslager Treblinka.

    Das Arbeitslager Treblinka wird am Sonnabend, den 11.7.42 betriebsfertig sein.

    Zur endgültigen Fertigstellung werden noch folgende Gegenstände benötigt:

      1000 Schellen für Lichtleitung 9 mm
       20 elektrische Fassungen mit Schalter
       20 elektrische Fassungen ohne Schalter
        3 m Treibriemen 6 cm breit
        3 Saugkörbe für Brunnen mit Rückschlagventil 1 1/2 Zoll
        1 Tischbohrmaschine
        3 kg Nussbaumbeize
        3 kg Beize Eiche hell
        1 Feldschmiede

    Um schnellste Lieferung wird gebeten. Der Betriebsbeginn wird durch den Termin der Lieferung obengenannter Gegenstände nicht berührt, da die Anlage bis Sonnabend bereits behelfsmässig arbeitsfähig wird.

                H e i l H i t l e r !

July 7, 1942: Dr. Irmfried Eberl, Commandant of Treblinka, notifies Dr. Heinz Auerswald, the Nazi Commissioner of the Warsaw ghetto, that Treblinka will be ready to start operations on July 11, 1942

July 22, 1942: The "resettlement" in Warsaw begins
Deportees on the way to Umschlagplatz

Warsaw Umschlagplatz: *Rounded-up Jews being loaded into boxcars destined for*
Treblinka

August 22, 1942, Siedlce: Transport bound for Treblinka. Photograph taken secretly by an Austrian soldier, Hubert Pfoch, now a Vienna City Councillor (Sereny)

Railroad siding leading from the Treblinka station to the extermination camp

August, 1942: A transport just arrived from Warsaw. Many had died from thirst and asphyxiation on the way in the overcrowded cars

Model of Treblinka exhibited in the Ghetto Fighters' Kibbutz (Israel). Model was created by the survivor Jankiel Wiernik

The Treblinka extermination camp. Mothers carrying children on their way to the gas chamber.

Naked women in front of the barber shop i

260

hair will be clipped before they are gassed

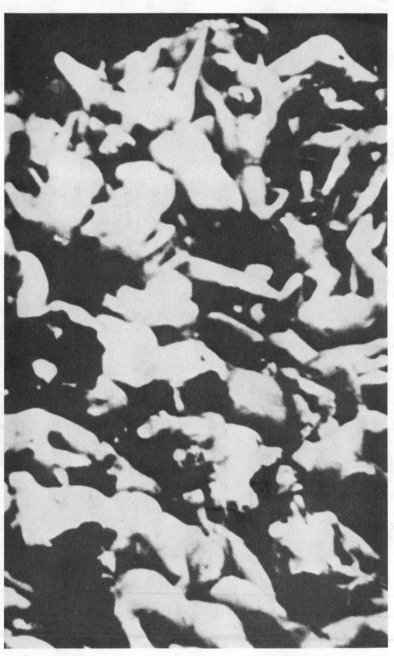

Corpses of victims asphyxiated in the gas chambers

Germans try to obliterate traces of the crime.
Graves opened for excavation and cremation.

(A German photo from 1943)

The excavator used to open the ditches and to transfer the corpses to the cremation grills.

(Photo from Kurt Franz's album)

August 2, 1943: Treblinka ablaze, set afire during the uprising.

(Photo by Zygmunt Ząbecki, given to Miriam Novitch by Franciszek Ząbecki in Düsseldorf during the Treblinka trial of 1964)

After the destruction of the camp, a farmhouse was built by the Germans on its site, and the Ukrainian guard Streibel was settled there. The farm lasted till the Russians arrived. (Photo from Kurt Franz's album)

1945: The Treblinka Gold Rush. Adventurers from all over Poland come to dig in the soil for hidden "treasures."

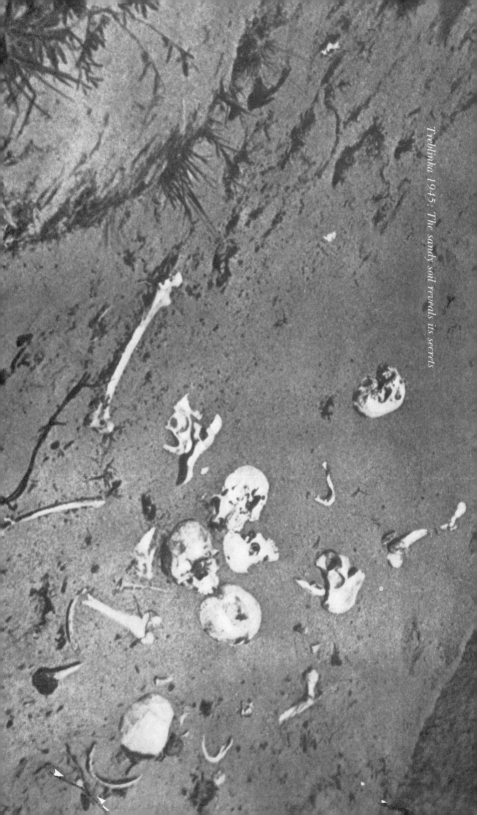

Treblinka 1945: The sandy soil reveals its secrets

Reunion of Treblinka survivors in 1944. From left to right (standing): Rosenthal, Brothandel, Shimon Goldberg, Chaim Ciechanowski, Wolf Schneiderman; (sitting): Jacob Domb, Gustav Boraks, Oscar Strawczynski, Samuel Rajzman, Arie Kudlik, Goldberg, Lejzer Ciechanowski (As identified by Samuel Rajzman)

The Treblinka monument created by the Polish sculptors Prof. Adam Haupt and Franciszek Duszenko was unveiled on May 10, 1964

DRAMATIS PERSONAE

DRAMATIS PERSONAE

THE HANGMEN

ODILO GLOBOCNIK
Commander of "Operation Reinhard"

Born on April 21, 1904 in Trieste (then part of the Hapsburg monarchy) as the son of an Austrian cavalry officer, Globocnik studied to become an architect but in 1922 he became involved in political activity. As early as 1932 he was a member of the SS (which was illegal in Austria). According to Eugen Kogon (*Der SS Staat*, p. 205), he had to flee to Germany in 1933 after murdering a Jewish jeweler in Vienna. He returned to Vienna only after the Nazi annexation of Austria when he was appointed (April 21, 1938) *Gauleiter* of the city.

He participated in the Nazi invasion of Poland and, on September 11, 1939, was appointed SS and Police Chief for Lublin. He soon became a favorite of Heinrich Himmler, who fondly called him "Globus." Late in April, 1942, Globocnik was appointed commander of "Operation Reinhard," thus becoming responsible for the murder and plundering of millions of Jews. His financial statement upon the completion of "Operation Reinhard" showed a "profit" of almost 180 million Reichsmarks in loot and valuables taken from the Jews. Since this report gave only very conservative estimates, it is safe to assume that the actual value of the loot was double the amount stated by Globocnik. Also, Globocnik's statement did not include items in short supply such as textiles, of which alone 1,900 boxcars were shipped from the extermination camps to German industries, nor does it account for property stolen "officially" and otherwise by the individuals who participated in the spoliation of the Jews. According to Spies and Gnichwitz, the prosecutors in the Düsseldorf trials, Treblinka's share in the loot amounted to 55%.

While the "mixed" camps of the type of Auschwitz and Maidanek were under the jurisdiction of the SS-WVHA (Main Office of

Economic Administration), the camps of "Operation Reinhard" (Bełżec, Sobibór and Treblinka) were the responsibility of Globocnik and Hitler's Reich Chancellery. According to Globocnik's report of October 27, 1943, the total personnel of "Operation Reinhard" consisted of 450 men, including 26 graduates of the Trawniki training camp and 92 men, mostly with experience in the euthanasia program, who had been assigned to the project directly by the Chancellery. Everyone involved in "Operation Reinhard" had to swear an oath of secrecy to SS-Hauptsturmführer Hermann Höfle. Kurt Gerstein quotes Globocnik as having said in this connection: "This is one of the most secret affairs, in fact, the *most secret*. Whoever talks about it will be shot immediately."

Globocnik exchanged visits with Rudolf Hoess, commandant of Auschwitz, to compare notes on the efficiency of their respective projects. When Himmler visited the Warsaw ghetto to expedite plans for its final liquidation, it was Globocnik who acted as his escort. Later, Globocnik helped crush the Warsaw ghetto revolt in April, 1943. Earlier, in Lublin, he had received a visit from Hitler himself. However, he also had many enemies and there were rumors that he had lined his own pockets and those of his friends with Jewish property which he had been supposed to turn over to the German Reich. As a result, he was relieved of his command and, on September 13, 1943, appointed top SS and Police Chief for the Adriatic coast, where his task was to fight the widespread Yugoslav partisan movement.

He was captured by British troops in Carinthia, Austria, and committed suicide by taking poison in Weissensee, Austria on May 21, 1945.

CHRISTIAN WIRTH
Inspector of "Operation Reinhard"

Wirth's career in the Nazi party began in 1922. Although he had very little formal education, he quickly climbed the SS career ladder, eventually attaining the rank of Hauptsturmführer. He became chief of the criminal police in Stuttgart, Germany and participated in the euthanasia program. After the termination of the euthanasia project on August 21, 1941, Wirth, as a specialist in methods of gassing, set up Chełmno, the pilot extermination camp in Poland and appointed Dr. Irmfried Eberl as commandant there. Wirth installed mobile gas chambers at Chełmno (the victims were placed into vans, into which carbon monoxide generated by the van's own engine was led, killing the victims). In the spring of 1942, Wirth was ordered to report to Globocnik in Lublin. Before leaving Chełmno, he had to give an oath of secrecy to Heinrich Himmler, who told Wirth that he, Himmler, expected him and his men to be "inhuman to a superhuman degree" (*er mute ihnen Übermenschlich-Unmenschliches zu*). Wirth and his crew then began to construct stationary gas chambers which utilized carbon monoxide generated by diesel engines. Wirth became commandant of Bełżec, a position he held until August, 1942, when he was appointed inspector of "Operation Reinhard," commuting between Bełżec, Sobibór and Treblinka to plan and assure the efficient operation of the mass murder program. "It was not possible to save even a child in Treblinka," Franz Stangl was to testify at his trial. "Wirth gave very specific instructions in this respect." It was Wirth who initiated the cremation of the victims, in line with the order of SS Standartenführer Paul Globel, chief of Kommando 1005, to obliterate every trace of the Nazi mass killings.

There was a competition between Wirth and Kurt Gerstein, SS chief disinfection officer, as to the comparative efficiency of carbon monoxide versus the hydrogen cyanide (Zyklon) gas used in Auschwitz. In August 1942 Gerstein arrived in Bełżec in order to change the method of gassing. Wirth prevailed upon him "not to ruin his reputation."

Wirth is remembered as a hot-tempered, brutal individual and ruthless careerist who was harsh and abrupt with his subordinates. He was nicknamed "Christian the Terrible" and "Christian the Savage." He has been described as running through the camps brandishing his whip and his gun, shouting and cursing. The SS historian Höhne characterized him as a "conceited ogre"; at Hitler's Chancellery he was known as the "chief executioner."

In the fall of 1943 Wirth was ordered to destroy the extermination camps and was transferred to the Istrian peninsula to fight against the Yugoslav partisans. He was killed by partisan fighters near Trieste on May 26, 1944.

DR. IRMFRIED EBERL
First Commandant of Treblinka

SS Obersturmführer Dr. Irmfried Eberl, a physician by training, directed the construction of Treblinka and served as the camp's first commandant. Like many other key figures in the implementation of the Final Solution (Eichmann, Globocnik, Heydrich, Franz Stangl, etc.), Eberl was of Austrian origin. Born in Bregenz, Austria, he made his career in the euthanasia program as officer in charge of the Bernberg Center near Hanover. After the establishment of Camp Chełmno, Eberl briefly served as its commandant, then was placed in charge of the construction of the Treblinka camp. The construction work was done by the Leipzig construction firm of Schönbrunn and the Warsaw branch of another German firm, Schmidt and Münstermann, both of which used Polish and Jewish slave labor.

On July 7, 1942, Eberl officially notified Dr. Heinz Auerswald, commissar of the Warsaw ghetto, that Treblinka would be ready for operation on July 11. As a result, the SS made arrangements with the German railroad authorities for the deportation of hundreds of thousands of Warsaw Jews to Treblinka.

The first transport of Jews from Warsaw arrived in Treblinka on July 23, 1942, after a journey of 12 hours. Eberl turned out to be unequal to his task. Because he was unable to complete the gassing and removal of victims with the required speed and efficiency, new transports on their arrival would see the corpses of earlier victims strewn about the camp grounds. The impact of the sight on the new arrivals impeded the smooth operation of the proceedings. As a result, Eberl was relieved of his command by Wirth and replaced by Franz Stangl.

Eberl committed suicide in 1948.

FRANZ STANGL
Second Commandant of Treblinka

Franz Paul Stangl was born on March 26, 1908 in the small Austrian town of Altmünster as the son of a night watchman. Stangl first worked as a weaver, then became a policeman and, in 1936, joined the (then illegal) Austrian Nazi party. After the annexation of Austria by Germany he was transferred to the Gestapo and assigned to the euthanasia program as a police supervisor stationed at the Hartheim killing center near Linz, Austria.

In 1942 he became commandant of Sobibór; on August 24 of that year, he was appointed commandant of Treblinka to replace Dr. Irmfried Eberl. He took with him to Treblinka his assistant, Kurt Hubert Franz ("The Doll").

ODILO GLOBOCNIK

DR. IRMFRIED EBERLE

FRANZ STANGL

KURT FRANZ ("The Doll")

Arrested in Austria after the war on charges of having killed mental patients at Hartheim, he escaped from prison in May, 1948 and made his way to Italy. An Austrian bishop attached to the Vatican was instrumental in procuring for Stangl a Nansen passport and an employment contract for work in Damascus, Syria. In 1951 he moved with his family to Brazil, where he worked first in the textile industry and later at the Volkswagen plant in São Paulo, living under his own name and registered with the Austrian consulate.

It was not until the mid-1960's that Simon Wiesenthal, head of the Jewish Documentation Center in Vienna, learned of Stangl's whereabouts. For a total of $7,000 ("one cent for every Jew killed") the informant agreed to divulge Stangl's address. Stangl was arrested in Brazil on February 28, 1967 and was extradited to the West German authorities on June 23 of that year. At his first hearing at the West German court, Stangl declared that while it was true that he had been the commandant at Treblinka, he had had nothing to do with the killing of Jews. His task, he said, had been solely to supervise the collection and shipment of valuables brought into the camp by the victims. The individual responsible for the killings had been Christian Wirth.

Stangl's trial before the Düsseldorf Court of Assizes (the "Second Treblinka Trial") began on May 13, 1970. On December 22, 1970 he was found guilty and sentenced to life imprisonment. In prison, he was interviewed by the British journalist Gitta Sereny, who asked him what he had thought at the time to be the Nazis' motivation in exterminating the Jews. According to Ms. Sereny (*Into That Darkness*, p. 101), Stangl gave the same reply twice. "They wanted their money," he asserted. "Have you any idea of the fantastic sums that were involved? That's how the steel was bought in Sweden."

Stangl appealed his sentence. He died in prison of a heart attack on June 28, 1971, while awaiting the results of his appeal.

KURT HUBERT FRANZ
"The Doll"—and His Dog

Kurt Hubert Franz was born in Düsseldorf in 1914, the son of a small businessman. At the age of 14 he left school to become an apprentice cook at a hotel in his native city. In 1932 he became an ardent follower of Adolf Hitler. At 22 he joined the German army, serving for two years, then joined the SS and was assigned to the

Buchenwald concentration camp. In 1939 he was assigned to the euthanasia program and served at the killing centers of Grafeneck, Linz and Sonnenstein, where hundreds of people regarded by the Nazi system as "unfit to live" were eliminated by gassing or injections.

After the cessation of the euthanasia program, Franz was assigned to Sobibor, where he was assistant to Franz Stangl. Late in August, 1942, Kurt Franz arrived with Stangl in Treblinka to serve as the camp's deputy commandant. Nicknamed *Lalka* (Polish for "The Doll") because of his physical beauty, he became a byword for sadism and moral turpitude. He came to Treblinka with his dog, Barry, who had been trained to attack the Jewish prisoners, particularly to maul the genitals of men. When Stangl was relieved of his post in Treblinka following the uprising of August 2, 1943, Franz was named commandant and supervised the liquidation of the camp. Afterwards, he was transferred to northern Italy to fight against the partisans.

After the war he returned to his native Düsseldorf, where he lived under his own name until his arrest on December 2, 1959. He and nine other hangmen of Treblinka were tried before the Düsseldorf Court of Assizes ("First Treblinka Trial"). The trial, which opened on October 12, 1964, ended on September 3, 1965. Franz was sentenced to life imprisonment. When Franz was arrested, a search of his apartment turned up an album containing numerous photographs from his days in Treblinka. The album was captioned *"Die schönsten Jahre meines Lebens"* (The Best Years of My Life).

THE ACCOMPLICES

Max Bielas, killed by an inmate, Meir Berliner, on September 11, 1942.

Josef Hirtreiter (nicknamed "Sepp") was the first of the Treblinka hangmen to be brought to trial. He was tried in Frankfort on the Main and on March 3, 1951 was sentenced to life imprisonment. Among the crimes of which he was found guilty were the following: beating two prisoners until they were unconscious, because money had been found on them, then hanging them by their feet and finally killing them with a shot in the head; killing many young children ages one and one-half to two, during the unloading of the transports, by seizing them by the feet and smashing their heads against the boxcars.

Kurt Küttner (nicknamed "Kiewe"). Chief officer at the "Lower Camp." Died before he could be brought to trial.

Another fourteen years were to pass before ten other Treblinka murderers were brought to trial ("First Treblinka Trial, Kurt Franz et al.," 1965).

Otto Richard Horn, worked at the incinerator where the corpses of victims were cremated. He was released.

Hermann Lambert (b. 1910), helped in the construction of the gas chambers. He was sentenced to four years in prison.

Arthur Matthes (b. 1902). Chief officer of Camp No. 2 and the gas chambers. Killer at the *lazaret*. Sentenced to life imprisonment.

Willy Mentz (b. 1904). Nicknamed "Frankenstein." Killer at the *lazaret*. Sentenced to life imprisonment.

August Miete (b. 1909, nicknamed "Malakh Ha-Moves," Yiddish for "Angel of Death"). Killer at the *lazaret*. Killed the prisoner Berliner after the latter had stabbed Max Bielas.

Gustav Münzberger (b. 1903), assistant to Matthes, operator of the gas chambers. Sentenced to twelve years.

Albert Rum (b. 1890). Chased the prisoners with whips to the gas chambers. Sentenced to three years in prison.

Otto Stadie (b. 1897). Chief in charge of the Ukrainian guards. Received incoming transports; killed the kapo Rakowski. Sentenced to six years in prison.

Franz Suchomel (b. 1908), was in charge of collecting and processing gold and valuables of Jewish prisoners. Sentenced to seven years in prison.

Out of the 35 to 40 ranking SS officers at the Treblinka death camp, only 15 have been accounted for. The names of the majority are unknown and they "couldn't be located."

CHRISTIAN WIRTH

THE REBELS

We know very little about the leaders of the Treblinka conspiracy. Extensive research conducted in Warsaw, Israel and in New York to find more biographical data about Dr. Julian Chorążycki has yielded no results whatsoever, not even a photograph of this man who undoubtedly belongs to the Pantheon of our resistance heroes.

A similar problem arose with the other leader of the uprising who fell in combat, the engineer Galewski. No one of the survivors seems to know his first name. When in 1945 he was posthumously awarded the Polish Cross of the Valiant (Krzyż Walecznych) by the then Polish Minister of Defense, General Rola-Żymierski, his first name in the citation was given as Alfred. His relatives in New York say it should be Stefan. But according to his brother, whom I located in Australia, it was neither Alfred nor Stefan. Both Alfred and Stefan were cousins, both were in Warsaw ghetto, but they perished there and were never in Treblinka. The "real" engineer Galewski's first name was Marceli. I therefore checked with my good friend Samuel Rajzman, who knew Galewski very well, and he seems to accept the Australian version.

Nobody is sure of the first name of Kurland, the tragic kapo of the *lazaret*. Some say it was Zev; others, Zvi.

These are, of course, just details but exactly these details make the difference between identification and anonymity, and they are the researcher's biggest problem.

The following leaders of the Treblinka uprising died before or during the revolt:

ZHELOMIR (ZELO) BLOCH
A photographer by profession, Bloch had been an officer in the Czech army prior to the fall of Czechoslavakia. Richard Glazar, one of the survivors (see p. 286), describes him as a "good-looking man of medium height with brown hair and a mustache, a strong,

square face and muscular body." Shalom Kohn, one of the leaders of the revolt who survived the war (see p. 287), recalls that after Galewski became ill "the title of chief of staff of the revolt went to Captain Zelo. The contribution of this highly educated military man substantially facilitated the realization of this difficult and complex undertaking."

At Treblinka, Zelo was appointed foreman of the labor detail which sorted out the clothing turned in by the victims upon their arrival. One day in March, 1943, a bundle of clothes ready for shipment to Germany fell apart and somehow the articles were listed twice in the inventory. The Germans noticed that there was only one bundle and made Zelo responsible for the discrepancy. Samuel Willenberg, who was a member of this labor detail, recalls: "A roll call was arranged. We were ordered to take off our own jackets, to bring our own shirts and overcoats and other pieces of clothing from the barrack. And so the missing bundle was replaced." SS man Küttner (Kiewe) punished Zelo and his assistants by transferring them to Camp No. 2, the Death Camp. It was a terrible blow for the conspiracy as well as for Zelo personally. He could no longer stay in touch with his comrades in arms at Camp No. 1 and was able to join them only on the day of the uprising. He fought like a hero and died in the revolt. "He was a real leader," Glazar remembers.

Dr. JULIAN CHORĄŻYCKI

Before the war, Dr. Julian [Ilya] Chorążycki (pron. Kho-ron-ZHITS-ky) had been a well-known laryngologist in Warsaw. Born in 1885 and admitted to medical practice in 1911, he was 57 years old when he was deported to Treblinka. However, he still looked robust and was therefore picked by the SS from the transport to head their own clinic, the *Revierstube*.

A former captain in the Polish army, Chorążycki was involved in the inmates' conspiracy from the very beginning. Since his *Revierstube* was almost exactly opposite the room in which the *Goldjuden* were processing the money and valuables of the prisoners, he was entrusted with the task of getting as much of this money as possible for the purchase of weapons.

The exact details of Chorążycki's death are not known. The extant testimonies of survivors show a number of discrepancies. The most likely account seems to be that of Samuel Willenberg (see p. 189 ff.)

We gathered about 750,000 zlotys for the purchase of arms. I brought the roll of bills to Dr. Chorążycki with my own hands. But here something unexpected occurred, which almost led to the exposure of our conspiracy. Before Dr. Chorążycki could hide the money in a safe place, "The Doll" burst into the clinic. The doctor was upset because he had so much money on him, and the SS man immediately noticed his embarrassment. In order to verify his suspicions, "The Doll" searched him, and, of course, found the roll of bills in the doctor's pocket. Chorążycki knew he was done for. . . . With a sudden blow he knocked Kurt Franz down, pushed him across the threshold and then swallowed a vial of poison which he had with him for any eventuality. It is not known whether it was luminal or potassium cyanide. Several of us worked directly alongside the barracks of the Germans and were witness to this unusual occurrence.

"Kurt Franz kept beating Chorążycki with his whip even after it was obvious that he was dead," Richard Glazar remembers. "He had him dragged to the *lazaret*—all the *Goldjuden* had been brought there; he told them they'd be shot, one after the other, unless they told where the doctor had gotten the cash. . . . Well, none of them told anything—the doctor was dead—and in the end Franz let them all go. He knew very well that these people were the most valuable experts they had [at Treblinka]."

After Dr. Chorążycki's death, his place in Treblinka and in the conspiracy was taken by Dr. Marius Leichert (or Leitner) from Wengrov.

In 1945, on the second anniversary of the Warsaw ghetto revolt, Dr. Chorążycki was posthumously awarded the Cross of the Valiant (Krzyż Walecznych) by Poland's then Minister of Defense, General Rola-Zymierski.

ENGINEER GALEWSKI

Galewski hailed from Lodz and was an engineer by profession. Richard Glazar remembers him as a man "in his forties, tall, slim, with dark hair. He looked and behaved like a Polish aristocrat — a very remarkable man." According to the Australian version his name was Marceli Galewski, born in Kutno on Oct. 10, 1899. He graduated from the Warsaw Polytechnic School in 1928 with the degree of electrical engineer. In 1929 he married in Warsaw Jadwiga Litauer, née Kobryner, a widow. They had a daughter Romana.

Another branch of the family is represented by Dr. Stefan Galewski, a physician now residing in London. He left his native

Lodz in 1935 and migrated to London via Switzerland. According to him the Treblinka hero was his cousin Bernard Galewski, born in Lodz around 1900. He studied civil engineering in Germany, lived in Lodz and was married.

When the Nazis set up a ghetto in Lodz, Galewski and his family fled to Warsaw, from where they were deported to Treblinka in 1942. Galewski was "selected" for work and was appointed *Lagerältester*. He was involved in the Treblinka inmate conspiracy from the very beginning, but he was able to keep his role so secret that not even Samuel Willenberg was aware of it. He fell in combat during the uprising.

In 1945 Galewski, along with Dr. Chorążycki, was posthumously awarded the Cross of the Valiant by Minister of Defense General Rola-Żymierski.

The photo we print was received from S. Willenberg (Israel). Its authenticity could not be verified so far.

Eng. GALEWSKI   *RUDOLF MASAREK*

ZEV (ZVI?) KURLAND

Kurland was one of the most tragic figures in Treblinka. He was assigned as kapo in charge of the *lazaret* where the aged, crippled and sick were "cured" by a bullet in the neck. In order to maintain the "hospital" camouflage, Kurland was forced to wear a Red Cross armband, so that many of the prisoners considered him a real doctor. Each evening, Kurland would recite the Kaddish for all the

Jews who died on that day. The anguish of his experiences turned his dark hair gray. He belonged to the inmates' conspiracy from the outset. Nevertheless, rumors were spread that he administered lethal injections to fellow prisoners and aided in the executions in other ways. This charge has been categorically denied by survivors. In a letter dated August 16, 1966, Karel Unger, one of the survivors, writes, "'Doctor' Kurland, kapo of the *lazaret*, was one of the best and most beautiful personalities I had ever known, one of the leaders in the revolt." In a letter dated September 4, 1966, Richard Glazar writes that Kurland "was a leader of the Committee of Liberation all along . . . An extraordinary man and a senior member of the revolutionary committee, to whom we prisoners swore an oath of secrecy and allegiance." He was killed in the uprising.

RUDOLF MASAREK

After Zelo Bloch had been transferred to Camp No. 2, the military command of the inmates' underground was taken over by Rudolf Masarek, who, like Bloch, had been an officer in the Czech army prior to the fall of Czechoslovakia; he had held the rank of lieutenant. Glazar remembers that when he had come to Treblinka he had been "twenty-eight years old, tall, blond, blue-eyed." They also recall that Masarek's family owned an exclusive men's shirts shop in Prague. Some accounts from Treblinka survivors spell Masarek's name as Masaryk. This erroneous spelling gave rise to the story that he had been a non-Jew and related to Thomas G. Masaryk, first President of the Czechoslovak Republic, and that he had voluntarily followed his Jewish wife to Treblinka. Actually, he was half-Jewish. His wife was a Jewish girl from Vienna whom he had married in October, 1942. Under Nazi law, this marriage put Masarek in the status of a full Jew. Together with his wife, Masarek went to Theresienstadt and from there to Treblinka.

Only six men from Masarek's entire transport were "selected" for work. The rest of the people who had arrived in Treblinka with him, including his wife, her mother, and his wife's thirteen-year old sister, were taken directly to the gas chambers.

According to Richard Glazar, Masarek played a key role in the planning and execution of the Treblinka uprising. Shalom Kohn remembers that Masarek manned the rebels' one machine gun and fired away at the Nazis from the roof of the camp's pigeon house. Masarek was killed in the uprising, but his mother and two sisters survived the war.

THE SURVIVORS

Over a million Jews from ten countries (Poland, Austria, Belgium, Bulgaria, Czechoslovakia, France, Germany, Greece, the Soviet Union and Yugoslavia) and from 150 cities and towns crossed the gates of Treblinka to disappear forever in ashes and smoke. Only 1,000 were still alive when the uprising on August 2, 1943 put an end to the infamous death factory. But of these, only 200 managed to break through to freedom on that day. And of these in turn, only some 60 survived the war to tell the horror story of Treblinka. The Yad Vashem has in its archives about fifty testimonies of Treblinka survivors, most of them facsimiles of material in the files of the Jewish Historical Institute in Warsaw. Many of them testified at different trials: the Nuremberg trial, the Eichmann trial, the two Treblinka trials. Out of this material six eyewitness stories were selected for this volume giving a most-panoramic and least-repetitious picture of Treblinka.

When I approached some of the survivors for authentic details about Treblinka, their reaction was by far not as enthusiastic as I had expected. Samuel Rajzman was willing and cordial. I spent two days with him in his cozy apartment in Montreal, and Treblinka came alive for us with hundreds of authentic details and allusions that only personal experience can give. He also gave me the sketch for the map which is attached to this volume.

Not everybody was so friendly. It took me a great deal of effort to convince the non-committal and suspicious Samuel Willenberg in Israel that I am not "another Steiner" who was out to take advantage of the survivors in order to manufacture a distorted account of Treblinka.

Some simply did not answer my inquiries. Below are recorded the available data on the survivors and, in parentheses, passages from such testimony as they gave of their experiences in Treblinka. They are anything but complete.

Czeslaw Augustyniak. Now living in Sweden.

(About August Miete, the "Angel of Death": "He was all over like a shadow, the 'Angel of Death.' Coldbloodedly he would select his victims and finish them off at the *lazaret!* One could see him return with a contented look on his face.")

Oskar Berger. Businessman from Czechoslovakia. Moved to Kielce early in World War II, and, with his wife and son, was deported to Treblinka in July, 1942. His wife and son were killed on the first day. In September, 1942, Berger escaped, hidden beneath a pile of prisoners' clothing that was being shipped to Germany. Arrested again in July, 1943, he was taken to Buchenwald, where he survived the war.

("The work was supervised by SS men who held a pistol or truncheon in one hand, a whiskey bottle in the other. Even now my memory stands aghast at the picture of little children seized by their feet and dashed against tree trunks.")

Abraham Bomba, barber, now living in Israel.

("In front of the entrance to the 'beauty salon' were the quarters of the so-called *Goldjuden*. There, each woman was ordered to lie down on a special examining table. They had to take off all their clothing, and their vaginas were searched. After this inspection the women were led, single file, into the 'beauty salon,' where their hair was clipped off close to the scalp by the barbers, who used small scissors for the work.")

Gustav Boraks (b. 1901), "barber" at Treblinka, now a barber in Israel.

("The barber shop was located in the barrack where the women had to undress. There were five benches and 20 barbers. The women disrobed in one room, stepped in through a door, had their hair cut off and then stepped out through another door into the gas chamber. We had one minute to grab the hair, make one single snip with the scissors, and that was that.")

Henoch Brener, now living in the United States. ("The transport consisted of 60 boxcars. In each car there were from 100 to 200 persons. Men, women, children—everybody went together. We traveled for 48 hours and one night, and all this time we did not receive one single drop of water.")

Chaim Ciechanowski, Buenos Aires.

Leizer Ciechanowski, Buenos Aires.

Josef Czarny (b. 1927), deported to Treblinka from Warsaw. Now a trade union clerk in Israel.

("I was fifteen years old and very poor. My entire family had died from starvation. I was hungry, so I went to the *Umschlagplatz* of my own free will so that I might receive the three kilograms of bread and one kilogram of marmalade promised [to those who reported voluntarily]. We were placed into cattle cars like so many salted fish. We drank our own sweat and urine. In the camp, I hid out in the barrack. I was small and thin, so the comrades gave me an extra pair of pants [to wear over my own prison clothing] so I would look heavier.")

Aaron Czechowicz. Arrived in Treblinka on September 9, 1942. He is now living in Caracas, Venezuela.

Jacob Domb. Now living in Israel.

Jacob Eisner. Escaped from Treblinka with Moshe Rappaport, January, 1943. Now living in Israel.

(About Kurt Franz, "The Doll": "Franz said to one of the inmates: 'Let's have a boxing match.' The latter had been a professional prizefighter in Cracow. The boxing gloves were put on the prisoner's hands. Franz had only one glove. on his right hand. A little gun was concealed in that glove. 'Start!' the SS man commanded. He moved toward the young prisoner, pretending that he was about to start the match, and fired straight into his face. The poor fellow collapsed and died on the spot.")

Pinchas Epstein (b. 1925). Now living in Israel.

("I was deported from Czestochowa on September 22, 1942. I was then 18 years old. For eleven months I carried corpses in Camp No. 2. . . . After the revolt I escaped [and returned] to my home town, got myself Aryan papers and enrolled as a Gentile for work in Germany. I arrived in Israel in July, 1948.")

Leon Finkelstein, Now a butcher in Paris.

("I arrived in Treblinka on July 22, 1942. As they chased the victims to the gas chambers, the Ukrainians Ivan and Nicholas cut off the women's breasts with swords.")

Aron Gelbard. Now living in Israel.

Richard Glazar (b. 1920). Now an engineer in Switzerland. Born in Prague, he was accepted at the University of Prague in 1939. In September, 1942 he was deported to Theresienstadt and the following month was taken to Treblinka in a passenger train, together with his close friend Karel Unger. He participated in the Treblinka uprising and managed to escape. Together with Unger he made his way across Poland to Czechoslovakia, and from there to Mannheim, Germany, where they worked as Gentiles in a German factory. After the war, he returned to Prague.

After the 1968 revolt in Czechoslovakia he escaped to Switzerland.

Szymon Goldberg (b. 1914). A Warsaw-born cabinet maker. Died in 1976.

Abraham Goldfarb. Now living in Israel.

Zygmunt Gostynski. Now living in Israel.

Sonia Grabinski. Now living in Israel.

("Stern [a fellow inmate] refused to name a comrade who had given us some money. He was killed by Franz.")

Tanhum Grinberg. See "The Revolt in Treblinka," p. 214 ff.

Eliahu Grinsbach. Now an electrician in Israel.

Yosef Gross. Now a machinist in Israel.

Shlomo Hellman. Now living in Israel.

("Whenever 'The Doll' came to the camp we knew there would be at least two dead.")

Jacob Jakubowicz. Present whereabouts unknown.

("'The Doll' couldn't sit down to breakfast or dinner without having knocked off at least two Jews.")

Kalman Jankowski.

Judah Kelin.

Shalom Kohn (Stanislaw Kon). See "The Treblinka Revolt," pp. 224 ff.

Abe Kon.

Jacob Koszycki.

Arie (Alexander) Kudlik. Now a draftsman in Israel.

("I remember Langner, a businessman from Czestochowa, on whom money was found. He was stripped naked and tortured by SS men. When he fainted, cold water was poured on him and the beatings continued. Finally they hanged him by his feet on the gallows. He was left hanging there about two hours for attempting to instigate a revolt. Eventually he was shot by an SS man.")

Lachman.

(About August Miete: "We were literally starving. A youngster near me found a can of sardines and tried to open it. At that moment, the 'Angel of Death' suddenly appeared. He was skulking around, with his head lowered and a smile on his brutal face. He had caught the thief red-handed. He chased the youngster to the *lazaret*. The boy's father, who was working nearby, pleaded with him, 'Take me in his place ... Let him live.' Miete thereupon killed both the father and the son."

Moszek (Mietek) Laks. Now living in Israel.

Leon Lewi.
Sonia Lewkowicz (b. 1922). Now a secretary in Israel.
Abraham Lindwasser (b. 1909). Now living in Israel. He was deported to Treblinka from Warsaw on August 28, 1942. After the uprising, he hid out in the woods, then volunteered for the Polish army. He emigrated to Israel in 1948.
("They made me a 'dentist.' I could not stand it, so I tried to hang myself. I was already swinging on my belt when a Jew with a beard—I don't know his name—took me down and chided me. [He said that] someone at least should survive it all, to describe later on what was going on here.")
Moshe Luck.
Markus.
M. Mitelberg.
Moshe Pacanowski. Now living in Israel.
Marek Petakowsky.
Maniek Platkiewicz. Now living in Israel.
("A youngster stole some wood in order to warm up a little 'coffee' for his comrades. SS man Stadie killed him for 'sabotage.'")
Moshe Porzecki.
("I arrived in Treblinka in a transport of 6,000 men, women and children. We were met by a crowd of SS men and Ukrainians, all armed. We got off the train. In the rush whoever happened to turn around or look behind him was beaten up at once. Women and children were led away in one direction, men in the other. We had to get on our knees. Whoever tried to get up was shot immediately. No resistance was possible. There was no help for us.")
Henryk Poswolski (Pazovalski). From Warsaw, now living in Rio de Janeiro.
("Franz . . . ran through the camp and hit the unfortunate workers in their faces with his whip. At night, during roll call, he made them step out of the ranks and turned them over to Miete, the 'Angel of Death,' who killed them with a bullet in the neck. One day SS man Küttner threw a baby into the air and Franz killed it with two shots from his gun. . . . About March, 1943, the camp was visited by Himmler. At 4 p.m. the whole camp crew and the Jewish workers were assembled in the roll call square, and a report was accepted by SS man Kiewe. He in turn reported to the camp commandant, who then reported to Himmler.")

Henryk Rajchman (Yechiel M. Reichman). Now living in Uruguay.

("The cremation of the corpses was begun on a larger scale only after January, 1943 when a new chief, who was a specialist in the cremation of corpses, arrived at Camp No. 2.")

Jerzy (Georg) Rajgrodzki. Born in Siedlce, he settled in Warsaw where he worked as a draftsman. Deported to Treblinka, he spent 11 months in the "Totenlager," participated in the revolt. Now living in West Germany.

Samuel Rajzman. See "The End of Treblinka," p. 231 ff.

Meir Rak.

Moshe Rappaport. Escaped from Treblinka with Jacob Eisner in January, 1943. He is now living in the United States.

("The doors of the cars open. A horde of SS hurl themselves on us. My wife is pregnant; she cannot run. Our little boy of 11 is with us. An SS man fires at my wife. She falls. Then he fires at the kid.")

Rojtman.

("My old parents, my three sisters, my three brothers and my brother-in-law—they all were murdered at the [camp] entrance. Shots, whistle of whips—all this in a matter of a few minutes.")

Berek Rojzman (b. 1910). Now a butcher in Warsaw. Rojzman is the only Treblinka survivor to have remained in Poland. Before the war he lived in Grodzisk Mazowiecki. In 1939 he joined the Polish army and fought against the German invaders. After the fall of Poland he went to Warsaw and then to Biala Rawska. In November, 1942 he was deported to Treblinka with his wife and two-year-old son. His wife and son were killed, but Rojzman, over six feet tall, survived. He was not one of the organizers of the uprising but fought in it, then hid out in the woods for more than one year. After the war he married a Gentile woman, the widow of one of his friends, and settled in Warsaw.

Eliahu Rosenberg. Now living in Israel.

After the uprising he escaped, tried to join a partisan unit, was turned down but was accepted by another group. He enlisted in the Polish army and was discharged in November, 1946. When asked whether he still thought about Treblinka, he replied, "I don't think about it; it's in me, like an indelible tattoo."

("I was 18 when I arrived in Treblinka with my mother and my three sisters. Until the day of the revolt I saw nothing but the sky and the sand, sky and sand, and corpses on the ground.")

Wolf Shneiderman. Now a butcher in New York City.

Joseph Siedlecki. Now maitre d'hôtel at Grossinger's, Grossinger, New York. Born in Warsaw, Siedlecki, a man over six feet tall, was in the Polish army when World War II began. Participated in the revolt.

With Gentile papers, he was able to obtain employment with a Polish construction unit attached to the German *Wehrmacht*. After the war he married a German woman named Erika, who converted to Judaism and emigrated with him to the United States.

Oscar Strawczynski. Died in Montreal in 1972.

("Your Honors: I was waiting for this moment for 20 years. I will recognize them [i.e., the Treblinka Nazis] always, and over and over again.")

Zygmunt Strawczynski. Died in Montreal in 1975.

Henryk Sperling. Deported from Czestochowa in September, 1942. Now living in Glasgow, Scotland.

Bronka Sukno. Now living in Israel.

("A transport arrives, a gang of SS is there. A little girl is holding a doll. SS man Suchomel wants to grab it from her; the mother protects the child. One shot, she falls. . . .")

Wolf Szejnberg. Now living in France.

Jacob Szmulowicz. Now living in Israel.

Haim Sztajer. Now living in Australia.

("For eleven long months I had to carry my dead fellow-Jews on my shoulders to the mass graves. Inside myself I carried one great prayer—not to die before I would be able to commit some slight act of revenge against the murderers of my people. One day I suddenly heard voices from inside the gas chamber. It seemed that four boys from Warsaw had survived inside the gas chamber because there hadn't been enough gas to kill them. They heard us talking in Yiddish and, through the walls, they told us the story of the uprising that took place in the Warsaw ghetto. It seemed to us as if death itself had acquired speech and spoke to us from inside the chamber and boasted of the heroism of the Jews.")

Kalman Taigman. Now living in Israel.

(Testimony at the Eichmann trial in Jerusalem, 1961: "Your Honors: The way in which facts are being presented here, one might come to the conclusion that the 700,000 Treblinka deportees were not gassed by the SS men but all [simply] committed suicide! . . .")

Mieczyslaw Tobias.

Eugen Turowski (b. 1914). Now living in Israel.

Karel (Charles) Unger. Now a chemical engineer in California. He was 21 when he came to Treblinka in October, 1942 from Theresienstadt. His entire family was killed. (See also Richard Glazar).

Szyja Warszawski. Arrived in Treblinka on July 23, 1942.

("Large-scale cremations began late in February, 1943. The ashes were thrown into the ditches from which the corpses had been exhumed. Vetch was sown and saplings from the woods were planted on the surface to camouflage these spots.")

Wasser.

Jankiel Wiernik. See "One Year in Treblinka," p. 147 ff.

Samuel Willenberg. See "I Survived Treblinka," p. 189 ff.

Ziegelman.

JUSTICE
IN DÜSSELDORF

JUSTICE IN DÜSSELDORF

The closing section of this volume consists of verbatim excerpts from the judgments (Urteilsbegründung) *handed down by the German courts in the trials of the Treblinka defendants. West Germany's slowness and leniency in dealing with these criminals had been a disappointment for many who hoped that the old Germany had yielded place to a "new" Germany of true justice and humanity. Men of good will throughout the world were distressed by the decision of the West German government to abolish the death penalty; some felt that this new legislation had been motivated by the desire to protect from execution those Nazi criminals who may yet be caught. According to figures supplied by the Main Office of Investigation of Nazi Crimes in Ludwigsburg, a total of 85,802 persons were investigated in connection with Nazi crimes since 1945; 6,440 persons were sentenced for Nazi and war crimes by West German courts. Only 166 received the maximum sentence of life imprisonment. As of June 30, 1979, there were still 3,078 cases under investigation.*

However, another 9,700 proceedings had to be discontinued because the accused could not be located, because there had been insufficient evidence, or because the defendants had either died or were considered too ill to stand trial. Kurt Franz was permitted to live unmolested in his native city for 14 years before he was finally arrested, and his immediate superior, Franz Stangl, though officially registered with the Austrian consulate in São Paulo, could not be "located" until 1967, or 22 years after the fall of Nazi Germany.

When the accused were finally brought to trial, the German machinery of justice did everything imaginable to help the defendants. Prosecutors, investigators, judges and defense attorneys missed no legal trick, no device of sophistry or hypocrisy to strengthen the position of the defendants, to harass and discourage the witnesses for the prosecution, and to hamstring the efforts of the honest public servants who wanted to see justice done. The very framework of the court procedure was designed to confine the trials to strictly personal guilt rather than emphasize the Nazi crimes in the context of history; the court stressed individual standards rather than the collective moral responsibility of the Nazi defendants. Behind the facade of court trials, everything was done to protect the Nazi criminals and to promote their reintegration into German society. When the crimes of these individuals were brought to the attention of the public, there was no reaction of collective outrage, no St. Bartholomew catharsis, only a collective effort to forget the past.

Nevertheless, the significance of the Nazi trials must not be underrated. With proverbial German thoroughness, the West German authorities collected a wealth of factual material. The documentary evidence gathered by the prosecution and rec-

orded by the courts is overwhelming and confirms basic historical facts which can neither be refuted nor obliterated. It represents the official German seal attesting to the authenticity of facts which seem unbelievable. It is with this in mind that the excerpts quoted in this section have been selected.

EXCERPTS FROM JUDGMENTS (URTEILSBEGRÜNDUNG)

Passed on September 3, 1965 in the trial of Kurt Franz and nine others at the Court of Assizes in Düsseldorf (First Treblinka Trial) (AZ-LG Düsseldorf: II-931638, p. 49 ff.), and the trial of Franz Stangl at the Court of Assizes at Düsseldorf (Second Treblinka Trial) on December 22, 1970 (pp. 111 ff., AZ-LG Düsseldorf, XI-148/69 S.)[1]

Number of Persons Killed at the Treblinka Extermination Camp:

At least 700,000 persons, predominantly Jews, but also a number of Gypsies, were killed at the Treblinka extermination camp.

These findings are based on the expert opinion submitted to the Court of Assizes by Dr. Helmut Krausnick, director of the Institute for Contemporary History (*Institut für Zeitgeschichte*) in Munich. In formulating his opinion, Dr. Krausnick consulted all the German and foreign archival material accessible to him and customarily studied in historical research. Among the documents he examined were the following: (1) the so-called Stroop Report, a report by SS Brigadeführer Jürgen Stroop[2] dealing with the destruction of the Warsaw ghetto. This report consists of three parts; namely, an introduction, a compilation of daily reports and a collection of photographs; (2) the record of the trial of the major war criminals before the International Military Tribunal in Nuremberg, and (3) the official transportation documents (train schedules, telegrams and train inventories)[3] relevant to the transports to Treblinka. The latter documents, of which only a part were recovered after the war, were the subject of the trial and were made available to Dr. Krausnick by the Court of Assizes.

Dr. Krausnick's report includes the following information:

According to the Stroop Report a total of approximately 310,000 Jews were transported in freight trains from the Warsaw ghetto to Treblinka during the period from July 22, 1942 to October 3, 1942. Approximately another 19,000 Jews made the same journey during the period from January, 1943 to the middle of May, 1943. During the period from August 21, 1942 to August 23, 1943, additional transports of Jews arrived at the Treblinka extermination camp, likewise by freight train, from other Polish cities, including Kielce, Międzyrzec, Łuków, Włoszczowa, Sędziszów, Częstochowa, Szydłowiec, Łochów, Kozienice, Białystok, Tomaszów, Grodno and Radom. Other Jews, who lived in the vicinity of Treblinka, arrived at Treblinka in horse-drawn wagons and in trucks, as did Gypsies, including some from countries other than Poland. In addition, Jews from Germany and other European countries, including Austria, Czechoslovakia, Bulgaria, Yugoslavia and Greece were transported to Treblinka, predominantly in passenger trains.

It has not been possible, of course, to establish the exact number of people transported to Treblinka in this fashion, because only part of the transportation documents, particularly those relevant to the railroad transports, are available. Still, assuming that each of the trains consisted of an average of 60 cars, with each freight car holding an average total of 100 persons and each passenger car an average total of 50 (i.e., that each freight train might have carried an approximate total of 6,000, and each passenger train an approximate total of 3,000 Jews to Treblinka), the total number of persons transported to Treblinka in freight trains and passenger trains might be estimated at approximately 271,000. This total would not include the approximately 329,000 Jews from Warsaw. Actually, however, these figures in many instances were much larger than the ones cited above. Besides, many additional thousands of Jews—and also Gypsies—arrived in Treblinka in horse-drawn wagons and on trucks. Accordingly, it must be assumed that the total number of Jews from Warsaw, from other parts of Poland, from Germany and from other European countries, who were taken to Treblinka, plus the total of at least 1,000 Gypsies who shared the same fate, amounted to far more than 700,000, even if one considers that several thousands of people were subsequently moved from Treblinka to other camps and that several hundred inmates succeeded in escaping from the camp, especially during the revolt of August 2, 1943. In view of the foregoing, it would be scientifically admissible to estimate the total number of persons killed in Treblinka at a minimum of 700,000.[4]

The Court of Assizes sees no reason to question the opinion of this expert, who is known in the scholarly world for his studies on the National Socialist persecution of the Jews. The expert opinion he has submitted is detailed, thorough, and therefore convincing. . . .

The expert's estimate of an average of 100 Jews per freight car arriving at Treblinka is, if anything, not too high but much too conservative, because many of the Jewish witnesses have testified before the Court of Assizes that the number of persons in the cars in which they had been transported to Treblinka had been far in excess of 100. According to the testimony of several trustworthy Jewish witnesses, some of the freight trains included French freight cars, which were larger than corresponding German and Polish rolling stock; these cars had an average passenger load of approximately 200. This fact was confirmed also by the witness Franz Z.,[5] a high administrative official with the Polish railroads, who had served as dispatcher at the Treblinka station from 1941 to 1945. He clearly remembers that most of the transport trains consisted of 60 freight cars, including some French cars, that each of the cars had the number of passengers within marked with chalk on the outside, and that these numbers ranged between 120 and 200. In view of the foregoing, there can be no doubt as to the accuracy of the opinion submitted by the expert, Dr. Krausnick, regarding the number of people killed at Treblinka.

Description of the Treblinka Extermination Camp:

The Treblinka extermination camp was intended primarily for the extermination of the Jews from the Warsaw ghetto; however, Jews from other parts of Poland and other European countries were also killed there. As evident from a letter dated July 7, 1942, and addressed by Dr. [Irmfried] Eberl, the first commandant of the camp, to the Commissioner for the Jewish Residential District of Warsaw, the camp had been set up by the summer of 1942 and was ready for operation on July 11, 1942. It was situated on an elongated, wooded elevation. This location had been selected because of its natural topography, which made the camp invisible both from the Kosów-Małkinia highway running parallel with the camp's northern boundary and from the Siedlce-Małkinia railroad line running parallel with the camp's western edge. The entire camp area, approximately 600 meters long and approximately 400 meters wide, was surrounded by a barbed wire fence approximately 3 to 4 meters high, which had been camouflaged with brushwood. Immediately behind this fence was a ditch approximately 3 meters wide, behind which in turn there was a completely bare strip of land approximately 40 to 50 meters wide. This strip of land was marked off from the surrounding area by barbed wire and "Spanish horses" resembling anti-tank obstacles. At each of the four corners of the camp were watchtowers approximately 8 meters high. Some of them had searchlights; all of them were manned by Ukrainian guards day and night. Originally, an additional watchtower had been set up at the southern edge of the camp, midway between the two corner towers, but this structure was subsequently moved into the center of the so-called "Death Camp" (*Totenlager*).

The layout of the camp was altered several times as the months went by. The camp may be divided into three areas of approximately equal dimensions:

a) Living quarters (*Wohnlager*)
b) Reception area (*Auffangslager*)
c) "Death Camp" (*Totenlager*)

The living quarters and the reception area together were also described as the "Lower Camp."

The sector described as "living quarters" included barracks for the German camp staff, administrative areas such as the office, infirmary, warehouses, workshops and farm buildings, quarters for the Ukrainian guard details, annexes, and finally, clearly separated and sealed off from the rest of the area by a barbed wire fence, the so-called ghetto. The ghetto contained the dormitory barracks and the work rooms, as well as the roll call square (*Appellplatz*) for the "work Jews" (*Arbeitsjuden*) and the "court Jews" (*Hofjuden*).

A railroad siding of approximately 300 meters branched off from the railroad tracks running alongside the western edge of the camp. This siding ran through a special gate into the reception area, where it terminated at a long unloading platform, which eventually was expanded to resemble a regular station platform. In front of the platform, off to one side, at the right, was the large sorting barrack in which the valuables, particularly the clothes and shoes, taken from the Jews on their arrival, were stored until they could be shipped to the SS Central Distribution and Administration Office (*SS Wirtschafts- und Verwaltungshauptamt*). Sometime during the Christmas season of 1942 a part of the sorting barrack was fitted up to look like a railroad station building, complete with a station clock, ticket windows, posted train schedules and arrival and departure signs. The intention was to give the arriving Jews the impression that they had stopped at a transit camp from which they would be moved on to their final destination.

In front of that part of the platform not occupied by the sorting barrack and the station there was a wide open square. After getting off the train, the Jews would be led across this square through a gate to another enclosed space, the so-called distribution center (*Umschlagplatz*). To the left of the distribution center (*Umschlagplatz*) was the so-called "women's disrobing room." On the right there was a barrack of about the same size, which served for a time as a shelter and "disrobing room" for the Jewish males. Later on, however, this building was used solely as a storehouse for clothing and as a sorting barrack. Situated between this area and the southern boundary of the camp was the so-called sorting square (*Sortierplatz*), where the clothes taken off by the Jews upon their arrival, and the baggage they had brought with them, were sorted according to kind and quality. Initially, there was in the southwest corner of the camp, behind the large sorting barrack already noted, a huge ditch, in which the bodies of those Jews who had died during the journey would be burned together with the refuse that had accumulated on the train. To the east of the ditch was the so-called "hospital" (*lazaret*).

The "lazaret" was surrounded by a tall barbed wire fence, camouflaged with brushwood to screen it from view. Within this area, which could be reached by way of an entrance on the side facing the train platform, was a big ditch which served as a mass grave. The soil excavated from this ditch was piled up to form a mound approximately one meter high, directly on the right-hand longitudinal side of the ditch. A flame was burning in the ditch almost all the time. The *lazaret* area also contained a small booth that served as a shelter in bad weather, and a bench. In order to justify the designation of *lazaret* for this area—which, in reality was simply the place where people were killed by a bullet in the neck—the three Jewish inmates assigned to duty at the *lazaret* wore Red Cross armbands. The Jewish *kapo* K.[6] also wore a white surgical gown to make him look like a doctor. The Red Cross sign was prominently displayed on the booth mentioned above.

Leading from the women's "disrobing room" in the reception area to the upper part of the camp was a path popularly called "the tube" (*Schlauch*), "road of no return" (*Weg ohne Rückkehr*) or "road to heaven" (*Himmelfahrtstrasse, Himmelfahrtsallee*). This path, which was approximately 80 to 90 meters long and approximately 4.5 to 5 meters wide, ran for about 30 meters toward the east side of the camp, then made an almost 90-degree turn and terminated exactly in front of the central passage of the new gas chamber building in the "upper camp." The path was enclosed on either side with barbed wire fencing of more than a man's height; this fence, too, was so thickly camouflaged with brushwood that it was impossible to see through it from the outside.

299

The third large area of the camp, the "Upper Camp" or the "Death Camp" (*Totenlager*), occupied the southeastern sector of the camp. This was the part in which the actual destruction of the Jewish individuals took place. It was partitioned off completely from the rest of the camp by tall barbed wire fences camouflaged with brushwood. Such passageways as existed to the "Upper Camp" were provided with special screens to conceal the area. At the western limits facing the sorting square there was a high mound of soil, covered with grass, to further conceal the existence of the camp from unauthorized persons.

At the core of the "Death Camp" (*Totenlager*) were the gas chambers, in which the Jews were killed by the exhaust fumes produced by a running Diesel engine. When the mass killings first began, there was only the so-called "old gas house." This massive brick structure, set atop a foundation of concrete, contained three gas chambers, each of them approximately 4 × 4 meters in area and approximately 2.6 meters high, a chamber for the Diesel engine, and the power plant that supplied the lighting for the entire camp. Each of the chambers opened onto a wooden passage built in front of the structure. Several steps led to this passage, from which doors approximately 1.80 meters high and approximately 90 centimeters wide led into the gas chambers. The chambers were constructed much like air raid shelters; when the doors were closed, the chambers were hermetically sealed. On the opposite wall of each chamber were trap doors made of thick wooden planks. Approximately 2.50 meters wide and approximately 1.80 meters high, these trap doors could be opened from the outside like modern garage doors. They opened onto a concrete platform which completely circled the building and which was approximately 70 centimeters above the ground. The floors of the gas chambers were tiled and slanted toward the platform. The walls, too, were set with tiles, at least up to a certain height. On the ceiling of each chamber there were pipes and shower heads to create the impression that the chambers were showers. Actually, however, the pipes served to introduce into the chambers the exhaust fumes produced by the Diesel engine in the engine room. The chambers did not have lighting fixtures of their own.

Soon after the camp had begun operations, it became clear that the capacity of the old gas house was not sufficient for the smooth liquidation of the transports of Jews arriving at the camp each day. Therefore, late in August or early in September, 1942, construction was begun on a new, large gas house containing more and bigger gas chambers than the older building. These chambers were completed and ready for use within about one month.

Like its older counterpart, this building, which was set at the junction of the "tube" (Schlauch) and the old gas house, was a massive brick structure set on a foundation of concrete. Five wide stone steps, lined with flower bowls, led up to the front entrance of the building. Inside, there was a wide passage, on either side of which there were doors leading directly into the gas chambers. . . .

The capacity of the new gas chambers was approximately double that of the chambers in the old gas house. Probably, then, the new gas chambers were approximately 8 meters long, 4 meters wide, and 2 meters high. The witnesses also differed with one another regarding the exact number of gas chambers in the new building. From the very outset, all the defendants agreed that there had been six chambers, while all the Jewish witnesses stated that there had been 10. The Court of Assizes was unable to determine the correct number. On the one hand, the fact that more and bigger gas chambers were required for a more efficient extermination process would support the testimony of the Jewish witnesses. But on the other hand there is no good reason to assume that defendants should have wanted to conceal the truth on a point which would not have altered the extent of their culpability, especially so since it is the impression of the Court that they made every effort throughout the trial to adhere to the truth in their descriptions of conditions at the camp.

The arrangement and fittings of the new gas chambers, including the doors and the trap doors, largely correspond to those in the chambers of the old building. At the end of the passage, which ran straight from the front to the rear of the building, was the engine room containing the Diesel engine that produced the gas. The gable on the front wall of the building bore a large Star of David. The entrance was screened by a heavy, dark curtain, which apparently had been taken from a synagogue and bore the following legend in the Hebrew script and language: "This is the gate through which the righteous shall enter."

The bodies of the Jews killed in the gas chambers were piled into huge mass graves, in which they were laid out in rows, each layer of corpses being covered with a thin sprinkling of sand or calcium chloride. Witnesses at the trial could not agree on the number and dimensions of the mass graves. However, some idea of the dimensions of these ditches can be obtained from the testimony of the defendant S., according to whom at least one of the ditches contained no less than approximately 80,000 corpses.

Initially, the corpses were transported to the mass graves in small-gauge railway cars. These cars were moved by inmates running in double-time tempo. As a result, there were frequent breakdowns when the cars jumped the tracks. Consequently, this mode of transportation was soon abandoned. For a time, the inmates were ordered to carry the bodies by hand to the mass graves, but later the arrangement was that teams of two inmates each would load one or two corpses at a time onto a wooden stretcher which they would carry, running in double-time tempo, to the mass grave. The corpses were then tipped into the mass grave, where they were neatly laid out by another labor detail.

In the spring of 1943 a basic change in the disposal of the corpses was instituted. The corpses were no longer buried but cremated. After various methods of cremation had been tested, a large grill was erected. It consisted of concrete pillars, each approximately 70 centimeters high, supporting 5–6 rails taken from railroad tracks, each approximately 25 to 30 meters long and arranged in close proximity to one another. The fire was lit directly underneath these rails, which thus served as a grill on which the bodies of the Jews killed in the gas chambers, 2,000 to 3,000 at one time, would be placed and cremated.

When this system was found to be working well, the corpses buried in the mass graves during the preceding months were exhumed with the aid of huge mechanical excavators and also cremated in the manner described above.

The ashes from the cremations were checked for bone particles, then mixed with soil and buried, or used to fill up the mass graves that had been excavated. Larger bone particles that turned up were pulverized or thrown back into the fire. The terrain from which the mass graves had been excavated was leveled and seeded with lupine to conceal every trace of the mass killings. . . .

Jews assigned to duty in the "Upper Camp" were also housed there, in an area surrounded and sealed off from the rest of the sector by a barbed wire fence. In addition to the housing, there were conveniences such as a kitchen, laundry room, and so forth. As in the "Lower Camp," so here, too, in addition to the male "work Jews," there was a special women's detail which primarily attended to the laundry of the inmates. This women's detail consisted of about 15 to 20 females.

The camp staff of Treblinka, which was responsible for the smooth performance of the mass killings, consisted of about 35 to 40 Germans, all of whom wore the field-gray uniform of the *Waffen-SS*. None of them held a rank lower than *SS Unterscharführer*. They came either from the *Waffen SS* or from the regular SS but some of them had previously served with the police. The male nurses and craftsmen among them had obtained practical experience in euthanasia operations performed at various euthanasia institutions. As a rule, the members of the German camp staff carried pistols and, on special occasions, also submachine guns. In addition, they all carried long leather whips.

In addition to this group of Germans who made up the camp staff, there were about 90 to 120 Ukrainian auxiliary servicemen, who were assigned mainly to guard duty, but who sometimes also had to assist in the mass killings. As distinct from the Germans, these men wore black uniforms and were armed with carbines or rifles. Most of them carried long leather whips and some also had side-arms. Furthermore, guard details could use machine guns and hand grenades which were stored in a special armory. In addition, Treblinka had an armored patrol vehicle.

The chief of the entire camp staff, who was responsible for the management of the whole camp area, was the camp commandant. He was assisted by an Unterführer, who acted as his adjutant or deputy. The administrative work was done in the office under the direction of an office manager. A Stabscharführer was in charge of the division of labor and supervised the actual work. In addition there was one chief officer for the "Lower Camp" and one for the "Upper Camp," each of whom was responsible for the smooth operation of the camp machinery in his province.

The other members of the German camp staff were assigned to duties as required by the operation of the camp at any given time, but they never had to perform physical work. In almost every instance they acted as foremen of labor details. They supervised the work of the Ukrainian auxiliary servicemen as well as that of the permanent Jewish labor details, the so-called "work Jews."

The Ukrainian squads were divided into platoons commanded by ethnic

Germans (*Volksdeutsche*). The Ukrainians were primarily engaged in guard duty, not only at the borders of the camp and on the watchtowers, but also, under the direction of the German detail foremen, with the various labor details working inside and outside the camp. In addition, they assisted in the reception and processing of newly-arrived transports.

The first commandant of the Treblinka extermination camp was SS Obersturmführer *Dr. med.* Irmfried Eberl, who was to die by his own hand in 1948. He was relieved of his command only a few weeks after the inception of the killings—probably late in August or early in September, 1942—because he was not equal to his duties. Conditions at his camp were indescribable because he kept on sending new Jews to be killed before the bodies of those killed in earlier operations had been removed, i.e., disposed of. Thus, the first sight the new Jewish arrivals saw as they got off the train at Treblinka was piles of corpses, partly in advanced stages of decomposition, so that they understood at once what was in store for them. As a result, it was extremely difficult to process them. . . .

Dr. Eberl was succeeded by SS Obersturmführer (later SS Hauptsturmführer) Franz Stangl, who had been camp commandant at Sobibor. For a period of several weeks (late September until early October, 1942) Stangl's place was taken by an older police officer, Captain Sch----- of Dresden, but after that time he remained in Treblinka without interruption until August, 1943.

In the early afternoon of August 2, 1943, approximately 400 Jewish inmates from the "Lower" and "Upper" camps, including several women, armed with carbines, pistols, hand grenades and other weapons, overpowered the Ukrainians and German guards and escaped from the camp. However, the terrain around the camp was subsequently searched and many of the fugitives were killed. This uprising had been carefully planned for months in advance by a committee of several inmates, including the witnesses Samuel R[ajzman] and Jankiel W[iernik], and the *Kapo* K[urland]. One of the reasons why the revolt was staged on August 2, 1943 was that this had been a very hot day and many of the Ukrainians were absent from the camp, having gone to bathe in the River Bug. The Jewish inmates had procured their weapons by bribing Ukrainians with cash and valuables; they had broken into the ammunition bunker with the aid of a picklock to obtain ammunition. Only about 100 Jews still remained in the camp. During the revolt the Jews, before escaping, poured gasoline on numerous camp buildings and set fire to them, so that the buildings were destroyed. However, both the old and the new gas chambers remained intact. For this reason the inmates who arrived at Treblinka after August 2, 1943 could be destroyed in the large gas house as before.

Stangl remained at the camp for another few days after the revolt. During the first half of August, 1943, he was transferred to Upper Italy. He was succeeded at Treblinka by the defendant Franz, who had been promoted to the rank of SS Untersturmführer on June 21, 1943 and who remained in charge of the camp until its final liquidation late in November, 1943.

While the Germans and Ukrainians on the camp staff, with few exceptions, performed only guard and supervisory functions, the physical tasks were performed only by Jews. A larger number of Jewish workers were always kept on reserve at the camp for this purpose; they would be selected from the transports as they arrived, and their ranks would be augmented whenever the need arose.

These "work Jews" were divided into groups according to the type of work they performed. Thus, in the "Lower Camp," there were, first of all, the "court Jews" (*Hofjuden*). This group included artisans such as tailors, locksmiths, blacksmiths, carpenters and cobblers but also the hairdressers and musicians who were assigned to the various workshops or played in the camp band.

The "gold Jews" (*Goldjuden*) worked at gathering, sorting and packing cash, foreign currency, jewelry and other valuables brought by the inmates. They were identified by a yellow cloth badge sewn onto their clothing. The members of the "blue group," identified by blue cloth badges, assisted the newly-arrived Jews in getting off the trains at the unloading platform, removed the baggage that had been left in the cars and, after all the passengers had been taken off the train, gave the cars a thorough cleaning.

The largest group among the "work Jews" was the sorting detail, whose members wore red badges. The function of this group was to gather up the belongings the new arrivals had left on the unloading platform, including the clothing they had taken off at the distribution center (*Umschlagplatz*), and to move them to the adjacent sorting square (*Sortierplatz*). There, they sorted the items, packed them and then either piled them up outdoors or sorted them neatly in the large sorting barrack for shipment. There were other labor details, too, of varying numerical strength, assigned to a variety of projects, such as road building, work on the camp farm, construction and maintenance of camp buildings, camouflaging of enclosures, care of the animals kept at the camp, and so forth.

In the "Upper Camp" there was, to begin with, the burial squad, which consisted of several hundred persons. The function of this unit was to remove the bodies of the dead Jews from the gas chambers and to take them to the place where the corpses would be disposed of. Initially, this meant transporting the bodies to the mass graves; later, it entailed removing the bodies to the grills in the manner already noted. There were other labor details, too, each with its own special duties; i.e., cleaning the gas chambers, laying out the corpses in the mass graves and, later, exhuming the corpses for cremation. Still other labor details attended to the cremation of the corpses on the grills, the sifting of the ashes, and the pulverization of bone particles found in the ashes.

A position of special importance in the "Upper Camp" was assigned to the so-called "dentists." As the corpses which had been removed from the gas chambers were transported to the mass grave (and later to the grills), the "dentists" checked each corpse for valuables, particularly dentures with gold teeth. If these were found on a corpse, the burial detail members bearing that corpse would be ordered to step to one side with the body so that the "dentists" could extract the gold teeth with large forceps. The "dentists" then cleaned the gold and sent it in lots to the collection depot for valuation. In many instances the inspection of the corpses was not confined to a search for dental gold but also entailed a checking of the rectums and, in women, of the vaginas, for other items of value.

Finally, the "Upper Camp," like the "Lower Camp," had a number of artisans to do occasional work, and a group of female inmates to attend to the laundry. Each Jewish labor detail was supervised by a Jewish kapo, who in turn reported to the SS man in charge. The kapo was assisted by an overseer, who acted as his deputy. In addition, each of the two camps had a chief kapo. Finally, each camp had a "camp elder" (*Lagerälteste*), who was the top Jewish inmate in the camp administration.

The chief kapo in the "Lower Camp" was the inmate B.; his counterpart in the "Upper Camp" was the inmate S. The first "camp elder" (*Lagerälteste*) was G[alewski], an engineer from Warsaw; he was succeeded by R[akowski], of Częstochowa. After R[akowski]'s death in May, 1943, G[alewski] took over again. These inmates, who had been assigned special functions, were responsible to the German camp administration for the strict enforcement of all orders and the smooth operation of the entire organization. For this reason they were exempt from day-to-day physical work and also exercised some disciplinary authority over their fellow inmates.

The living quarters for the "work Jews," whose numbers kept changing but probably averaged between 500 and 1,000, were very primitive. In both the "Lower" and the "Upper" camps these people were housed in special barracks, which were totally bare except for the wooden plank beds on which the inmates slept. During the night the inmates were locked in the barracks; toilet facilities consisted of a few buckets placed in the barracks for that purpose. However, these buckets were not adequate and before long the stench in the barracks became unbearable. There were no other sanitary facilities. Medical care and an infirmary were instituted only at a rather late date, and even these were grossly inadequate. The only cure that the camp administration had to offer to working inmates with serious illnesses was death dealt at the *lazaret* by a bullet in the neck.

The daily routine of the inmates began with reveille soon after sunrise. The usual cleanup of the barracks and a skimpy breakfast were followed by the first roll call of the day, the so-called "morning roll call." For this roll call the inmates had to line up in closed ranks, section by section. After a complicated counting procedure the Jewish camp elder reported the number of inmates on hand, the number of inmates sick, and so forth, to the *Unterführer* on duty for that day. That *Unterführer* in turn conveyed the report to the chief officer of the camp, who then passed the information to the camp commandant or the latter's deputy. After the report, the orders for the day were issued and the details marched off to their duties.

The working day lasted from early morning until the evening and was interrupted only by a lunch break of about an hour. At night, before the inmates returned to their living quarters, there was the evening roll call, which was dreaded by all the inmates. This affair was frequently dragged out over several hours. After a repetition of the morning's complicated counting procedure, the sick, the debilitated and the *Gestempelten*, i.e., those inmates who had been "stamped" or "marked" by welts or wounds from floggings or other causes during that day, were separated from the others and sent to the *lazaret* for liquidation. The evening roll call was also the time when corporal punishment was administered to inmates for whom floggings had been ordered, often on very flimsy pretexts such as reports that the inmate had not worked hard enough, had failed to give the proper salute to some Unterführer or did not know the "Treblinka Song."

This song, written by the defendant Franz, had been set to music on Franz's orders by [Arthur] Gold, the conductor of the orchestra in the "Lower Camp." Its text was as follows:

We look straight out at the world;
The columns are marching off to their work.
All we have left is Treblinka;
It is our destiny.

We heed the commandant's voice,
Obeying his every nod and sign.
We march along together
To do what duty demands.

Work, obedience and duty
Must be our whole existence,
Until we, too, will catch a glimpse at last
Of a modest bit of luck.

There were no standard specifications for corporal punishment. The floggings would be administered at the "Lower Camp" on a special whipping rack to which the inmate would be strapped. The lashes were given by members of the German camp staff, occasionally also by the Ukrainian guards, using the leather whips which were part of their personal gear. The victim was whipped on the buttocks—in many cases on the bared buttocks. Usually—depending on the seriousness of the alleged offense and on the mood of the SS man administering the punishment—the number of lashes ranged between 25 and 50, but in some cases there were more. The inmate had to count out each of the lashes aloud as they rained down on his body. If he lost count or if the pain stopped him from counting, the whole procedure was started all over again until he did it properly. Those inmates whose physical efficiency was impaired by the whippings would be transferred to the *lazaret* for liquidation, either immediately after the whipping or on the next morning when they were unable to report for work.

Even while they worked, the "work Jews" were in danger of their lives. There was always the chance that they might be whipped or otherwise abused, perhaps even shot or beaten to death, by their overseers on the most trivial pretext. The members of the supervisory staff could do with them as they pleased. If they summarily killed an inmate who for some reason had unfavorably attracted their attention, or sent him to the *lazaret* to be shot, they did not have to answer to anyone for their action.

Under these circumstances, it was only natural that the working inmates made every conceivable effort never to attract unfavorable attention and, above all, never to give the impression that they were sick. In view of the fact that these inmates had been completely exhausted by the heavy physical labor and enfeebled as the results of inadequate nourishment, the effort of holding out even for a limited period required maximum concentration.

Aside from these "separations" or "eliminations," as the liquidations of individual inmates were described in camp parlance, there also were frequent "selections" on a larger scale, made on a variety of pretexts. Thus, selections might be held when a temporary slowdown in the arrival of new transports left some of the work Jews unwanted because there was too little for them to do. Selections might also be held in retaliation for attacks on the guards, if a conspiracy was exposed, if inmates had attempted to escape, or for any number of other reasons.

The treatment meted out to the "work Jews" was essentially the same in both the "Lower" and the "Upper" camps. In the "Upper Camp," too, the customary roll calls were held, and abuses, "eliminations" and killings were the order of the day. However, unlike the "Lower Camp," the "Upper Camp" did not have a whipping rack for floggings. But the camp presented an entirely different picture when it came to "recreational activities." The German camp administration, with the approval of Inspector Christian Wirth, was anxious to provide its people with the sort of recreation during off-duty hours calculated to inspire them with renewed zest for their work. While the "Upper Camp" had only a small ensemble of three or four musicians, the "Lower Camp" had a regular orchestra consisting of about ten professional musicians under the baton of Arthur Gold, who had been a noted conductor in Poland before the war. This orchestra was assigned special hours for practice during which the players were excused from all other work. Later they were even outfitted with new uniforms, full-dress suits made of white and blue silk.

During the first few weeks of the camp's operations the orchestra was stationed near the "tube" (*Schlauch*), where it played lively operetta tunes to drown out the screams of the victims in the gas chambers. Later on this practice was stopped and the orchestra played marches and Polish or Jewish folk tunes mostly during the evening roll call. In 1943 the orchestra performed at several major functions (boxing matches, short plays, dances, etc.). These were macabre scenes, for even as these functions were going on, the flames from the cremation grills lit up the sky high above the camp. Entertainment of this type for the German camp staff was organized mostly by the defendant Franz. For some time during 1943 the transports were reduced; during that period marriage ceremonies between male and female inmates were arranged for the entertainment of the German camp staff, who encouraged these festivities with extra rations of food and drink.

For the German camp staff there was a canteen and plenty of hard liquor. As a result, German SS men frequently got drunk. The Germans also received excellent food, because the Jewish deportees would bring with them both fresh and canned groceries and delicacies, all of which they would be ordered to turn in before being led to the gas chambers. However, the nourishment obtained by the inmates, particularly at the "Lower Camp," was also not bad as long as transports continued to arrive, because then the working inmates were able to pocket some of the food turned in while they sorted out the clothing of the new arrivals. The German SS men at the camp enjoyed numerous perquisites. Their rooms were cleaned by female inmates. Their shoes were polished and their uniforms brushed and pressed. Their linens were washed at the camp laundry. Any special requests could be filled at the workshops in the camp where tailors, shoemakers, furriers, shirtmakers, locksmiths, etc. were employed. Thus, for example, every German SS man was entitled to one free hand-tailored civilian coat. Good fabrics, taken from the victims, were in ample supply.

Also, the German SS men working at the camp received a special bonus in addition to their regular pay. The amount of this bonus can no longer be determined.

There were at the camp two saddle horses and one draft horse, but only the defendant Franz availed himself of this opportunity for horseback riding. The horses were given the same painstaking care by the inmates as was Barry, the dog. The animals in the camp zoo (especially foxes, deer and other animals indigenous to Poland) were also carefully tended, and the zoo was fashioned into a little showplace for the enjoyment of the German SS men.

The German staff received a generous allowance of furloughs and days off. After they had completed their daily work shift, German SS men not assigned to night duty were permitted to leave the camp grounds without special formalities. Their days off afforded the staff opportunities for contacts with male and female staff members of the German Reserve Hospital in Ostrow, which was near Treblinka. Thus, the defendant Franz formed a friendship with Dr. St., the chief medical officer of that hospital, whom he addressed with the intimate *du*. In addition, he had a love affair with a German Red Cross nurse, the witness N., who was then working at the Ostrow hospital and with whom he once made a weekend trip to the southern part of East Prussia.

Every German SS man received two to three weeks' furlough at three-month intervals. Moreover, those Germans who had come to Treblinka from T-4[7] were given the option of spending their furloughs with their wives at the rest center maintained by T-4 at Lake Atter in Austria. . . .

How the Mass Killings Were Performed

The directions for the mass killings (the so-called "processing of transports") were set down in minute detail by [Odilo] Globocnik and his associates, particularly [Christian] Wirth, the inspector of the extermination camps of Belzec, Treblinka and Sobibor. Globocnik and particularly Wirth made repeated inspections to satisfy themselves that all their directives were followed in the mass killings.

The mass killings at Treblinka were carried out as follows in accordance with these directives. The Jews fated to be murdered were transported to Treblinka, mostly by train, from the ghettos of the Polish cities, particularly Warsaw, Częstochowa, Białystok and Kielce, but also from Germany and other parts of Europe. Only freight trains were used for transports from Poland. All these trains consisted of 50 to 60 cars. Since the unloading platform at the camp could accommodate no more than 20 cars at a time, 20 cars at a time would be detached from the train and pushed from the rear by a shunting engine over the siding to the camp's unloading platform, while the remaining cars of the train waited at the Treblinka station. The railroad employees and the train escorts, who for reasons of secrecy were absolutely forbidden admittance to the camp grounds, did not proceed beyond the station. As soon as a whistle from the engine pushing the uncoupled train section signalled the arrival of the cars at the camp, the guards and the Jewish labor details from the camp took their assigned places. Especially the administrative staff of the camp and, if possible, all the SS men, proceeded to the platform where some of the Ukrainians had already lined up.

After the cars had stopped at the camp's unloading platform the doors were opened and orders were shouted to the passengers to get off as quickly as possible with their luggage.

In order to encourage the impression among the new arrivals that Treblinka was merely a transfer point on their journey to employment elsewhere in the East, large signs had been placed on or near the unloading platform with the following text in German and Polish:

> Attention, Jews from Warsaw!
>
> You are now at a transit camp, from which you will continue your journey to labor camps.
>
> In order to prevent epidemics, clothing as well as luggage must be turned in for disinfection.
>
> Gold, cash, foreign currency and jewelry must be turned in at the ticket office. You will be given receipts for these valuables. Your valuables will be returned to you later, on presentation of your receipts.
>
> For reasons of personal cleanliness, all new arrivals must bathe before continuing the journey.

In many cases—at least during the early period of the mass killings—a member of the German camp staff would address the new arrivals gathered at the station landing. He would reiterate approximately the same directions printed on the signs. Next, he would request the old, the sick, the infirm and others unable to walk, to proceed to the *lazaret*—with assistance from members of the Jewish labor detail, if necessary—where he said that they would receive medical aid. Numerous people in the transports took this explanation at its face value and reported to the *lazaret* for treatment. But as soon as they arrived there, they were ordered to take off all their clothes. Next, they were ordered to sit together on the mound of soil piled up alongside the mass grave, or to lie down at the edge of the mass grave. Then they would be shot by the guards on duty at the *lazaret*. Initially, the killing was done by a bullet from a carbine or a rifle. Later, however, it was done exclusively with a bullet in the neck from a pistol. This was in accordance with orders from Wirth himself. He personally killed several Jews in the *lazaret* with a bullet in the neck to show the defendant M. how it should be done. Meanwhile, the victims seated together atop the mound were facing the mass grave and so were forced to watch the bodies of earlier victims burning and smoldering in the ditch before they themselves were killed. The shootings at the *lazaret* were always done by the German Unterführers. But when things were going full blast, Ukrainians might be drafted to lend a hand.

This barbaric method of killing was intended to accomplish a dual purpose. First, by being told that they would be given medical aid, the victims were encouraged to believe that the whole operation was merely one of resettlement. Secondly, the separation of the sick and the infirm from the others was meant to assure the smooth performance of the mass killings.

After they had got off the trains, those victims not eligible for special treatment in the *lazaret* were taken to an area between the women's disrobing barrack and the smaller sorting barrack. This area was called the "distribution center" (*Umschlagplatz*). By commands from the guards on duty in that area, accompanied by shouts, beatings and frequently also by random shots for added emphasis, the women and young children were separated from the men and adolescents. The former were herded into the "disrobing room" while the latter still remained in the distribution center. Next, all the new arrivals were ordered to undress; they were instructed to fold their clothes into small bundles, to tuck their stockings into their shoes, and to tie their shoes into pairs with bits of string handed to them for this purpose by a working inmate. At the same time the valuation process began: all cash, gold, jewelry and such valuables as fountain pens, eyeglasses, watches and so forth had to be handed over to the so-called "gold Jews," whose function it was to collect and valuate all these items.

After disrobing and giving up their valuables, the women at the head of the barrack had to pass through the so-called "beauty salon," where their hair was cut off by members of the "hairdresser detail." The hair was collected and, after proper treatment, sent to the SS Central Economic-Administrative Office (*SS Wirtschafts- und Verwaltungshauptamt*) along with the other personal effects collected from the new arrivals.

After passing through the "beauty salon," the women proceeded to the "tube" already described earlier. In many cases they were ordered to hurry up because "the water was getting cold." In that way they set out on their path to final destruction.

Meanwhile, another selection was made from among the males who had remained in the distribution center. The strongest and most vigorous among them were picked out and assigned to various labor details throughout the camp, either as replacements for other inmates or as additional workers. Initially, these selections offered the selectees only a very slight chance of survival, for once they had completed the work to which they had been assigned, they, too, would be killed. Only later on, when the camp administration came to realize the usefulness of experienced labor details in the smooth performance of the killings, and to understand that such well-trained workers also made the work of the guards easier, the "work Jews" had greater prospects of remaining alive at least a little longer.

The males and adolescents who were left for extermination after the selection were also herded into the "tube," which they had to enter by way of a special entrance at the head of the women's disrobing barrack.

From that stage on, both male and female victims received the same treatment. So that these people should have no time to think or to offer resistance, they were driven through the "tube" by guards stationed there, who struck out at them with canes, whips, rifle butts and with their fists to hurry them along. The victims had to run through the "tube" four and five abreast, completely naked and with arms raised; this was the way in which they were herded into the gas chambers. The capacity of each gas chamber

310

was utilized down to the last square centimeter. Under a rain of constant blows and abuse so many people were squeezed into the chamber that no one was able to move any more. Often, infants and young children would simply be tossed into the rooms above the heads of the adults standing in the chambers. When it was no longer possible to squeeze additional people into the chambers, the doors were sealed and the German squad leader ordered the Ukrainian in the engine room (he might say, "Ivan, water!") to switch on the engine, whose exhaust fumes were then conducted into the chambers. The killing process itself lasted about 30 to 40 minutes. After that time the engine was shut off and someone went to the doors to listen for signs of life in the chambers. If no sign of life could be detected, the command was given to open the trap doors on the outer walls, and the transfer of the corpses began. On occasion some victims showed signs of life even after the gassing had been completed. Such people would be shot on the platform or perhaps on the way to the ditch or the cremation grill. The shooting was done either by the German squad leader or by one of the Ukrainian guards. Others shot at the mass graves included newcomers who could not be pushed into the already overcrowded gas chambers, but who were too few in number to warrant the expense of a separate gassing operation.

While the gas chambers were cleared and then cleaned by members of the so-called cleanup detail, the next group of victims would have to wait their turn at a distance of about 50 to 60 meters from the gas chambers. They were unable to see what was transpiring inside; while the gassing went on, the door of the old gas house was closed, and in the new gas chambers the entrance was screened by the dark curtain already described earlier. The wait until the gas chambers were ready to admit the next group was particularly agonizing because the people waiting outside could hear the screams and moans of the people already in the chambers, so that they were left in no doubt about what was in store for them also. The agony reached a climax when, as often happened at least during the early period, the engine broke down and some time passed before it could be started again.

The court could not establish with certainty the exact number of persons killed in any one gassing operation. The testimonies from the various defendants as well as from the Jewish witnesses who were cross-examined diverged with regard to the number of persons who could be crammed into a gas chamber at one time and the number of chambers used in any one operation. It can be said with certainty only that, first, not all of the 6 or 10 chambers of the new gas house were ever in use simultaneously at any one time, and secondly, that the capacity of the chambers that were used was utilized to the utmost. The most likely figures would be a capacity of approximately 200 to 350 persons per gas chamber in the old building and approximately 400 to 700 persons per gas chamber in the new building.

As a rule the interval between the arrival of a transport at the unloading platform and the completion of the killings of the new arrivals was not longer than about an hour and a half. This may be seen from the still extant train schedules that were issued by the office of the general manager of the Eastern Railway (*Ostbahn*). These schedules in many instances allowed for no more than 2½ to 3½ hours between the time the train arrived and the time the train left again, completely emptied and cleaned. The schedules included directives to the effect that the hours listed in them had to be strictly observed.

It is obvious that these schedules had to be observed not only on paper, but also in practice, if one considers that during the period of peak activity three and sometimes as many as four or five transport trains would arrive with their horrible cargo each day and would have to be processed. Since each transport brought an average of 6,000 new arrivals, it is obvious that the camp administration as well as the entire German camp staff had to make it their business—and indeed made it so—that the systematic processing, i.e., the mass killings, should go on smoothly, and strictly on schedule.

* * *

Late in 1942 and early in 1943 a number of hangings took place as object lessons, primarily following abortive attempts at escape or other "serious offenses." The victims, usually several of them at a time, were hanged by their feet, naked, their hands tied behind their backs. They remained in that position until they died or at least became unconscious. Sometimes they were whipped while they hung from the gallows. Sometimes they were shot in the head after they had lost consciousness. The corpses were left hanging for several hours, sometimes even until the next day, as a deterrent. When such hangings took place, there usually was a special roll call for the "work Jews," who had to stand in line for a longer period of time and see the victims hang. The officers predominantly involved in these executions were Franz and K[üttner]. . . .

* * *

The dog Barry was brought to the Treblinka extermination camp either late in 1942 or early in 1943. He was the size of a calf, with a black and white spotted coat, a mixed breed but with the physical characteristics of a Saint Bernard predominating. At Treblinka he attached himself to the defendant Franz and adopted him as his master.

Mostly, when Franz made the rounds of the "Lower" and "Upper" camps, Barry would accompany him. Depending on his mood, Franz would set the dog on inmates who for some reason had attracted his attention. The command to which the dog responded was, "Man, go get that dog!" By "Man" Franz meant Barry; the "dog" was the inmate whom Barry was supposed to attack. But Barry would attack an inmate even if he merely heard Franz shouting at that individual. In other words, the command "Man, go get that dog!" was not always necessary to galvanize Barry into action. Barry would bite his victim wherever he could catch him. Barry was the size of a calf so that, unlike smaller dogs, his shoulders reached to the buttocks and abdomen of a man of average size. For this reason he frequently bit his victims in the buttocks, in the abdomen and often, in the case of male inmates, in the genitals, sometimes partially biting them off.

312

When the inmate was not very strong, the dog could knock him to the ground and maul him beyond recognition.

But when the defendant Franz was not around, Barry was a different dog. With Franz not there to influence him, he allowed himself to be petted and even teased, without harming anyone.

Franz had entrusted the care of his dog Barry to M., an inmate from Czechoslovakia. M. had to care for the animal and to see that he got his food, which was much better than that of the working inmates.

The Court of Assizes was able to substantiate only three of the many cases in point described by the witnesses. On one occasion, in 1942, while he was helping load textiles aboard a freight train at night, the witness Gl[azar] personally heard Franz set his dog Barry on a working inmate. He personally observed how Barry bit the man in his genitals and how the injured man was taken away to the *lazaret* to be shot. The witness J[akubowicz] gave an account of how, on one occasion, Franz set Barry on a naked inmate at the entrance of the "tube" and how Barry bit off the genitals of one inmate. On another occasion he saw Barry, at the command of Franz, tear a piece of flesh from the body of an inmate near the Ukrainian kitchen. The co-defendant Mi[ete] had confirmed these accounts. After first refusing to discuss the matter, he finally admitted that among the inmates whom he had shot at the *lazaret* on Franz's orders there had been individuals whom Barry had bitten in the genitals and in other parts of the body.

At the same time, the witnesses Gl., St., J., T., T., K., C., S., R., K., and L. testified that Barry was a different dog when he was not under the influence of Franz. When Franz was not around, he was good-natured and lazy. Furthermore, the witness Dr. St. testified that in Ostrow he had frequently taken Barry with him when he passed among hundreds of naked soldiers to examine them for fitness to return to front-line duty, and that Barry had never harmed any of these soldiers.

The Court of Assizes requested the internationally known scientist Prof. Dr. L., director of the Max Planck Institute for Behavioral Research in Seewiesen, Upper Bavaria, to submit a sworn expert opinion on the question whether Barry could have been a ferocious beast one day, and a good-natured, playful house pet the next. The convincing expert opinion submitted by Dr. L. includes, among other items, the following statements:

According to the photographs of Barry made available to him by the Court of Assizes, Barry, though he predominantly showed the physical characteristics of a Saint Bernard, was not a pure-bred Saint Bernard, but a mongrel. Mongrels are much more sensitive than pure-bred animals. If mongrels attach themselves to a human and enter into a dog-master relationship with him, they are literally able to sense the wishes of their master. A dog's behavior is a "reflection of his master's subconscious mind," and this is particularly true in the case of mongrels. Behavioral psychologists have accepted it as a fact that one and the same dog can be good and harmless on some occasions, but dangerous and vicious at other times. The latter can happen if the dog is set by his master at another person. Sometimes the dog will attack a person if he merely hears his master shouting at that person. A little later, that same dog may be playing quite innocently

313

with children, without any need to fear for the children's safety. He will also be nice to grownups when he hears his master address them in a friendly manner. In other words, the dog is completely attuned to his master's moods and frame of mind.

If a dog then enters into a new dog-master relationship, his personality can undergo a complete change. Hence, if Barry, under his new master, the witness Dr. St., no longer showed tendencies to bite, this in itself was nothing unusual. Similar experiences have been cogently confirmed by experiments conducted with dogs.

According to these convincing explanations from Prof. Dr. L., then, there is no logical contradiction between the reports that, on the one hand, Barry was dangerous when Franz set him at Jews, while, on the other hand, he was lazy, good-natured and harmless on the camp grounds when Franz was away, and later, when he lived with Dr. St. in Ostrow.

The Court of Assizes further interrogated Prof. Dr. D., the well-known professor in ordinary for Surgery at the Academy of Medicine in Düsseldorf, on the effect of dog bites on the male genitals. Prof. D.'s sworn expert opinion includes the following statements:

Injuries to the male genitals are especially painful, the pain of injuries to the scrotum being even more intense than that of injuries to the penis. If a male genital is completely torn from the body, the victim as a rule will not be able to walk. On the other hand, males who suffer an injury only to part of their genitals are able to walk even though they are in intense pain. But neither an injury to part of the male genitals, nor the complete loss of these organs, is fatal. There is also no reason to assume that the victim of such an injury will rapidly bleed to death. On the contrary, the victim will not bleed to death even in cases where the male genitals have been completely amputated by a dog bite. The blood vessels in the male genitals are much narrower than those in other parts of the body, and therefore the smaller blood vessels in the male genitals seal themselves off in a relatively short time.

This precise and cogent scientific presentation by the expert, Prof. Dr. D., proves that the inmates whom Barry bit in their genitals did not necessarily have to die from an injury of this kind, and that therefore it was not necessary to liquidate them either on the spot or at the *lazaret*, as the co-defendant Mi[ete] admits was actually done on orders from Franz.

According to the witnesses Gl., C., S. and R., Barry attacked not only male genitals, but also other parts of the body (buttocks, thighs, and so forth). If it happened with relative frequency that Barry attacked the male genitals of his victims, this was attributable to his height, which was that of a calf. While smaller dogs preponderantly attack the lower parts of the leg, Barry, due to his height, was able to reach the male genitals of his victims with his muzzle and hence also to injure them. No special training from the defendant Franz was required for that. This does not exclude the possibility that Franz may not have been sorry to see Barry attack the male genitals of the inmates.

According to numerous Jewish witnesses, including the engineer Gl[azar], the mechanic T., and the hotel office worker S[iedlecki], Franz was a "sadist of exquisite cruelty," who derived particular pleasure from "special refinements" in the abuse and killing of Jews. Certainly attacks and amputations of the male genitals of an inmate by Barry could be classed as such a "special refinement."

* * *

On August 2, 1943 a long-planned revolt of the "work Jews" broke out in the camp. The inmates had succeeded in procuring weapons and ammunition from the arsenal without being noticed. On that day part of the Ukrainian guard units were absent from the camp, having left the camp grounds with Franz to bathe in the river Bug. The camp was set on fire with gasoline. The bulk of the Jews succeeded in escaping from the camp, but most of them were recaptured by search patrols and shot summarily. Only a few managed to escape permanently and to survive in the woods or at some other hiding places until the end of the war.

Following the revolt, the camp was not rebuilt in its original form. During the month of August, several additional small transports from Bialystok were killed in the gas chambers that had remained intact. The buildings, including the gas house, which had survived the revolt, were eventually demolished. The landscape was leveled and seeded with lupine. Every trace of the existence of a death camp was to be eliminated. On the camp grounds a farmhouse was built in which a former member of the Ukrainian guards was assigned to stay and to guard the area. Some of the Jews who were still left in Treblinka at the time were transferred to Sobibor.

After the demolition of the camp toward the end of November, 1943 there still were on the camp grounds, aside from several German and Ukrainian guards, no less than 25 but no more than 30 Jewish inmates, including two women, who had been working in the kitchen of the homestead. The remaining inmates were housed in two freight cars which were either under guard or locked. When the defendant received orders to close the camp down completely and to move with the rest of the squads to the Sobibor extermination camp, he made arrangements for the liquidation of the last remaining Jewish inmates.

For this purpose all the male Jewish inmates were locked up in the two freight cars, where they were guarded by the co-defendant R. One of the Jewish inmates hanged himself inside the car; the others waited to be shot. With the help of a squad of Ukrainians commanded by a German SS *Unterführer*, loaned by the Treblinka labor camp about 2 kilometers away, a sentry-line was set up in the space between the freight cars and the homestead to prevent the inmates from escaping. First, SS *Unterscharführer* Br[edow] got out the two Jewish women who had been working in the kitchen of the homestead. At the same time five male inmates were taken out from one of the two cars. These seven people, who remained fully clothed, were ordered to kneel down in a little hollow to the left of the homestead and to lower their heads. They were then killed with a bullet in the neck. The shooting was done by the co-defendant Me[ntz], SS *Unterscharführer* Br[edow] and the SS *Unterführer* from the Treblinka labor camp, in the presence of the defendant Franz. The bullets came from Finnish submachine guns adjusted to discharge only one bullet at a time. The division of labor among the three SS *Unterführers* who participated in the shootings was as follows: One of the men started shooting the victims at

315

the left, the other at the right, and the third in the middle. When that group of victims had been finished off, another five men were taken from the cars. First, they were ordered to carry the bodies of those already killed to a makeshift grill for cremation. Afterwards, these five men, too, were shot in the manner just described. This continued until all the inmates had been killed. The last group of inmates shot was taken to the grill by Ukrainians and cremated.

After the last Jewish inmates of the Treblinka extermination camp had been eliminated in this manner, the defendant Franz drove his truck to the Sobibor extermination camp, taking with him the members of the guard detail, including the co-defendant Me. and R. Earlier, the defendant Me., on orders of the defendant Franz, had delivered the dog Barry to the witness Dr. med. St., chief medical officer at the Reserve Hospital in Ostrow.

The evidence produced at the trial did not indicate that Franz had personally participated in these shootings. However, the evidence has established beyond doubt that he personally ordered and supervised the execution of the last Jewish detail that still remained at the camp.

These facts, which, of course, no Jewish witnesses have survived to confirm, have been confirmed to the satisfaction of the Court of Assizes by the testimony of the defendants Me[ntz] and R[um].

Translated from the German

1. Quoted after Dr. Adalbert Rückerl, head of the Main Office for Investigation of Nazi Crimes in Ludwigsburg.

2. Stroop was sentenced to death in Poland and was executed on July 9, 1952.

3. *Translator's Note:* The German term used by the court for "train inventories" is *Wagenzettel*. The *Wagenzettel* is a document listing the number of cars, weight of cars, etc. in a train.

4. In the fall of 1969 another expert, Dr. Scheffler, submitted for the second Treblinka trial an opinion which was based on more recent research. According to Dr. Scheffler's findings a total of over 900,000 persons, almost all of Jewish origin, were killed at the Treblinka extermination camp.

5. Franciszek Ząbecki.

6. Zev (Zvi) Kurland.

7. *Translator's Note:* Code name for the euthanasia organization camouflaged as the "National Coordinating Agency for Therapeutic and Medical Establishments." T-4 referred to 4 Tiergartenstrasse in Berlin, where the organization had its headquarters.

TABLE OF SS RANKS

SS	Approximate Equivalent British Army	U.S. Army
Reichsführer-SS	Field Marshal	General of the Army
SS-Oberstgruppenführer	General	General
SS-Obergruppenführer	Lieutenant General	Lieutenant General
SS-Gruppenführer	Major General	Major General
SS-Brigadeführer	Brigadier	Brigadier General
SS-Oberführer	Senior Colonel	
SS-Standartenführer	Colonel	Colonel
SS-Obersturmbannführer	Lieutenant Colonel	Lieutenant Colonel
SS-Sturmbannführer	Major	Major
SS-Hauptsturmführer	Captain	Captain
SS-Obersturmführer	Lieutenant	1st Lieutenant
SS-Untersturmführer	2nd Lieutenant	2nd Lieutenant
SS-Sturmscharführer	Regimental Sergeant-Major	Sergeant-Major
SS-Hauptscharführer	Sergeant-Major	Master Sergeant
SS-Oberscharführer	Quartermaster-Sergeant	Technical Sergeant
SS-Scharführer	Staff Sergeant	Staff Sergeant
SS-Unterscharführer	Sergeant	Sergeant
SS-Rottenführer	Corporal	Corporal
SS-Sturmmann	Lance-Corporal	Private 1st Class
SS-Mann	Private	Private

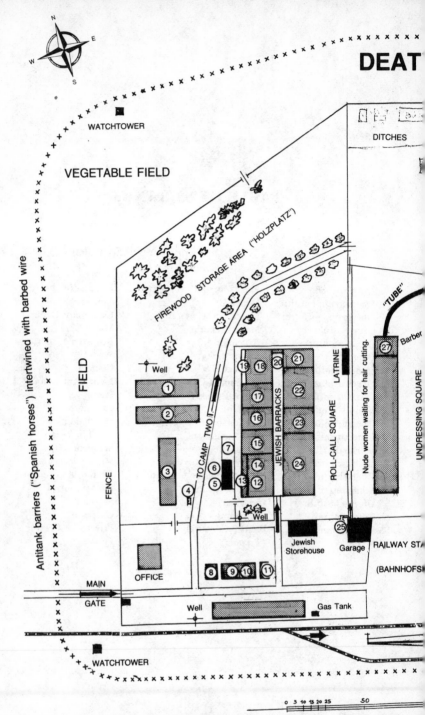

DEAT

1–3. Ukrainian barracks (In front of them a large sign "Max Biela Barracks"). 4. Zoo. 5. Stable. 6. P
7. Chicken Coop. 8. Chest for money, jewels, etc. 9. German storehouse. 10. German infir
("Revierstube"). 11. Bakery 12. Jewish kitchen. 13. SS laundry. 14. Jewish infirmary. 15. Kapo bar
16. Saddlery and shoemaker shop. 17. Tailor shop. 18. Carpenter shop. 19. Jewish women's bar

AMP TREBLINKA

(PLAN AS OF JULY 31, 1943)

FIELD

WATCHTOWER

ION GRIDS

CAMP TWO ("TOTENLAGER")
(Upper Camp)

GAS CHAMBERS

5-meter high wall

LATRINE

30

31 "LAZARET"

Antitank barriers ("Spanish horses") intertwined with barbed wire

FIELD

CAMP ONE (Lower Camp)

SORTING SQUARE
(SORTIERPLATZ)

PLATFORM   PLATFORM

LE 1:3300

150   200   250   300 M

WATCHTOWER

. Smithery. 21. Tool storehouse. 22. Jewish barrack I. 23. Washroom. 24. Jewish barrack II. 25. Street to
amp II. 26. Railway station (Big sign: "Treblinka=Obermajdan", and arrows: "To trains for Bialystok-
olkowysk", "To bathhouse".) 27. Barber shop. 28. Small chest for documents and valuables before entrance to
s chamber. 29. Lumber storage. 30. Lazaret, the fake hospital. 31. Small hut at the Lazaret.

Bibliography

Books

Ainsztein, Reuben, *Jewish Resistance in Nazi-Occupied Eastern Europe*, London–New York, 1974.

Elkins, Michael, *Forged in Fury*, New York, 1971.

Grossman, Vassili, *The Treblinka Hell*, Moscow, 1946.

Gutkowski, J. and Rutkowski, A., *Treblinka*, Warsaw, 1962.

Hilberg, Raul, *The Destruction of European Jewry*, Chicago, 1961

Łukaszkiewicz, Zdzisław, *Obóz śmierci w Treblince*, Warsaw, 1946.

Novitch, Miriam, *La Vérité sur Treblinka*, Paris, 1967.

——————, *Sobibor, Martyre et Révolte*, Paris, 1967.

Obozy, Tom I., *Dokumenty i materiały*, Warsaw, 1946.

Poliakov, Léon, *Harvest of Hate*, New York, 1979.

Poznanski, Stanislaw, *Struggle, Death, Memory 1939–1945*, Warsaw, 1963.

Roiter, Howard, *Voices From The Holocaust*, New York, 1975.

Rückerl, Dr. Adalbert, *NS Vernichtungslager im Spiegel deutscher Strafprozesse*, Munich, 1977.

Rüter-Ehlermann, A.L. and Rüter, C.F., *Justiz und NS-Verbrechen*, Amsterdam, 1968–75 (continuing) on J. Hirtreiter, Vol. II, pp. 270–308.

Rutkowski, Adam, *Męczeństwo, Walka, Zagłada Żydów w Polsce, 1939–1945*, Warsaw, 1960.

Sereny, Gitta, *Into That Darkness*, New York, 1970.

Steiner, Jean-François, *Treblinka*, New York, 1967.

Other Literature

Hilberg, Raul, "German Railroads/Jewish Souls," *Society*, 1976, pp. 60–76.

Biuletyn Żydowskiego Instytutu Historycznego, Warsaw.

Bleter far Geshikhte, Warsaw.

Yalkut Moreshet, Tel Aviv.